Contributions to Economics

For further volumes:
http://www.springer.com/series/1262

Samia Mohamed Nour

Technological Change and Skill Development in Arab Gulf Countries

Springer

Samia Mohamed Nour
Department of Economics
University of Khartoum
Khartoum
Sudan
and
UNU-MERIT - School of Business and Economics
Maastricht University
Maastricht
The Netherlands

ISSN 1431-1933 ISSN 2197-7178 (electronic)
ISBN 978-3-319-01915-4 ISBN 978-3-319-01916-1 (eBook)
DOI 10.1007/978-3-319-01916-1
Springer Cham Heidelberg New York Dordrecht London

Library of Congress Control Number: 2013952960

Printed on acid-free paper

Springer is part of Springer Science+Business Media (www.springer.com)

Acknowledgements[1]

I sincerely thank Allah, my God, the Most Gracious, Most Merciful, for enabling me to complete this Ph.D. thesis book successfully and for often putting so many good people in my way.

In completing my Ph.D. thesis book I owe a great debt to many people. I wish to extend my deep thanks, gratitude and appreciation to everyone who contributed to its successful completion.

First and foremost, I would like to express my sincere thanks, gratitude and deep appreciation to my promoter Professor Joan Muysken and co-promoter Dr. Thomas Ziesemer for their sincere efforts, interest and time they have kindly spent to guide my research. I am extremely grateful and indebted to Professor Muysken for his excellent supervision, intellectual guidance and invaluable comments, without which it would have been impossible to complete my thesis. I had the good fortune and honour to train with and work under his supervision. I am very grateful to him for the time he spent to teach me, and sincerely thank him for his interest, as well as his extraordinary cooperation and amazing patience in correcting my mistakes and restructuring my inconsistent writing. I hope that for every Ph.D. candidate there are excellent professors and supervisors like Prof. Muysken, who practically implement the learning by doing approach or problem-based learning method, a unique distinction characterizing Maastricht university among the other Dutch universities. I wish to extend my extreme gratitude and thanks to Dr. Ziesemer for his excellent supervision and support during the final stage of my thesis. I am very grateful to him for the time he spent in reviewing my thesis with great care and attention, and for

[1] The Study presented in this book was conducted at Maastricht Economic and Social Research Institute on Innovation and Technology (UNU-MERIT), School of Business and Economics, Maastricht University, Maastricht, the Netherlands, and fully sponsored by the United Nations University-Institute for New Technologies (UNU-INTECH), Maastricht, The Netherlands. The views, analysis and policy recommendations of this book are those of the author and do not necessarily reflect the views and policies of the United Nations University, Maastricht Economic and Social Research Institute on Innovation and Technology (UNU-MERIT), or UNU Affiliated Institutes.

his invaluable comments and suggestions that contributed much to the improvement and completion of my thesis. I also thank Dr. Abbas Abdelkarim for his comments, suggestions and supervision, which contributed to my thesis at its early stage. I am grateful to him for facilitating the fieldwork visit.

I also thank the members of the scientific examining committee: Prof. Robin Cowan, Prof Hans Heijke and Prof Lynn Mytelka, for their comments and for the time and effort they spent in reviewing my thesis.

I gratefully acknowledge the United Nations University-Institute for New Technologies (UNU-INTECH) for the 4-year fellowship award and also for the continued generous support through the duration of my Ph.D. study. The study presented in this book was conducted at Maastricht Economic Research Institute on Innovation and Technology (MERIT), Faculty of Economic and Business Administration, Maastricht University, and fully sponsored by the United Nations University- Institute for New Technologies (UNU-INTECH), Maastricht, the Netherlands. I am grateful to the United Nations University-World Institute for Development Economics Research for the 3 months' internship, the Ford Foundation and the Lebanese Center for Policy Studies for the Middle East Research Competition (MERC) Grant offered to partially support me in the midst of my research.

I would like to acknowledge that the successful completion, production and publication of this book would not have been possible without the extraordinary cooperation and full support of UNU-INTECH, Professor Joan Muysken, UNU-MERIT of the School of Business and Economics, Maastricht University, the Netherlands and Khartoum University, Sudan.

I would like to express my gratitude to all the staff members of UNU/INTECH and MERIT of the University of Maastricht. I deeply thank Prof. Luc Soete (Director of MERIT and UNU-INTECH) and Prof. Robin Cowan (Dean of students, MERIT-UNU/INTECH Ph.D. Programme) both for giving me a good opportunity to be a part of the interesting MERIT/UNU-INTECH Ph.D. programme and for their continuous cooperation and support during my study. My thank are extended to Prof. Lynn Mytelka (former director) and Dr. Lea Velho (former dean of students), Marc Vleugels (chief administrative staff), Ad Notten (senior library assistant) and Mourik Jan Heupink (computer systems assistant), I am very grateful to them for their help, kind cooperation and assistance during my study and stay at UNU-INTECH. Many special thanks are extended to all colleagues working at UNU-INTECH, especially, Yvonne de Groot, Eveline in de Braek, Ann Kelledy, Monique Raedts, Marijke Roolvink-Batty, Raeleen Waasdorp and Jacqueline van Kesteren, for the warm generous support they have kindly given to me and for making INTECH a warm comfortable home for all INTECH people. I would also like to extend my gratitude and special thanks to Corien Gijsbers, Silvana de Sanctis, Wilma Coenegrachts and the secretaries to Prof. Muysken at the Department of Economics, Faculty of Economic and Business Administration, Céline Rondagh, Susan Roggen and Fleur Keune for their kind cooperation. I thank Jane Williams for her kind support and Sophia Gross for her help in editing my thesis.

Special gratitude goes to my roommate Mamata Parhi for her good friendship and kind cooperation. I deeply thank her and Preeti Soni for their warm support, pleasant company, and the nice time we spent during our stay in Maastricht. I am very thankful to my fellow Ph.D. students, class of 1999, Minh, Geoffrey, Pedro, Poala, Oxana, Muge, Elad and Bulat. I also thank Marcia, Noi, Ekin, Kristen and all students. I am very pleased to have been involved in the University of Maastricht MERIT-UNU/INTECH Ph.D. programme.

My research benefited from my stay at UNU-WIDER in Helsinki (2002). I thank Prof. Matti Pohjola for his helpful supervision during my stay there. I also thank Dr. Maiju Perala and all staff for their hospitality and cooperation.

During the field visit and data collection I received considerable help from many people. I thank the directors and staff of the National Human Resources Development Authority and the Centre for Labour Market Research and Information in Dubai, the United Arab Emirates, for their hospitality, cooperation and support during the fieldwork. I thank Mr. Yousef Abdulgheni, Dr. Mohamed Osman and Mr. Abdullah Al Marzoqui for their cooperation, comments and the time they spent in filling in the questionnaires. Thanks also to Mr. Omran Tahboub for his valuable assistance during the survey, and Mr. Abdul Azeem Osman for preparing the Arabic translation of the macro survey questionnaire. I thank Mr. Saeed Al-Shaali, Ministry of Labour, and the part-time researchers Azhary, Tilal, Hatem and Amin for their helpful cooperation in the collection of the questionnaires from firms. I also thank Dr. Hector Morada for his valuable comments to improve the design of the questionnaires and Anthony Arundel from MERIT, for his comments on an earlier draft of the questionnaire. I thank all the respondents to both surveys. Special thanks also go to Ms. Inam Mubarak and her family for facilitating access to Ministry of Industry industrial database, and to Khawla Abdulrahman, Fatima, and Hesham Zaki for facilitating access to secondary data. Many thanks are extended to Prof. Ali Abdel Gadir Ali, Dr. Khalid Affan, Dr. Mohammed Attaitallah, Mr. Omer Sharfi, Dr. Omer Bizri, Dr. Yuhanna Aboona and Mr. Hag Ahmed for facilitating access to GOIC and ESCWA database.

I wish to thank Prof. Ali Abdel Gadir Ali, Prof. Suleiman Cohen, Dr. John Cameron and the participants at the UNU/INTECH and MERIT workshops 2001, 2005, UNU-WIDER seminar 2002, ETIC European Doctoral Training Programme 2003, CAPORDE 2004 and DRUID Winter 2005 Ph.D. conference for their useful comments to improve my thesis.

I would like to thank Prof. Mohamed Hashim Awad and all my colleagues at the Faculty of Economic and Social Studies, University of Khartoum. My deep thanks go to my friends Ahlam Hamza and Fatma Osman for their continuous support during my study. I also extend my thanks to Mr. Tariq Kafeel, Mr. Khalid Kafeel and Dr. Malik Alabasi and all the Sudanese friends in the Netherlands, particularly in Maastricht, for their helpful, continuous support during my stay there.

I also thank my grandparents, my aunts, my uncles and my brothers- and sisters-in-law and their families for their support. Last but not least, my everlasting gratitude, appreciation and sincere deep thanks go to my kind, beloved, wonderful mother Alawia and father Satti, my beloved sisters, Rashida, Khalda, Eiman and Lana and my kind brothers, Rashid, Osman, Khalid, Sami and their families for their sincere prayers for their warm, generous and steady support and faithful encouragement throughout my long learning expedition in Sudan and the Netherlands.

Maastricht
July 13, 2013

Samia Satti Osman Mohamed-Nour

List of Abbreviations

ADNOC	Abu Dhabi National Oil Company
AHDR	Arab Human Development Report
API	Arab Planning Institute
CIS	Community Innovation Survey
DUBAL	Dubai Aluminium Company
EPO	European Patents Office
ERF	Economic Research Forum for the Arab Countries, Iran and Turkey
ESCWA	Economic and Social Commission for Western Asia
FDI	Foreign Direct Investment
FTER	Full–time equivalent researcher
GCC	Gulf Cooperation Council
GDP	Gross Domestic Products
GOIC	Gulf Organization for Industrial Consulting
GNP	Gross National Product
HCT	Higher Colleges of Technology
ICT	Information and Communication Technology
ILO	International Labour Organization
IMF	International Monetary Fund
ISCO	International Standards Classification of Occupations
ISIC	International Standard Industrial Classification
IT	Information Technology
ITU	International Telecommunication Union
JULPHAR	Gulf Pharmaceutical Industries
KSA	The Kingdom of Saudi Arabia
MENA	Middle East and North Africa
MOL	Ministry of Labour and Social Affairs
MNC	Multinational Corporations
MOP	Ministry of Planning
OECD	Organisation for Economic Co-operation and Development

OPEC	Organisation of the Petroleum Exporting countries
R&D	Research and Development
S&T	Science and Technology
SITC	Standard International Trade Classification (SITC)
TAI	Technology Achievement Index
TANMIA	The National Human Resources Development and Employment Authority
TFP	Total Factor Productivity
TNCs	Transnational Corporations
UAE	The United Arab Emirates
UIS	UNESCO Institute of Statistics
UN	The United Nations
UNCOMTRAD	UNCTAD COMTRADE Database
UNCTAD	The United Nations Conference on Trade and Development
UNDP	United Nations Development Programme
UNESCO	United Nations Educational, Scientific and Cultural Organization
USPTO	US Patent and Trademark office web site
WB	World Bank
WDI	World Development Indicators – World Bank
WEO	World Economic Outlook –International Monetary Fund
WITSA	World Information Technology and Services Alliance

Contents

List of Figures

List of Tables

List of Schemes

Abstract (English Abstract)

Technological Change and Skill Development in Arab Gulf Countries

The central themes of discussion in this research are the required skill formation and upskilling of workers, together with their interaction with technological change in the Gulf countries. The Gulf countries have strategic importance in the global economy because the region holds 40% of the world's oil reserves and therefore affects the trends of oil supply and market. While the heavy dependence on oil has contributed to the enhancement of economic development in the region, it has also led to serious challenges now confronting the Gulf countries since oil is an exhaustible resource and, because of the instability of oil prices, the revenue from oil is uncertain and volatile. Other serious structural problems relate to the Dutch Disease and the high incidence of unskilled foreign workers that have caused serious structural imbalances in the labour market in the Gulf. Hence, long run economic growth and sustainable development strategy in the Gulf depends on both a shift in the focus from resources-oil based economy to a technology and skill based economy and on economic diversification. A key part of this strategy is to also manage the economy away from the dependency on the import of highly skilled workers in favour of domestic skilled workers.

In our view, the success of these strategies – local technological development, economic diversification and self-reliance on domestic workers to restructuring the labour market – is contingent upon the development of adequate and appropriate skills in the Gulf.

In our opinion, the implementation of these strategies is eminently impeded by the deficient educational system, the large amount of unskilled foreign workers and the lack of incentives in the Gulf countries. A new element in our research is that we confirm the role and impacts of the deficiencies in the educational system alongside the well-investigated role of the excessive use of uneducated foreign workers and lack of incentives in the labour market. We provide a more comprehensive investigation since we discuss the skill problem from two different perspectives, combining the impacts of the deficient educational system and the high incidence of uneducated foreign workers. In addition, we present a more elaborate and in-depth analysis to assess the causes, consequences and relationships between poor skill and technological performance in the Gulf from both the supply and demand sides and the macro–micro perspectives, since we use a very comprehensive set of indicators compared to the ones usually used in the literature. Finally, our analysis fills the gap in the Gulf literature since we highlight the importance of knowledge and external effects of schooling/the transfer of knowledge and we explore the factors hindering and those contributing toward enhancing the transfer of knowledge at both the macro and micro levels.

We focus on the UAE as a case study of the Gulf countries and use the results from new survey data both at the macro and micro/firm levels. We show that the interaction between the deficient educational system – at the macro level – and the high incidence of unskilled foreign workers – at the micro level – leads to low skill and technology levels and many serious consequences. These include the poor provision of training, severe skills mismatch, low transfer of knowledge, public–private duality, poor technology indicators and a heavy dependence on foreign technologies. We explain that the lack of local efforts for technology development is basically related to low R&D efforts that can be attributed to low skill levels, lack of networks systems, weak linkages/co-operation between universities and firms, lack of resources and low transfer of knowledge.

Our results show two surprising, contradicting views concerning the incidence and transfer of knowledge, the self-reliance on local skill and the role of both technological upgrading and upskilling in reinforcing these at both the macro–micro levels and the public–private sectors. Our findings imply that the transfer of knowledge/the external effects of schooling are probably successful within firms but unsuccessful within society at large. Our results indicate that the self-reliance strategy is probably a preferred government strategy, but not necessarily one favoured by private firms. We show that, in contrast to private firms, the large public firms seem successful/committed to implementing public policies for skill upgrading.

Our findings confirm the stylized facts in the new growth literature concerning the positive correlations between actual education, experience and wages and the complementary relationships between technical progress/technology (ICT), human capital/skill and upskilling (ICT training). We corroborate the importance of knowledge and the complementary relationship between tacit and codified sources of knowledge.

We confirm that the Gulf countries need to improve skills through the reform of educational and training systems, transfer of knowledge and the provision of further incentives to improve tacit and codified sources of knowledge at the macro and micro levels. They need to develop the local technologies through the promotion of skill; R&D activities; transfer of knowledge; networks system; collaboration between universities, firms, public sectors and private sectors; and implementation of explicit technology policy.

Abstract (Arabic Abstract)

بسم الله الرحمن الرحيم
خلاصة الدراسة (باللغة العربية)
تطوير المهارات والتغيرات التكنولوجية فى دول الخليج العربية

يناقش هذا البحث أهمية تنمية المهارات والتفاعل مع التغيرات التكنولوجية في دول الخليج العربية. وقد أكدت نتائج البحث على الأهمية الاستراتيجية لدول الخليج العربية في الاقتصاد العالمي، حيث أن منطقة الخليج العربية تمتلك 40٪ من احتياطيات النفط العالمية، وبالتالي تؤثر على اتجاهات إمدادات وعرض وسوق النفط. وبينت الدراسة ان الاعتماد الكبير على النفط قد ساهم في تعزيز التنمية الاقتصادية في منطقة الخليج، الا ان الاعتماد الكبير على النفط قد أدى أيضاً إلى التحديات الخطيرة التي تواجه دول الخليج الآن. حيث ان النفط مورداً قابلاً للنضوب، وكما ان عدم استقرار أسعار النفط، قد تسبب في تقلب وتذبذب عائدات النفط. بالاضافة الى مشاكل أخرى هيكلية خطيرة تتعلق بحدوث المرض الهولندي، وارتفاع نسبة العمال الأجانب غير المهرة التي تسببت في اختلالات هيكلية خطيرة في سوق العمل في دول الخليج العربية. وبالتالي، فان استراتيجية النمو الاقتصادي والتنمية المستدامة في منطقة الخليج العربية على المدى الطويل تعتمد على التحول من التركيز على الاقتصاد القائم على الموارد النفطية الى الاقتصاد القائم على التكنولوجيا والمهارات وعلى التنويع الاقتصادي. وترتكز هذه الاستراتيجية أيضاً على إدارة الاقتصاد بعيداً عن الاعتماد على استيراد العمالة الاجنبية ذات المهارات العالية وذلك بتحسين مهارات العمالة المحلية وزيادة الاعتماد عليها.

في تقديرنا، فإن نجاح هذه الاستراتيجيات- تنمية التكنولوجية المحلية، والتنويع الاقتصادي والاعتماد على الذات وعلى العمالة المحلية لإعادة هيكلة سوق العمل- جميعها تتوقف على تنمية المهارات الكافية والمناسبة في دول الخليج العربية. وقد أكدت الدراسة على أهمية تحسين المهارات كشرط ضروري لتحقيق التنويع الاقتصادي، والتطور التكنولوجي، وتخفيف حدة عدم التوازن في سوق العمل، والحد من استيراد العمالة الاجنبية وإعادة هيكلة سوق العمل فى دول الخليج العربية.

في تقديرنا، ابرز المعوقات التى تواجه تنفيذ هذه الاستراتيجيات تتعلق بقصور النظام التعليمي، والاستخدام المفرط للعمال الأجانب غير المهرة وعدم وجود حوافز في دول الخليج. وتتميز هذه الدراسة بمناقشة عنصر جديد يتمثل في التأكيد على أهمية دور وآثار القصور في النظام التعليمي، بالاضافة الى التأكيد على أهمية دور العامل الاخر الذى تناولته الادبيات ويتمثل في الاستخدام المفرط للعمال الأجانب غير المتعلمين وعدم وجود حوافز في سوق العمل. وتقدم هذه الدراسة تحليلاً أكثر شمولاً حيث تناقش مشكلة قصور المهارات من منظورين مختلفين، وتجمع بين آثار قصور النظام التعليمي والاستخدام المفرط للعمال الأجانب غير المهرة والذى يتمثل في ارتفاع نسبة العمال الأجانب غير المتعلمين. واختلاف هذه الدراسة عن الدراسات المشابهة فى الأدبيات الخليجية تأتي من خلال تميزها بتقديم مساهمة اصيلة وجديدة لملء فجوة كبيرة في الأدبيات الخليجية، حيث أنها قدمت تحليلاً كمياً ونوعياً لجانبى العرض والطلب وكذلك تحليلاً اكثر شمولاً للأسباب والنتائج المترتبة على تدنى مستوى المهارات ومؤشرات التكنولوجيا ونقل المعرفة والعلاقة بينهما على المستويين الكلي والجزئي في

الخليج. وقد استخدمت الدراسة تعريفاً ومنهجاً اكثر شمولاً باعتماد العديد من المؤشرات لقياس مستوى المهارات ومؤشرات التكنولوجيا، وإعتمدت على استخدام البيانات الأولية من المسوحات على المستويين الكلي والجزئي والتي أجريت في دولة الامارات العربية المتحدة في العام 2002. وكما إن المساهمة الاصيلة والجديدة لهذه الدراسة أنها سلطت الضوء على أهمية الآثار الخارجية للتعليم ونقل المعرفة ودراسة العوامل التي تعوق، والاخرى المساهمة في تعزيز الآثار الخارجية للتعليم ونقل المعرفة، هذا وقد أكدت نتائج الدراسة على أهمية تعزيز الآثار الخارجية للتعليم ونقل المعرفة.

وتركز هذه الدراسة على دولة الإمارات العربية المتحدة كدراسة حالة لدول الخليج العربية وتستخدم النتائج من بيانات المسوحات على المستويين الكلي والجزئي / المنشات. وقد بينت الدراسة أن التفاعل بين قصور النظام التعليمي بسبب تدني جودة التعليم – على المستوى الكلي – والاستخدام المفرط للعمالة الاجنبية غير الماهرة بوجود نسبة عالية من العمالة الاجنبية غير الماهرة – على المستوى الجزئي – قد أدى الى تدنى مستويات المهارات ومؤشرات التكنولوجيا، وقلة فرص التدريب، وعدم تطابق المهارات، وقلة المقدرة التكنولوجية، والاعتماد الكبير على التكنولوجيا الأجنبية على المستويين الكلي والجزئي والازدواجية بين القطاعين العام والخاص. والمساهمة الاصيلة والجديدة لهذه الدراسة لملء فجوة لمثل هذه الدراسات في الادبيات الخليجية أنها أوضحت أن ضعف المقدرة التكنولوجية يُعزى إلى قلة جهود البحث والتطوير (R&D) لتدنى مستوى المهارات، وقلة نظم الشبكات، وضعف الروابط / التعاون بين الجامعات والمنشات ونقص الموارد، ومحدودية نقل المعرفة.

كما أظهرت نتائج الدراسة التناقض المثير للدهشة فى وجهات النظر بشأن حدوث ونقل المعرفة على المستويين الكلي والجزئي، والاعتماد على الذات وعلى المهارات المحلية ودور كل من رفع المستوى التكنولوجي ورفع مستوى المهارات في تعزيز الاعتماد على الذات وعلى المهارات المحلية على المستويين الكلي والجزئي والقطاعين العام والخاص. بينت نتائج الدراسة أن نقل المعرفة / الآثار الخارجية من التعليم هى على الارجح اكثر نجاحاً داخل المنشات ولكنها غير ناجحة على مستوى المجتمع. واشارت نتائج الدراسة إلى أن استراتيجية الاعتماد على الذات هي على الارجح الاستراتيجية المفضلة لدى الحكومة، ولكنها ليست بالضرورة الاستراتيجية المفضلة للمنشات الخاصة. وبينت الدراسة أنه، وعلى العكس من المنشات الخاصة، فان المنشات الكبيرة العامة تبدو ناجحة / وملتزمة بتنفيذ السياسات العامة لتحسين المهارات.

تؤكد النتائج التي توصلت إليها الدراسة الحقائق البديهية التى تناولتها أدبيات النمو الحديثة بشأن الارتباط الإيجابي بين التعليم، والخبرة والأجور والعلاقات التكاملية بين التقدم التقني / التكنولوجي (تكنولوجيا المعلومات والاتصالات) (ICT) ، رأس المال البشري / المهارات وتحسين المهارات (التدريب على تكنولوجيا المعلومات والاتصالات) وتؤكد الدراسة على أهمية المعرفة والعلاقة التكاملية بين مصادر المعرفة الحسية والمدونة.

وتؤكد هذه الدراسة أن دول الخليج العربية تحتاج إلى تحسين المهارات من خلال إصلاح نظم التعليم والتدريب، ونقل المعرفة وتوفير المزيد من الحوافز لتحسين مصادر المعرفة الحسية والمدونة على المستويين الكلي والجزئي. وتحتاج إلي تطوير التكنولوجية المحلية من خلال تعزيز المهارات وأنشطة البحث والتطوير (R&D)، ونقل المعرفة، ونظام الشبكات، والتعاون بين الجامعات والمنشات والقطاعين العام والخاص وتنفيذ سياسة صريحة لتطوير التكنولوجيا.

بناءً على نتائج هذه الدراسة توصي الدراسة ببذل مزيد من الجهود لتحسين توفير فرص وجودة التعليم والتدريب، تقليل الاعتماد على العمالة الأجنبية، وتطوير المهارات، وتحسين اداء مؤشرات التكنولوجيا وتشجيع الآثار الخارجية للتعليم وتعزيز نقل المعرفة وتحسين التوافق بين مؤسسات القطاعيين العام والخاص على المستويين الكلي والجزئي من اجل تحسين النمو الاقتصادي، والتنويع الاقتصادى، والتنمية المستدامة في دول الخليج العربية.

Part I
Introduction

Chapter 1
General Introduction

1.1 Introduction

The aim of this introductory chapter is to give a brief general overview of the research problem and to briefly show the importance, relevance, objectives, questions, hypotheses and the general structure of the thesis.

1.2 Research Problem, Importance, Relevance and Method

Economists have long recognized the essential role of technical progress in the creation, acceleration and sustainability of economic growth and improvement of the quality of life in any society. Both the endogenous growth theories and empirical literature acknowledge the importance of human capital accumulation for economic growth. Endogenous growth literature also elaborates on the interaction and complementary relationship between technological progress and human capital to create, reinforce, accelerate and sustain economic growth (cf. Lucas, 1988; Romer, 1990). Moreover, economists also highlight the role of high levels and quality of skills as critical factors for competitiveness associated with the rapid progress of globalization and fast technological progress in the developed and developing countries. Considerable debate in the literature is on the effects of human capital and the diffusion and transfer of technology to the developing countries to accelerate the catching-up process. For instance, the Nelson and Phelps (1966) model allows human capital levels to affect the speed of technological catch-up and diffusion. Romer (1990) has also argued that the level of human capital may have an influence on growth of technological innovation both directly and through its effect on the speed of the "catch-up" process. Benhabib and Speigel (1994) adapted the Nelson and Phelps (1966) framework to allow for the catching-up of technology with those of the leading countries. In their view, the level of education not only enhances the ability of a country to develop its own

S. Mohamed Nour, *Technological Change and Skill Development in Arab Gulf Countries*, Contributions to Economics, DOI 10.1007/978-3-319-01916-1_1,

technological innovations, but also its ability to adapt and implement technologies developed elsewhere.

In this research we use the framework of and perspectives from the new growth literature to investigate the relevance and importance of skill upgrading and technological development and the interaction between these for economic development in the Gulf countries.[1] The Gulf countries have strategic importance in the global economy because the region holds 40% of world oil supplies (Devlin, 1998) and, therefore, affects the trends of oil supply and market. While oil has contributed to the enhancement of economic development in the region, the heavy dependence on it has led to serious challenges now confronting the Gulf countries since oil is an exhaustible resource and, because of the instability of oil prices, the revenue from oil is uncertain and volatile. Moreover, both the growing employment opportunities and the increased wealth from oil encourages migration to these countries – consequently, migrants, especially unskilled workers, have dominated and caused serious structural imbalances in the labour market in the Gulf.

The GDP of the United Arab Emirates (UAE) is still growing, but GDP per capita is stagnant.[2] So far, the falling contribution of the oil sector has been compensated by other sectors, but, in our view, the big question is whether or not this will work in the future. We feel that may be somewhat doubtful in light of current stagnation in education, particularly tertiary education. In addition, the high share of foreign workers indicates that the UAE is currently an agglomeration economy. But it may lose this position and become poor if both the oil industry and the complementary ones decline and/or if foreigners move out and there is less work in the government sector. While it is unclear which sector can fill the gap, it is evidently one that will need high levels of education. Therefore, it is quite essential for the government to improve investment and enrolment in education and skill upgrading.

So, the economic growth and sustainable development strategy in the Gulf depends on both a shift in the focus from an oil resources based economy to a technology and skill based economy and on economic diversification. A key part of this strategy is also to shift or to manage the economy away from dependency on the import of high skilled workers in favour of domestic skilled workers. Overcoming these strategic problems and challenges confronting economic development and thereby achieving long run economic growth and sustainable development in the Gulf depends on three main strategies: economic diversification, local technological development and self-reliance on domestic workers to restructuring the labour market. In our opinion the success/fulfilment of these strategies is contingent upon the development of adequate and appropriate skills, skill upgrading and efficient

[1] The economies of Bahrain, Kuwait, Oman, Qatar, Saudi Arabia and the United Arab Emirates (UAE) constitute the Gulf countries and also known as the Gulf Cooperation Council (GCC) countries.

[2] For the empirical investigation in Chaps. 5, 6, 7 and 8 we focus on the UAE as a case study of the Gulf countries, due to easy accessibility to data and information and facilities for the fulfilment of the fieldwork.

educational and training policies and building of local technological capabilities in the Gulf countries.

In our view, although the development of local technologies is a costly process, it can be funded from the oil revenues and by offering further incentives to motivate private investment in skills, technology and technical education. Moreover, to some extent, the Gulf countries have an option to remain importing technologies and to specialize in fields other than producing machinery and transport equipment (SITC 7). The Gulf countries show deficient skill and technology indicators and a substantial gap when compared to rapidly advanced countries. Therefore, the need for the development of local skills and building local technologies are important not only for fulfilling the above strategies, but also for shortening the gap, building local capacity, improving productivity and competitiveness in the international market (UAE University, 1997; El Sabaa, 1997; Alfakhery, 1999).

In our view, the implementation of these strategies is eminently impeded by the deficient educational system, the large share of unskilled foreign workers and the lack of incentives in the Gulf countries. One should note that many previous studies in the Gulf literature have well- investigated the implications of the excessive use of uneducated foreign workers and lack of incentives in the labour market. However, the impacts of the deficiencies in the educational system have not received an adequate investigation in these studies, despite the well known stylized facts in the endogenous growth literature that highlight the essential endogenous effect of education for accumulation of human capital and economic growth.

For that reason, our analysis in this research provides many new and interesting results. Different from other Gulf literature, we identify upskilling as a key element for the fulfilment of the three current strategies in the Gulf. Furthermore, we provide a more comprehensive investigation since we discuss the skills problem from two different perspectives: combining the impacts of the deficient educational system and the high incidence of uneducated foreign workers. In addition, our analysis goes beyond the available Gulf literature and presents a more elaborate and in-depth analysis to assess skill and technological performance in the Gulf since we use a very comprehensive set of indicators than often used in the new growth literature. We use these indicators to analyse the causes and consequences of low skills and technology levels, the link between them and the implications on skills mismatch, and the lack of local efforts for technological development and the consequent dependence on foreign technologies at both the macro and micro levels. In addition, in light of the recent literature that highlights the role of diffused technologies, our analysis uses a broader definition of technological change that considers the role of diffusion in fostering economic growth; and we assess the role of imported technologies and skill in promoting local technologies and local skills. This definition is particularly relevant for our analysis since the Gulf countries are highly dependent on both imported technologies and imported skilled workers to manage them. Our analysis also addresses the policy issues, stresses the role of both public and private educational and training policies and the need for incentives, harmony and collaboration between public-private institutions in upgrading skill and fostering human capital accumulation in the Gulf countries. Finally, our analysis fills the gap in the Gulf literature since we highlight the importance of knowledge and external effects of schooling/the transfer of knowledge and we explore the factors hindering and those contributing toward enhancing the transfer of knowledge at both the macro and micro levels.

Moreover, our research contributes to the few recent studies in the Gulf countries that call for upskilling and the interaction between skills and technology. We investigate the deficiencies in the educational and training systems (UAE University, 1994; Al-Sulayti, 2002; Gray, 1999; Abdelkarim and Haan, 2002); their impacts on skills mismatch; and the duality between public and private sectors (Gray, 1999; Khorshid, 2000; Abdelkarim and Haan, 2002). In addition, we show the impacts on poor technological level, dependence on foreign technologies and the impacts of technologies transfer (Elsabaa, 1997; Haan, 1999). Our analysis presents three new and additional aspects of the duality between public and private sectors with regard to knowledge transfer, upskilling and training policies.

To investigate the research problem we focus on the UAE as a case study of the Gulf countries, and we use a combination of primary and secondary data covering both the macro and micro levels and the results from the macro and firm surveys held in the UAE in 2002. In addition, the survey's data is supported by ten face-to-face interviews with firm managers and five interviews with the officials. The Firm Survey (2002) on "Technological change and skill development in the UAE manufacturing sector" aims to assess skill and technology indicators and the impacts of unskilled foreign workers amongst the chemical and metal medium and large size establishments in the UAE. The macro survey (2002) on "Skill creation, human resources development and policy intervention" was sent to policy makers and experts in the public and university institutions to examine the causes and consequences of low skills and the deficient educational system in the UAE. We collected all primary and secondary data personally.

1.3 Objectives, Hypotheses and Questions of the Research

Based on the above background, the central themes of this research are: the required skill formation and upskilling of the workers, together with their interaction with technological change; and the interaction between the deficient educational system and the excessive share of uneducated foreign workers and their implications. First, our analysis aims to provide an empirical investigation of the causes and consequences of low skill and technology indicators, in particular, the causes and consequences of the deficient educational system at the macro level and the implications of the excessive use of uneducated foreign workers at the micro level. Second, we examine the interaction between the low skill and technology indicators, the relationships between skill, upskilling and technology indicators, skills mismatch, the uses and impacts of ICT and differences defined by firm size (large and medium size) and industry (chemical and metal) at the micro/firm level. Third, we analyse the impacts of tacit and codified knowledge at the micro and macro levels respectively and examine the factors hindering and those contributing toward enhancing the transfer of knowledge/external schooling effects at the macro and micro levels. Finally, we highlight the need for implementation of consistent policies, increasing incentives and collaboration between public and private educational and training institutions to enhance skill upgrading, local technological development, economic development and transfer of knowledge.

Grounded on these objectives, our research attempts to answer three sets of questions:

1. What are the major causes and consequences of low skill and technological levels in the Gulf countries? What are the major implications of the interaction between the deficient educational system and the high incidence of uneducated foreign workers at the macro–micro levels in the Gulf countries?
2. Does the external effect of schooling/transfer of knowledge occur in the Gulf countries? If not, why does it not yet occur? What are the major factors hindering and those contributing toward enhancing the transfer of knowledge at both the macro and micro levels in the Gulf countries?
3. What are the major policies and mechanisms for upgrading skill, reforming the educational system, enhancing the provision of training and the development of local technologies at both the macro and micro levels in the Gulf countries?

Based on the research questions and objectives, the major hypotheses to be tested in this research are:

1. The Gulf countries need to promote local skills and local technologies in order to implement the three strategies of diversification, building local technological capacity and restructuring the labour market to achieve long term economic growth and sustainable economic development.
2. In the short and medium term, the Gulf countries are unable to rely on local skills and local technologies and will remain heavily dependent on both foreign skills and foreign technologies.
3. The interaction between the deficient educational system and the high incidence of uneducated foreign workers leads to low skill and technology levels and many other serious implications.

3.a. The deficient educational system is caused by low quality of education and leads to: (a) poor provision of training; (b) low skill levels; (c) skills mismatch; (d) low transfer of knowledge/external schooling effect; (e) weak technology indicators; and (f) dependence on foreign technologies at the macro level.

3.b. The excessive share of low educated foreign workers leads to: (a) low skill levels; (b) serious skills mismatch; (c) poor provision of training; (d) poor technology indicators; (e) weak adaptation of imported technologies; (f) dependence on foreign technologies; and (g) public-private duality at the micro level.

3.c. The major causes of low levels of local technology are low/a lack of R&D activities due to a lack of skills, transfer of knowledge, networks and collaboration between universities and industry/firms.

4.a. Irrespective of the observed differences in skill levels and requirements, the high skill requirements and the prevalent low skill levels – due to high share of unskilled foreign workers –lead to skills mismatch, public-private duality and contribute to productivity decline across private firms.

4.b. An increase in skill level– share of high skilled in total employment and in firm size– leads to improved relationships between actual and required education and experience and wages.

4.c. An increase in skill level– share of high skilled in total employment and in firm size– leads to improvements in the complementary relationships between skill, upskilling and technology (ICT).

5. The use of ICT has positive but insignificant/inconclusive effect at the micro level/across firms.

6. The transfer of knowledge/external schooling effects is unsuccessful at the micro and macro levels. The major reasons behind the low transfer of knowledge/external schooling effects are low educational qualifications, and deficient educational and training systems. The major consequences are the lack of networks and collaboration between universities and firms, low R&D efforts and low technology indicators.

7. Knowledge has positive impacts at the macro–micro levels; it can be enhanced by many factors.

7.a. At the macro level codified knowledge is positively correlated with economic growth (GDP); and tacit knowledge is positively correlated with schooling.

7.b. At the macro level codified knowledge and FTER show positive complementary relationships with each other and with technology (patents), publications and cooperation.

7.c. At the micro (firm) level tacit knowledge is positively correlated with technology (expenditures on ICT), upskilling (expenditures on training), profit, productivity, output and output diversification.

7.d. At the micro (firm) level tacit knowledge is positively correlated with market size (firm size, capital, and investment) and firm age.

8. The Gulf countries need to enhance their public- private educational and training policies:

8.a. Skill development depends on: (a) reforming the educational system; (b) enhancing the provision of training; (c) planning skill needs and matching educational output with market needs; (e) enhancing the transfer of knowledge/schooling effect; and (d) incentives and collaboration between public and private institutions.

8.b. The promotion of local technology and adoption of appropriate foreign technologies and the interaction between both to foster economic growth in the Gulf countries depends on skill development. In particular, an enhancement of: (a) skill upgrading: educational and training systems; (b) R&D activities; (c) the transfer of knowledge/schooling effects; (d) networks systems; and (e) incentives to motivate collaboration between universities and firms and between public and private institutions.

8.c. Both upskilling policies (educational and training policies) and transfer of knowledge are consistent at both the macro–micro levels and across public-private sectors.

1.4 Structure of the Research

Considering the research problem, aims, questions and hypotheses, it is convenient in this initial chapter to set out the structure of the thesis. This research is composed of four parts and nine chapters structured in the following way. Part I presents the introduction and motivation of the research and includes both Chaps. 1 and 2. Chapter 1 presents an introduction and briefly shows the aims, importance, relevance, hypotheses, questions and the general structure of the research. Chapter 2 explains some stylized facts about the Gulf countries that help to investigate more extensively the research problem along with other strategic problems and challenges confronting economic development, the impacts of oil and the Dutch disease in the structure of the labour markets and economies in the Gulf countries. In addition, this chapter aims to assess and elaborate the low skill and technology indicators and the gap in the Gulf compared to rapidly advanced countries and to show some stylized facts that justify and highlight the need for skill upgrading and technological development in these countries.

Part II presents the conceptual and theoretical framework and includes Chap. 3, which defines the concepts and describes the measures of technological change and human capital (education) and briefly explains the theoretical and empirical literature on the relationship between human capital, technological changes and economic growth. The purpose of this survey is to provide a background for our study, mainly to highlight the endogenous effects of technical change and human capital as confirmed in the endogenous growth literature to motivate the empirical analysis in the next chapters.

Part III presents the empirical application and includes Chaps. 4, 5, 6 and 7. Chapter 4 defines the methods of data collection; identifies the motives for performing the macro and firm surveys and selection of a case study; specifies the selection of the sample and the composition, operation, coverage, advantages and limitations of the survey's data; and shows the structure and design of the questionnaire. Next, Chap. 5 uses the data and results from the firm and macro surveys to examine the serious implications of the interaction between the deficient educational system and the high incidence of unskilled foreign workers. In particular, we use the results from the macro survey to show the causes of the deficient educational system and consequences on low skill levels, poor provision of training, skills mismatch and lack of/low transfer of knowledge at the macro level. In addition, we use the results from the firm survey to illustrate the implications of the high incidence of unskilled foreign workers on causing a low skill levels, poor provision

Research aims	Research Hypotheses	Research Chapters
		Chapter 1
1. To show why the Gulf countries need to promote the local skill and local technologies.	1. The Gulf countries need to promote the local skills and local technologies in order to implement the three strategies of diversification, building local technological capacity and restructuring the labour market to achieve long term economic growth and sustainable economic development.	Chapter 2
2. To examine whether the Gulf countries are able to rely on local skills and local technologies.	2. In the short and medium term, the Gulf countries are unable to rely on local skill and local technologies and will remain heavily dependent on both foreign skills and foreign technologies.	Chapters 2 and 5
3. To show deficiencies in this respect. To show the causes and consequences behind a low level of skills and technologies: causes and consequences of deficient educational system and high use of unskilled foreign workers.	3. The interaction between the deficient educational system and the high incidence of uneducated foreign workers leads to low skill and technology levels and many other serious implications: 3.a. The deficient educational system is caused by low quality of education and leads to: (a) poor provision of training; (b) low skill levels; (c) skills mismatch; (d) low transfer of knowledge/external schooling effect; (e) weak technology indicators; and (f) dependence on foreign technologies at the macro level. 3.b. The excessive share of low educated foreign workers leads to: (a) low skill levels; (b) serious skills mismatch; (c) poor provision of training; (d) poor technology indicators; (e) weak adaptation of imported technologies; (f) dependence on foreign technologies; and (g) public-private duality at the micro level. 3.c. The major causes of low levels of local technology are low/ a lack of R&D activities due to a lack of skills, transfer of knowledge, networks and collaboration between universities and industry/firms.	Chapters 2, 5, 6 and 8
4. To compare the relationships between technology, upskilling, skill and growth across firms.	4.a. Irrespective of the observed differences in skill levels and requirements, the high skill requirements and the prevalent low skill levels–due to high share of unskilled foreign workers-lead to skills mismatch, public-private duality and contribute to productivity decline across private firms. 4.b. An increase in skill level-share of high skilled in total employment and in firm size leads to improved relationships between actual and required education and experience and wages. 4.c. An increase in skill level-share of high skilled in total employment and in firm size leads to improvements in the complementary relationships between skill, upskilling and technology (ICT).	Chapters 5, 6 based on 3
5. To examine the effect of ICT at the micro level/ across firms.	5. The use of ICT has positive but insignificant/inconclusive effect at the micro level/across firms.	Chapter 6
6. To test the incidence of external schooling effect/ transfer of knowledge and to show the major factors hindering the transfer of knowledge and consequences at both macro and micro levels.	6. The transfer of knowledge/external schooling effects is unsuccessful at the micro and macro levels. The major reasons behind the low transfer of knowledge/external schooling effects are low educational qualifications, and deficient educational and training systems. The major consequences are the lack of networks and collaboration between universities and firms, low R&D efforts and low technology indicators.	Chapters 5
7. To illustrate the impacts of knowledge at both the micro and macro levels and the factors enhancing tacit knowledge at the micro level.	7. Knowledge has positive impacts at the macro-micro levels; it can be enhanced by many factors. 7.a. At the macro level codified knowledge is positively correlated with economic growth (GDP); and tacit knowledge is positively correlated with schooling. 7.b. At the macro level codified knowledge and FTER show positive complementary relationships with each other and with technology (patents), publications and cooperation. 7.c. At the micro (firm) level tacit knowledge is positively correlated with technology (expenditures on ICT), upskilling (expenditures on training), profit, productivity, output and output diversification. 7.d. At the micro (firm) level tacit knowledge is positively correlated with market size (firm size, capital and investment) and firm age.	Chapter 7
8. To suggest some relevant mechanisms and policies for enhancing skill development and upgrading of local technologies.	8. The Gulf countries need to enhance their public-private educational and training policies: 8.a. Skill development depends on: (a) reforming the educational system; (b) enhancing the provision of training; (c) planning skill needs and matching educational output with market needs; (e) enhancing the transfer of knowledge/schooling effect; and (d) incentives and collaboration between public and private institutions. 8.b. The promotion of local technology and adoption of appropriate foreign technologies and the interaction between both to foster economic growth in the Gulf countries depends on: skill development. In particular, an enhancement of: (a) skill upgrading: educational and training systems; (b) R&D activities; (c) the transfer of knowledge/schooling effects; (d) networks systems; and (e) incentives to motivate collaboration between universities and firms and between public and private institutions. 8.c. Both upskilling policies (educational and training policies) and transfer of knowledge are consistent at both the macro-micro levels and across public-private sectors.	Chapters 8 and 9

Scheme 1.1 Research Outline: summary of research aims, hypotheses and structure of the chapters

of training, skills mismatch, poor technology indicators and a heavy dependence on foreign technologies. Furthermore, we investigate from the micro–macro perspectives the transfer of knowledge, upgrading of skill and technology and their potential implications, and we also present a more comprehensive assessment of technology and skill indicators at the micro level. Chapter 6 aims to broaden our analysis in Chap. 5 by providing an in-depth analysis of skill and technology indicators, the relationship between them, and the implications of the prevalence of low-skilled foreign workers on skills mismatch and the public-private duality at the micro level. We use the data from the Firm Survey (2002) to examine the relationships between skills (actual and required education and experience) and wages; between skill, upskilling (ICT training) and technology (ICT); and between technology (ICT) and input–output indicators across firms. We also compare the relevance of our results to the theoretical framework in Chap. 3 and the findings concerning these relationships in the new growth literature. Chapter 7 extends our analysis in Chap. 5 on the transfer of knowledge. We use the data from the Firm Survey (2002) at the micro level and some secondary data at the macro level to discuss the importance (impacts) of knowledge in the UAE/Gulf countries. In particular, we check the relevance of some stylized facts about the importance (impacts) of knowledge at the micro–macro levels to the findings in knowledge literature.

Finally, Part IV presents the policies, recommendations and conclusions and includes Chaps. 8 and 9. Chapter 8 concludes our analysis by discussing educational policies, since our earlier analysis in Chap. 5 investigates the causes and consequences of deficient educational and training systems, the lack of knowledge transfer and upskilling, and the results set in Chaps. 6 and 7 imply the importance of a good education. From that perspective, therefore, Chap. 8 discusses the supply–demand sides and implications of educational policies in the Gulf countries. In addition, we use the results from the macro and Firm Surveys (2002) to examine the macro–micro views and suggestions for relevant mechanisms and policies for skill upgrading via an enhancement of the educational system and the provision of training and transfer of knowledge/external schooling effects at the macro–micro levels in the UAE. Finally, Chap. 9 summarizes the major findings, compares the main results with the findings in the general literature and contributions to the Gulf literature and concludes with policy recommendations.

Scheme 1.1 summarizes the main outline of research aims, hypotheses and structure of the chapters.

References

Abdelkarim, A., & Haan, H. (2002). *Skills and training in the UAE: The need for and the dimensions of institutional intervention* (Policy Research, Vol. 5). Dubai, UAE: Centre for Labour Market Research and Information.

Alfakhery, J. J. (1999). *Human development indicators in the UAE: A comparative study of UNDP Human development reports 1994–1998* (Labour and Social Research and Studies Series, Vol. 1, pp. 81–82). Dubai, UAE: The UAE Ministry of Labour and Social Affairs – Department of studies, research and statistics. (in Arabic).

Al-Sulayti, H. A. (2002). *Education and human development in the GCC Countries: An analytical study* (ECSSR Strategic Studies, Vol. 71). Abu Dhabi, UAE: ECSSR. (in Arabic).

Benhabib, J., & Spiegel, M. M. (1994). The role of human capital in economic development: Evidence from aggregate cross-country data. *Journal of Monetary Economics, 34*, 143–173. New York.

Devlin, J. (Ed.). (1998). *Gulf economies: Strategies for growth in the 21st century* (ECSSR international studies, Vol. 20). Washington, DC: Center for Contemporary Arab Studies.

El Sabaa, S. (1997). Linking technology to industrial development in the United Arab Emirates. *Trade and Industry Magazine, 22*(263), 16–29.

Firm Survey. (2002, April). *Technological change and skill development: A comparative study of chemical and metal medium and large scale enterprises in the UAE*. UAE: Firm Survey.

Gray, L. (1999). Private sector training and employment: Evaluation and intervention strategies (Specialist Report, Vol.4). Dubai, UAE: The Ministry of Labour and Social Affairs National Strategy for Labour Force Development and Employment Project.

Haan, H. (1999). The UAE: Assessment of technology use in some selected sectors- towards introduction and explaining capital and skill intensive technologies (Specialist Report, Vol.6). Dubai/Amsterdam: National Human Resources Development and Employment Strategy Project.

Khorshid, M. (2000, October 26–29). *A prototype labour market economic interaction modle for a gulf cooperation council country: Impact of structural imbalances and policy measures on medium term performance*. Paper presented at the Seventh Annual Conference of the Economic Research Forum (ERF), Jordan.

Lucas, R. E. (1988). On the mechanics of economic development. *Journal of Monetary Economics, 22*, 3–42. North Holland.

Macro Survey. (2002, April). *Skill creation, human resources development and policy intervention: Interviews with policy makers and experts in the UAE*. UAE: Macro Survey.

Nelson, R., & Phelps E. (1966). Investment in humans, technological diffusion and economic growth. *American Economic Review*: Papers and Proceedings, Vol. LVI, Vol. 61: 69–75.

Romer, P. M. (1990). Endogenous technological change. *Journal of Political Economy, 98*(5, Part 2), 71–102.

The UAE University. (1994). *The UAE education assessment report*. Al-Ain, UAE: The UAE University.

The UAE University. (1997). *Private sector employment and labour market in the UAE*. Al-Ain, UAE: The UAE University.

Chapter 2
Economic Development Challenges in the Gulf and the Need for Skill Upgrading and Technological Development

2.1 Introduction

In Chap. 1 we introduced the research problem, the aim of this chapter is twofold: first, to present a background to motivate the research by explaining some stylized facts to examine more extensively the research problem along with other strategic problems confronting economic development in the Gulf countries. Second, to highlight the need for upskilling and technological development in these countries.

The Gulf countries have strategic importance in the global economy because the region holds 40 % of world oil supplies (Devlin, 1998) and therefore affects the trends of oil supply and market.[1] At the regional level, oil provides a significant contribution for developing the economies and social welfare in the Gulf, in particular, it leads to higher per capita income. However, the Gulf countries are now confronted with serious challenges posed by oil being an exhaustible resource as well as the uncertain and volatile revenues from oil, because of instability of oil prices. Hence, economic growth and sustainable development strategy in the Gulf depends on both a shift in the focus from an oil resources based economy to a technology and skill based economy and on economic diversification. Also part of this strategy is a shift away from the import of high skilled workers in favour of domestic skilled workers.

Moreover, both the growing employment opportunities and the increased wealth from oil has encouraged migration to the Gulf countries. Consequently, migrant workers have dominated the labour market, particularly in the private sector, which leads to several problematic features such as the low skill levels, duality due to concentration of domestic workers in the public sector and foreign workers in the private sector and a growing unemployment rate. In addition, the Gulf countries

[1] Fasano and Iqbal (2003) indicate that the Gulf region accounts for about 45 % of the world's proven oil reserves and 25 % of crude oil exports (Saudi Arabia is the largest oil exporter). The region possesses at least 17 % of the proven global natural gas reserves (Qatar has become the fourth-largest exporter of liquefied natural gas).

S. Mohamed Nour, *Technological Change and Skill Development in Arab Gulf Countries*, Contributions to Economics, DOI 10.1007/978-3-319-01916-1_2,

suffer from structural problem related to the Dutch disease and lack of incentives, which has also affected the structure of labour market.[2] Moreover, skill and technology indicators in the Gulf countries show poor performance and a substantial gap when compared to international standards. Hence, the upskilling and technological development become imperative to overcome the strategic problems and challenges confronting economic development in the Gulf countries.

The rest of this chapter is organized in the following way. Section 2.2 explains the role of oil in the Gulf economies, discusses the strategic problems facing the labour market in the Gulf and highlights the need for skill upgrading and technological development; Sect. 2.3 concludes.

2.2 Economic Characteristics and Strategic Problems for Development in the Gulf Countries

Since the structure of the Gulf economies is related to oil, it will be useful to start by explaining the role of oil in creating opportunities and challenging economic development in these countries. Next, we show the structural problems related to the labour market, skills, technology and productivity.

2.2.1 Oil and the Opportunities for Development in the Gulf Countries

The Gulf countries are characterized by a small population (except Saudi Arabia) and a high GDP per capita. According to the UNDP human development indicators the average GDP per capita in all Gulf countries is higher than the world average. Moreover, according to the World Bank classification of economies four of the Gulf countries are amongst the higher income and the other two are amongst the upper medium income economies – see Table 2.1 below.

Although the GDP of the UAE is still growing – see Table 2.1 above – as is the foreign and domestic labour force, GDP per capita remains stagnant – see Fig. 2.1 below. This implies that the falling contribution of the oil sector has been compensated so far by other sectors – see Table 2.2 below. However, the big question from Chap. 1 above is whether or not this will work in the future. The stagnation in education, particularly in tertiary education – see our discussion in

[2] "The Dutch Disease is a process in which the discovery of natural resources causes a country to experience a 'change in the group of reference' from one that aim at generating a trade surplus in manufacturing to one that able to generate a trade surplus in primary commodities. The country experiencing this disease also shows differences between employment in manufacturing. The process of de-industrialisation due to the discovery of natural resources, mainly natural gas apparent from the case of Holland". (cf. Palma, 2003, p. 21)

Table 2.1 Population, GDP per-capita, real GDP growth and unemployment in the Gulf countries (1990–2002)

	Population size (million)[a]	GDP/capita (PPP US $)[a]	Real GDP growth (average annual change in per cent)[b]				Unemployment (in per cent of total labour force)[b]			
Country	2002	2002	1995–2000 average	1999	2000	2001	1990	1995	2000	2001
Bahrain	0.7	17,170	4.3	4.3	5.3	4.8	n/a	10.0	12.0	12.0
Kuwait	2.4	16,240	3.8	−2.9	2.9	−0.6	0.5	1.5	2.1	2.3
Oman	2.8	13,340	3.6	−0.2	5.1	7.3	n/a	n/a	n/a	n/a
Qatar	0.6	19,844	9.4	5.3	11.6	7.2	n/a	n/a	n/a	n/a
KSA	23.5	12,650	1.9	−0.8	4.9	1.2	n/a	n/a	n/a	n/a
UAE	2.9	22,420	5.7	3.9	5.0	5.1	n/a	n/a	n/a	n/a
Total GCC	32.9	16,944	3.3	0.3	5.1	2.5	0.5	5.8	7.1	7.2

[a]UNDP (2004) Human Development Report (2004)
[b]The International Monetary Fund (IMF): World Economic Outlook. September 2002; IMF; staff estimates. I/Simple average: nationals only for Bahrain

Chap. 8 below – makes us fairly sceptical, as we argue in the introductory chapter too. In particular, because investment in human capital is going on all over the world, mainly because a sufficiently high quality of education is essential prerequisite for high value added. In addition, as we explain below, the high share of foreign workers indicates that currently the UAE is an agglomeration economy. But it may lose this position and become poor if the oil industry and the complementary ones decline and/or if foreigners leave the country and there is less work in the government sector. Although it is unclear which sector could possibly fill the gap, it is clearly one that will need high levels of education. Therefore, it is quite essential for the government to adopt measures to improve investment and enrolment in education and to upgrade skills.

One should observe that during the past decades the increasing exploitation and development of oil and natural gas reserves have played an important role in developing the economies and raising government revenues, total exports, GDP and GDP per capita in the Gulf countries.[3] Tables 2.2 and 2.3 show that despite the declining share of the oil sector compared to the non-oil sector for all Gulf countries, the share of oil sector remains significant and exceeds 30 % of total GDP, 61 % of total government revenues and 68 % of total exports during the period 1975–1995.[4, 5]

[3] Expect in Bahrain, which shows decreasing trends with respect to both total oil and natural gas reserves.

[4] The share of oil sector refers to the total share of crude oil and oil industries, including refineries, downstream processing and petrochemical, etc. Fasano and Iqbal (2003) indicate that oil contributes about one-third to total GDP and three-fourths to annual government revenues and exports. See also Fasano (2002).

[5] Except in the case of Bahrain, where the share of oil in GDP declines from 26 % in 1975 to 18 % in 1995.

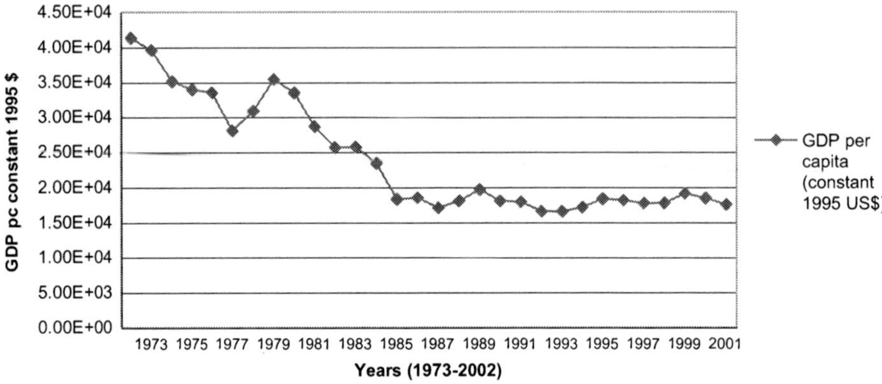

Fig. 2.1 Trend of GDP per capita in the United Arab Emirates (1973–2002) (Constant 1995 US$) (Source: The World Bank, World Development Indicators database (WDI) (2005))

Table 2.2 Proven crude oil and natural gas reserves and the share of oil and non – oil sector in GDP in the Gulf countries (1980–2002)

	Crude oil reserves (in million barrels)				Crude natural gas reserve (in billion cubic meters)			
Country/year	1980[a]	1990[a]	2000[b]	2002[b]	1980[a]	1990[a]	2000[b]	2002[b]
Bahrain	225	100	160[a, c]	160[a, c]	255	173	118[a, c]	118[a, c]
Kuwait	67,930	97,025	96,500	96,500	940	1,518	1,557	1,557
Oman	2,340	4,300	5,240[a, c]	5,240[a, c]	71	204	807[a, c]	807[a, c]
Qatar	3,585	2,993	13,157	15,207	2,800	4,621	14,443	25,768
KSA	168,030	260,004	262,766	262,790	3,183	5,223	6,301	6,646
UAE	30,410	98,100	97,800	97,800	2,730	5,675	6,060	6,060
GCC	272,520	462,522	470,223[d]	472,297[d]	9,979	17,414	28,361[d]	40,031[d]
The share of oil and non – oil sector in GDP (%)								
Year		1974	1985	1990	1995	1998		
Oil sector		75.2	36.1	38.8	34.3	27.2		
Non- oil sector		24.8	63.9	61.2	65.7	72.8		

[a]GOIC Industrial Data Bank (2000b)
[b]OPEC (2002)
[c]Data refers to 1998
[d]Data excludes Bahrain and Oman

Moreover, the concentration of oil reserves is the motivating factor for the bulk of the investments in manufacturing and industrial activities in the Gulf countries being concentrated in Saudi Arabia and the UAE. For instance, Table 2.4 shows that these two countries account for 68.3 % of total number of factories, 80.4 % of total capital investment and 77.1 %, of total employment. Consequently, they account for 78 % of total chemical, petroleum, coal and plastic products; 57 % of total non-metallic mineral products; 76 % of total basic metallic industries and 73 % of

Table 2.3 Oil reserves, share of oil in GDP, government revenues and exports in the Gulf countries (1975–1998)

Country	Years of oil reserves[a]	Share of oil in GDP (%)[a]		Share of oil revenues in total government revenues (%)[a]		Share of oil and gas exports in total exports (%)[a]	Share of oil, chemical, machinery, equipment and manufactured products in total imports (%)[b]	
		1975	1995	1975	1995	1975	1995	1998
Bahrain	5	26	18	77	62	86	70	53.3
Kuwait	136	70	48	74	78	92	95	81
Oman	17	67	37	90	76	98	85	79
Qatar	20	68	36	89	68	96	76	86.6
KSA	82	71	38	80	71	99	95	75.7
UAE	110	68	32	85	88	96	69	86.4
GCC	61.67	61.67	34.83	82.5	73.83	94.5	81.67	79.8

[a]Askari, Nowshirvani and Jaber (1997)
[b]World Development Indicators and GOIC Industrial Data Bank (2000b)

total fabricated metal products, machinery and equipment industrial activities in the Gulf countries.

More recently, the cheap and abundant availability of oil and natural gas in the Gulf region has contributed to an enhancement of the industrial and manufacturing sector; oil, in particular, has promoted the development of the petroleum and petrochemical industries in the Gulf countries. Tables 2.4 and 2.5 indicate that the chemical, petroleum, coal and plastic products; the fabricated metal products, machinery and equipment; and the non-metallic mineral products are the major manufacturing activities in the Gulf and their shares in total number of factories are respectively 18.5 %, 26.7 % and 17 %. In addition, the chemical, petroleum, coal and plastic products category has the highest share among manufacturing industries in terms of capital investment, followed by the fabricated metal industries in terms of the total number of factories and employment.

2.2.2 *Oil and the Challenges of Development in the Gulf Countries*

On the other hand, the heavy dependence on oil has created several serious challenges for development in the Gulf countries. One serious challenge following the discovery of oil is that the Gulf countries suffer from structural problems related to the Dutch Disease phenomenon. For instance, the World Bank (2004) indicates that despite massive efforts to promote industrialization in many of the MENA (including the Gulf) countries, the manufacturing share in employment and output

Table 2.4 Total number and distribution of operating establishments (factories), capital investment and employment in selected industries in the Gulf countries (1998)

	Number of factory (%)[a]					Total capital investment (million dollars) (%)[a]	Total number of workers (%)[a]
Country	All industries (%)[a]	Chemical, petroleum, coal and plastic products (%)[b]	Non-metallic mineral products (%)[b]	Basic metallic industries (%)[b]	Fabricated metal products, machinery and equipment (%)[b]	All industries (%)[a]	All industries (%)[a]
Bahrain	393 (5.5)	54 (4)	58 (5)	9 (10)	81 (4)	5,293 (6.5)	25,554 (4.6)
Kuwait	720 (10.2)	103 (8)	181 (15)	3 (3)	200 (11)	6,659 (8.2)	47,802 (8.6)
Oman	751 (10.6)	86 (6)	183 (15)	8 (9)	151 (8)	1,690 (2.1)	31,737 (5.7)
Qatar	382 (5.4)	55 (4)	96 (8)	3 (3)	67 (4)	2,322 (2.9)	22,195 (4)
KSA	2,996 (42.3)	639 (48)	444 (36)	34 (37)	877 (46)	57,042 (70.1)	282,700 (50.5)
UAE	1,846 (26.0)	407 (30)	261 (21)	36 (39)	520 (27)	8,362 (10.3)	148,509 (26.6)
GCC	7,088	1,344	1,223	93	1,896	81,367	559,352

Note: Figures between brackets represent the share in total Gulf countries
[a]Shiha, M. (2000), p. 21
[b]GOIC Industrial Data Bank (2000b)

was either stagnant or declining in 1970s and 1980s, a result of the Dutch Disease phenomenon.[6] A general increase in expenditures and appreciation of the real exchange rate brought about by the oil windfall resulted in a boom in nontradables, adversely affecting the production of tradable goods (World Bank, p. 104; Corden, 1984; Richards & Waterbury, 1998). The Dutch Disease or deindustrialization appears from the declining share of manufacturing and industry in total exports, GDP and employment – see Figs. 2.2, 2.3, and 2.4 below.

In contrast to the World Bank (2004) argument presented above, a study by Goyal (2003) provides a conflicting argument against the Dutch disease and indicates that the UAE managed to avoid the Dutch disease. "Access to expatriate workers at internationally competitive wages also contributed to avoiding the consequences of a "Dutch disease" usually observed in oil (or other natural

[6] According to the World Bank classification of world regions the Middle East and North Africa (MENA) region is composed of 14 countries, including Algeria, Djibouti, Egypt, Iran, Iraq, Jordan, Lebanon, Libya, Morocco, Oman, West Bank and Gaza: Occupied Palestine Territories, Syrian Arab Republic, Tunisia and Yemen.

Table 2.5 Total number and distribution of establishments (factories), capital investment and employment in the manufacturing industries in the Gulf countries 1998 (defined by industrial categorization)

Industrial category	Number of factory	%	Total capital investment (million dollars)	%	Total number of workers	%
31. Food, beverages and tobacco	1,048	14.8	6,012	7.4	73,471	13.4
32. Textile, wearing, apparel and leather	483	6.8	1,103	1.4	56,990	10.4
33. Wood products including furniture	452	6.4	736	0.9	25,587	4.7
34. Paper products, printing and publishing	455	6.4	1,794	2.2	28,853	5.3
35. Chemical, petroleum, coal and plastic products	1,314	18.5	49,605	61.0	117,805	21.6
36. Non-metallic mineral products	1,173	16.5	9.54	11.1	77,645	14.2
37. Basic metallic industries	93	1.3	6,013	7.4	18,221	3.3
38. Fabricated metal products, machinery and equipment	1,891	26.7	6,730	8.3	137,769	25.2
39. Other manufacturing industries	179	2.5	321	0.4	10,011	1.8
Total	7,088	100	81,368	100	546,352	100

Sources: GOIC Industrial Data Bank (2000b, p. 79) and Shiha, M. (2000, p. 20)

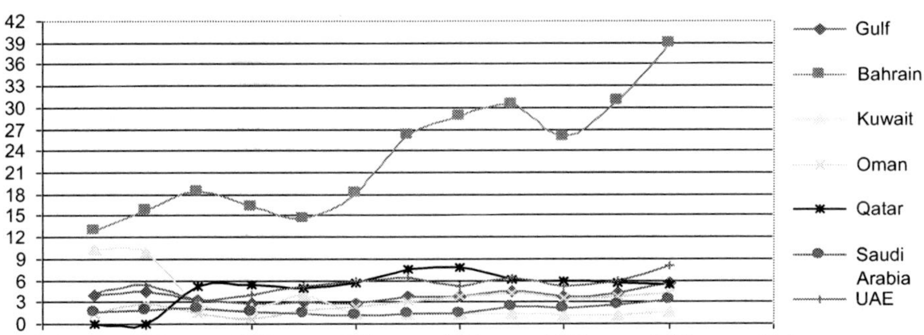

Fig. 2.2 The share of manufacturing in total exports in the Gulf countries (1987–1998) (Source: Adapted from GOIC (1998, 2000a))

resource) rich economies like the UAE. In most of these economies, the formal or organized labor market comprises mainly national. Thus when the world price of oil rises, the wages of these nationals increase, making the non-oil export sector less competitive and encouraging the adoption of import substitution policies. In contrast, the UAE economy has been able to avoid "this disease" because it faces a highly elastic supply of foreign labor at competitive international wages and flexible contracts. In fact, the exogenous decline in real and relative wages of

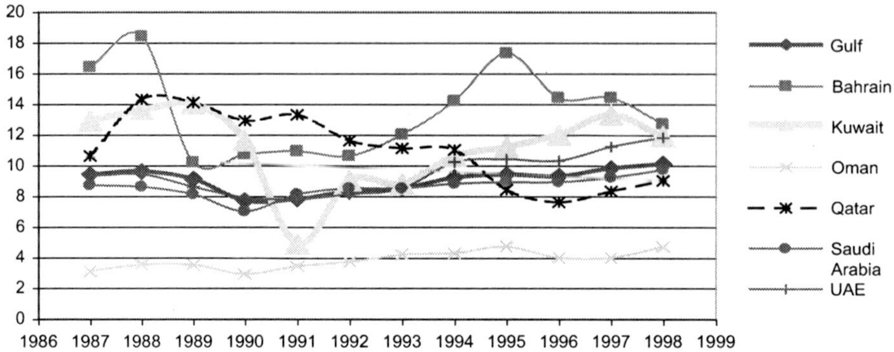

Fig. 2.3 The share of manufacturing in GDP in the Gulf countries (1987–1998) (Source: Adapted from GOIC (1998, 2000a))

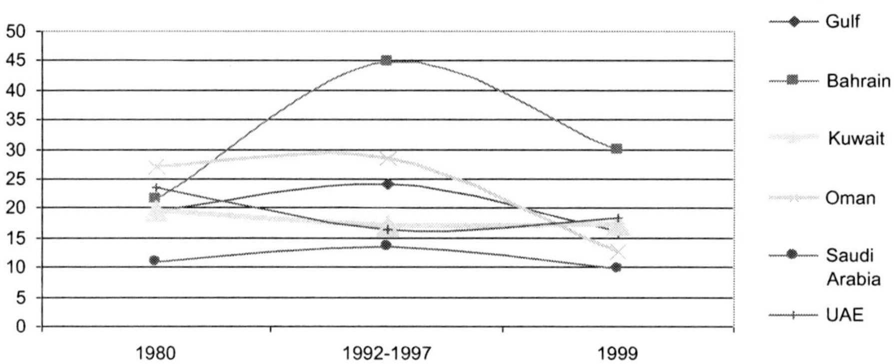

Fig. 2.4 The share of industry in total employment in the Gulf countries (1980–1999) (Sources: Adapted from ERF (2002a, b) and the Joint Arab Economic Report (2001))

low-skilled expatriate workers over the 1990s contributed to boosting employment and output growth by lowering relative labor costs. As a result, employment of low skilled workers was especially strong in that period, as was the growth of sectors such as trade and construction that use low-skilled workers more intensively" (cf. Goyal, p. 46).

Moreover, although oil has contributed to the enhancement of economic development in the Gulf, the general instability of oil prices in the world market and the extreme dependence on uncertain oil revenues lead to serious fluctuations and challenges confronting economic development in the Gulf region - see Fig. 2.5 below. Hence, economic diversification in the Gulf becomes more pressing. The success of the diversification strategy is contingent upon availability of appropriate skills and human resources development.

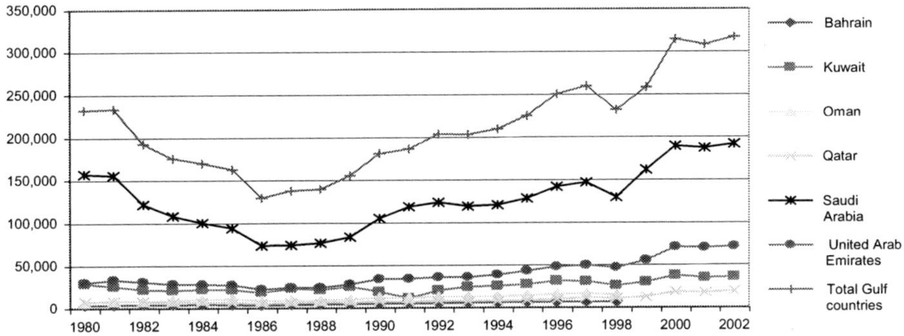

Fig. 2.5 The trend of total GDP in the Gulf countries at current prices (1980–2002) (Million US$) (Sources: (a) GOIC Industrial Data Bank (2000b) and (b) OPEC (2002))

Furthermore, other serious problems facing the Gulf economies appear from the declining reserves of oil and natural gas. Table 2.3 above predicts that oil reserves are likely to last for a century only for a half of the Gulf countries, namely, Saudi Arabia, Kuwait and the UAE, whereas for the other half, Bahrain, Oman and Qatar, proven reserves are likely to be exhausted within the next two decades. In order to avoid the risks of over dependence on diminishing oil resources, the Gulf countries are determined to decrease their dependence on oil revenues and diversify their sources of income. A diversification strategy, mainly industrial diversification, is required to shift to non-oil industries to encourage the development of a wide range of manufacturing industries. Table 2.6 indicates that in the last decade the extent of economic diversification – measured by exports diversification index (excluding oil) – varies across the Gulf countries and shows only a relative success in both Oman and Qatar. However, in general, the average performance for all Gulf countries has declined over the same period of time (Economic Research Forum for the Arab Countries, Iran and Turkey [ERF], 2002a).[7]

Our results presented above indicate that although the Gulf countries share many economic characteristics, there are important differences among these countries. For instance, the per capita income ranges from less than $13,000 in Saudi Arabia to $22,420 in the United Arab Emirates. The structure and composition of the economy and the degree of diversification also vary across the Gulf countries. For instance, the weight of the manufacturing sector has been growing very rapidly in Saudi Arabia, as with the trade and related activities sector in the United Arab Emirates, the banking and insurance sector in Bahrain, the natural gas sector in Qatar, and natural gas resources and tourism in Oman (cf. Fasano & Iqbal, 2003).

[7] The exports diversification index is a measure of products diversification -it assigns a value of zero to the most diversified economies and a value of one to the least. It aims to widen the range of the exports products, to expand exports base and reduce the concentration in a few commodities such as agricultural or raw materials and minerals. For the Gulf countries, the exports diversification index especially defines the move away from primary exports or the dependency on oil exports (ERF, 2002a, p. 53).

Table 2.6 Exports diversification index in the Gulf countries (1980–1990)

	Including oil		Excluding oil	
Countries	Mid 1980	Mid 1990	Mid 1980	Mid 1990
Bahrain	n/a	0.56	n/a	0.55
Kuwait	n/a	0.59	n/a	0.63
Oman	0.91	0.74	0.33	0.27
Qatar	0.71	0.64	0.41	0.34
Saudi Arabia	0.77	0.75	0.57	0.57
United Arab Emirates	n/a	0.36	n/a	0.36
Average Gulf countries	0.7966	0.6066	0.43666	0.4533

Source: ERF (2002a, p. 53)

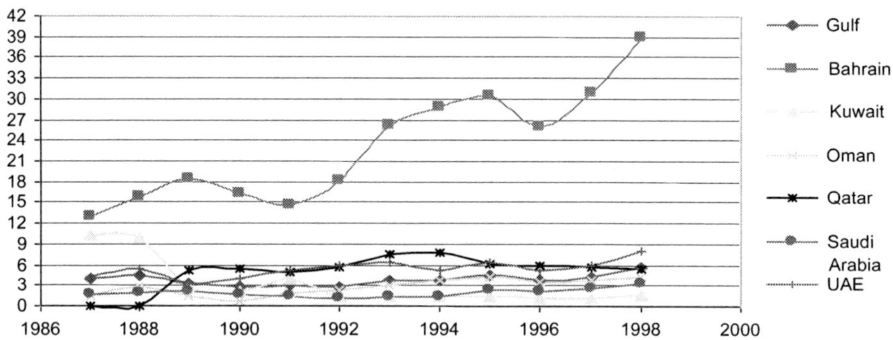

Source: Adapted from GOIC (1998, 2000a)

Differences also remain in the degree of industrialization and the role of manufacturing sector. For instance, Figs. 2.2, 2.3, and 2.4 above indicate that Bahrain seems to be different from the other Gulf countries in terms of the share of industry in total employment (1980–1999) and the share of manufacturing sector in total exports and in GDP (1987–1998). Bahrain seems to have opted to invest more in manufacturing to diversify the economy, probably because of the more sound institutional settings and policies that were adopted to increase industrialization, Bahrain being compelled to act by the fast depletion of its oil resources as compared to the other Gulf countries.

2.2.3 *Structural Problems of the Labour Market in the Gulf Countries*

In addition to the challenges associated with the heavy dependence on oil, the structure of the labour markets in the Gulf countries shares several problematic features. One serious structural problem related to oil, and probably also to the Dutch disease, is the minor share of the manufacturing sector in total

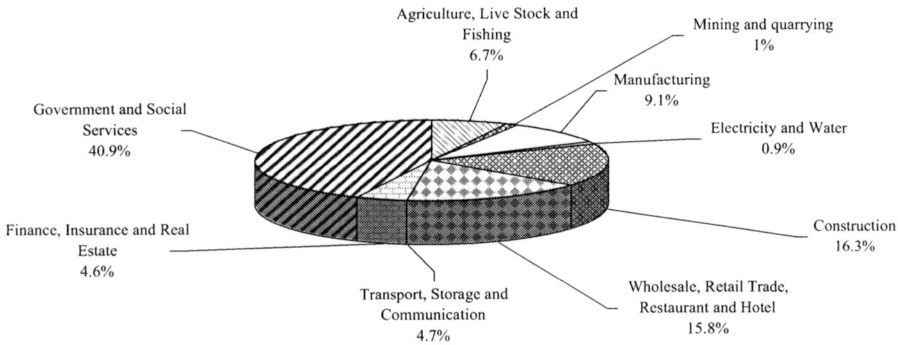

Fig. 2.6 The share of economically active population in economic activities in the Gulf countries 1998 (Source: GOIC Industrial Data Bank (2000b))

employment as the majority of the economically active population is employed by the services sectors. For instance, Fig. 2.6 below illustrates that the services, construction, sales and trade sectors employ 73 % of total economically active population, the government and social services sector alone accounts for 40.9 %, while the manufacturing sector absorbs only 9.1 % of the total economically active population.

Moreover, the labour market in the Gulf countries is characterized by serious structural imbalances due to the minor and declining share of nationals workers in the total labour force when compared to foreign workers – see Table 2.7 below.[8] Several studies (cf. Gray, 1999; Haan, 1999; Issawi, 1982; Serageldin, Socknat, Birks, Li, & Sinclair, 1983) interpret the imbalanced structure in both population and labour market as consequences of the low density of population, shortage of domestic workers, the influx of migrants and a heavy dependence on foreign workers. The migration to the Gulf countries during the last three decades was encouraged in response to the increasing demand for workers to support development projects established following the increasing wealth from oil revenues in the Gulf. The major implication of the dominance of foreign workers in the labour market is the increasing competition for employment opportunities available for national workers, particularly in the private sector of the economy in the Gulf countries. For instance, despite the high share of private sector workers in total

[8] During 1975–1995, the percentage of national to total manpower has decreased in all Gulf countries except in Bahrain. "Available data indicate that the number of expatriate workers is about 7.8 million in 1999, of whom 3.5 million are Arabs (or about 45 %) and 4.3 million are Asians. The former group is dominated by workers from Egypt and, to a lesser extent, Palestine and Sudan. The latter group is made up primarily of workers from India and Pakistan and to a much lesser extent, Iran." ERF (2000, Chap. 5).

Table 2.7 The share of national and foreign labour in total labour force in the Gulf countries (1975–1995)

	Share of foreign labour in total labour force (%)[a]				Share of national labour in total labour force (%)[b]			Annual growth rate of national labour (%)[b]		Annual growth rate of foreign labour (%)[b]	
Country/year	1975	1980	1985	1990	1975	1985	1995	1975–1985	1985–1995	1975–1985	1985–1995
Bahrain*	80.3	59.3	67.7	75.0	18.2	42.1	40	6.6	2.4	11	2.9
Kuwait	69.8	78.1	81.1	82.0	18.2	14.3	16.6	5.6	6.2	8.2	4.6
Oman	45.5	40.0	56.6	75.4	68.9	48.2	35.8	1.4	3	5.1	6.2
Qatar	85.5	81.6	75.5	81.0	17	23.5	17.9	7.3	5.2	3.8	8.1
KSA	25.2	58.3	64.2	78.6	74.8	37.5	36.5	1.2	1.4	8.5	4
UAE	81.4	89.7	87.6	83.5	16	12.4	11.6	3.9	5.5	6.5	6.2
Weighted average Gulf	64.6	67.8	72.1	79.3	61	33.2	26.4	1.7	2.1	8	4.5

Footnote: (*) Data for Bahrain is in respect of census years 1971, 1981, 1985 (estimate) and 1991

[a]Figures through 1990 are from Gameldin (1994)

[b]Girgis (2000)

employment in both Kuwait (70 %) and the UAE (83 %), the share of national workers in the private sector does not exceed 2 % (Khorshid, 2000, p. 6, p. 3).[9]

In addition, the heavy and increasing dependence on foreign workers, especially in the private sector, result in contrasting implications: on the one hand, the high skilled foreign workers have positive impacts on enhancing productivity and output in the private sector. On the other hand, one major drawback related to the heavy dependence on foreign workers is the leakage of foreign remittances away from the Gulf countries, which results in a drain on the current account balance and GNP. For example, in 1990 the remittances from the foreign workers accounted for 20–66 % of the total import bills of the Gulf countries (Datta, Nugent, & Samman, 2000, p. 5; Girgis, 2000). In addition, the excessive use of unskilled foreign workers leads to low skill levels and contributes to declining productivity of labour, as we will explain below and in Chaps. 5 and 6.

Moreover, another common characteristic challenging the labour market in each of the Gulf countries is the dualistic feature that appears from the concentration of domestic workers in the public sector and foreign workers in the private sector. A fact that has been well documented in the Gulf literature is that the national workers lack incentives to work in the private sector and prefer to work in the public sector because the public sector offers higher salaries, subsidies, shorter working hours and other benefits. For instance, Gray (1999) finds that in the UAE, the private sector prefers to employ foreign workers, because they are more productive, less expensive and accept flexible employment contracts. In contrast, the national workers are considered less productive, more expensive and do not possess the prerequisite skills. Both subsidy and wage premiums offered to domestic workers lead to considerable variations in the distribution of average wages between domestic and foreign workers. Further evidence of the dualistic nature and differences in wage premiums and average working hours for both domestic and foreign workers in Kuwait appears from the results of Wadi's study (2001). These results imply the duality and inequality characterizing the distribution of average wages in the Gulf countries.

Furthermore, Table 2.1 above indicates that the average rate of unemployment increased rapidly from 0.5 in 1990 to 7.2 % in 2001. "The labour markets in the Gulf countries are experiencing serious growing trend of both structural and cyclical unemployment. The incidence of structural unemployment is related to discrepancy between the demand for and the supply of workers due to changes in the structure of the economy and the mismatch in both skills and wages premium

[9] See Khorshid (1997, 2000), Gray (1999), Haan (1999) and Cohen (2000) respectively. Gray (1999) finds that the UAE is more dependent on non-national workers than its neighbours, particularly in the private sector. Private sector employers in the UAE are distinctive in their dependence on importing ready-made skills, rather than investing in training nationals in the requisite skills, the sector is currently staffed almost entirely by expatriate workers, with nationals comprising only 2 % of its workforce (Gray, p. 5). The UAE Population Census data (1995) indicates that the non-national constitutes about 75.6 % of total population and 90.9 % of total work force.

for national workers. The major interpretation is related to the failure of the demand to respond to the recent increase in the supply of new national job seekers, (majority of whom do not possess the skill much in demand by private sector)" (ERF, 2000; Girgis, 2000; Khorshid, 2000). "The rapid increase in domestic work force of the Gulf nationals is attributed to the rapid growth in the domestic population, rising participation rates of female workers and projected increase in the share of the economically active population. For instance, during the period (1985–1995), the supply of national manpower in Kuwait, Qatar and the UAE grew by 6.2 %, 5.2 % and 5 % respectively, while, the average growth rate of the national job seekers increased from 1.7 % during the period (1975–1985) to 2.1 % during the period (1985–1995)" (Khorshid, p. 3, p. 6). Moreover, "the Gulf countries suffer from cyclical unemployment that attributed to economic slowdown caused mainly by the instability of the oil prices and revenues. That leads to decline in government spending and had caused serious reduction in the demand for workers and growth rate of employment, particularly in the public sector. The failure of the private sector to fill the gap, due to preference for hiring foreign rather than national workers in the sector created an open unemployment phenomenon especially among the national workers in the Gulf countries" (ERF, p. 118; Girgis; Khorshid, p. 3, p. 5).

Therefore, the Gulf countries need to restructure the labour market, to create more jobs to absorb the growing supply of workers, especially skilled national workers, reduce the unemployment rate and dependence on foreign workers. To that end, more attention needs to be paid to enhancing investment and incentives for public and private sector education and training, mainly tertiary and technical education, and training to promote adequate and appropriate local skills.

2.2.4 The Low Skill Levels in the Gulf Countries

Further to the challenges associated with the extreme dependence on oil and structure of labour market, other serious problem for economic development in the Gulf countries is the low skill levels or educational qualifications of both domestic and foreign population.[10] As we will explain below and in the Chaps. 5 and 8, the low skill levels that appear from several indicators at both macro and micro levels can be attributed to both the deficient educational system and the excess supply of unskilled foreign workers in the Gulf countries. For instance, 67 % of the UAE foreign population have educational qualifications below secondary schooling, 68 % and 72 % of Kuwait foreign workers were either unskilled or low skilled in 1989 and 1999 respectively (cf. Al-Tony, 2002; UAE, 1998, 1999). At the macro level, Table 2.8 indicates that the low skill levels in the Gulf when compared

[10] Similar to other developing countries, the Gulf countries have low skill levels. The more specific feature of the Gulf countries is the low skill levels in a majority of foreign workers.

to World advanced countries are evident from several indicators, including the Harbison Myers Index, the technical enrolment index, the engineering index, the share of tertiary students in science, math and engineering, gross enrolment at tertiary education and school life expectancy.[11] Skill indicators vary enormously across the Gulf countries, for instance, skill indices and gross enrolment ratios in Kuwait and Saudi Arabia are higher than the UAE, while the opposite is true with respect to the share of tertiary students in science, math and engineering. In addition, school life expectancy is higher in Bahrain and Qatar compared to the UAE, Saudi Arabia and Kuwait.

Moreover, Fig. 2.7 illustrates the low skill levels – measured by occupational classification – as the share of white collar/high skilled class accounts for only 16.4 % of total Gulf population, compared to 83.6 % for blue collar/low skilled class. The occupational classification indicates the low share of skilled foreign and national workers; Khorshid (2000) finds that in both the UAE and Kuwait the share of skilled and semi skilled national workers in the total supply are below 5 %. The national workers are greatly biased towards clerical work, military occupations, teachers and non scientific professions, and senior managers. For instance, in Kuwait the share of clerical and policemen; managers and supervisor professions; and teachers represent 41 %, 17 % and 13 % of total labour force respectively, whereas the share in remaining professions does not reach 7 %. The national workers participation rates in four occupational groups: teachers, social scientists, managers and supervisors and clerical exceed 50 % of the total number of workers. Similarly, the UAE shows a low share of national workers in most of occupational

[11] We use many indicators to measure skill levels. For instance, the Harbison Myers Index is sum of secondary enrolment and tertiary enrolment times 5, both as % of age group. Technical enrolment index is tertiary total enrolment (times 1,000) plus tertiary enrolment in technical subjects (times 5,000), both as % of population, Engineering skills index is the same as previous index, with tertiary enrolment in engineering instead of enrolment in technical subjects (Lall, 1999, p. 52). In addition, we use school life expectancy as another measure of skill; according to the UNESCO technical specifications, school life expectancy is one indicator on access to schooling, and is defined as "the total number of years of schooling which a child of a certain age can expect to receive in the future, assuming that the probability of his or her being enrolled in school at any particular age is equal to the current enrolment ratio for that age"- cf. the UNESCO web site. This indicator shows the overall level of development of an educational system in terms of the number of years of education that a child can expect to achieve. We observe that the data used for the estimation of the UNESCO school life expectancy refers to enrolment by age at all levels of education. For that reason, these figures are higher than those of Barro and Lee (2000), which have been used in the UNDP (2001) figures on mean/average years of schooling and refer to age 15 and above. For instance, the UNESCO school life expectancy accounts for 13 and 8.7 in both Bahrain and Kuwait respectively, while Barro and Lee (2000) and the UNDP (2001) mean years of schooling accounts for 6.1 and 6.2 in both Bahrain and Kuwait respectively. However, we use the UNESCO figures in our analysis because Barro and Lee (2000) and the UNDP (2001) figures are available only for Bahrain and Kuwait.

Table 2.8 Skill indicators in the Gulf countries compared to World countries (1992–2000)

	Skill indices (1995)[a]			Gross enrolment ratio (%) at tertiary education	Share tertiary students in science, math and engineering	School life expectancy	
Country	Harbison Myers Index[a]	Technical enrolment index[a]	Engineering enrolment index[a]	1998–2002/2003[b]	1994–1997[c]	1992[d]	2000[e]
Bahrain	n/a	n/a	n/a	21	n/a	13.5	13.0
Kuwait	19.10	36.49	30.57	21	23	7.0	8.7
Oman	8.95	5.35	4.44	7	30	n/a	8.7
Qatar	n/a	n/a	n/a	23	n/a	11.8	13.1
KSA	13.45	18.96	14.42	22	18	8.5	n/a
UAE	12.20	7.51	5.70	10	27	10.6	10.7
Average Gulf	13.425	17.0775	13.7825	17.33	24.5	10.3	10.8
Norway	38.85	73.52	60.25	74	18	n/a	17
Sweden	34.45	64.50	49.94	62.3	31	13.7	16
USA	50.25	88.10	68.98	81	n/a	16.0	15
UK	37.55	68.69	49.83	64	29	15.7	16
Japan	30.05	63.54	63.54	49	23	13.3	14
Korea	36.10	132.06	113.83	85	34	13.5	15
Singapore	23.05	48.81	44.76	n/a	n/a	n/a	n/a
Mexico	12.95	37.53	31.83	21	31	n/a	12
Brazil	10.15	19.87	15.50	18	22	10.7	15

[a]Lall (1999)
[b]UNESCO – UIS (2004b) Educational statistics (1998–2002/2003): most recent data on gross enrolment in tertiary education
[c]UNDP (2002), Human Development Report (2002)
[d]UNESCO (1996)
[e]UNESCO – UIS (2003): www.unesco.org

classifications except military occupations, where national represents 56 % of the total workers (Khorshid, pp. 6–7).

Therefore, these results highlight the need for reforming the educational and training systems in the Gulf in order to ensure more balanced occupational structure. As we elaborate below and in the next Chapters, the low skill level in the Gulf countries hinders the development of local technologies, productivity and hence economic growth. Since the supply of skills (as shaped by systems of education and training) has not responded fully to the rising demand, skill development has become even more pressing for enhancing productivity of labour, replacing foreign workers with domestic workers, reforming the labour market and developing local technologies.

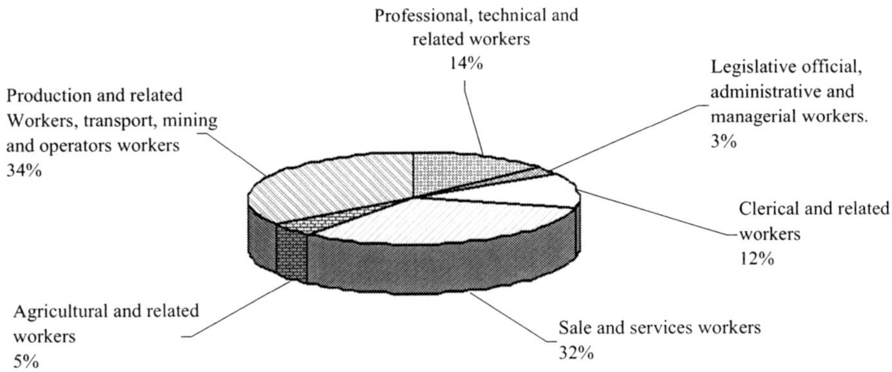

Fig. 2.7 The share of economically active population in the Gulf countries 1998 (defined by occupational level) (Source: GOIC Industrial Data Bank (2000b))

2.2.5 The Low Technological Level and Technological Gap in the Gulf Countries

The low skill levels in the Gulf countries have resulted in poor technological performance and a wide technological gap or distance from the world's rapidly advanced countries such as Singapore, Korea and Malaysia.[12, 13] Table 2.9 illustrates the poor technological performance and technological gap that is manifested in the percentage share of spending on R&D in GDP, the number of scientists and engineers in R&D, patent and population access to Internet, telephone

---

[12] In recent years there is a growing body of literature focusing on technological capability building in the developing countries, for early references, see e.g. Fransman and King (1987), Lall (1987), Enos (1991), Hillebrand, Messner and Meyer-Stamer (1994), United Nations Conference on Trade and Development [UNCTAD] (1996) and Romijn (1999). Early studies on Trinidad and Tobago, Costa Rica and Iran have brief observations indicating that technological capability building is related to current resources based industries, and that governments work only on static capability building. Another earlier study on the Andean countries in 1979 contains a brief remark on multinationals discouraging capability building.

[13] Several indicators have been used to measure the technological distance between nations. Such as the number of patent registrations; per capita expenditure on R&D, or its share in GDP; the number of skilled persons engaged therein; or the ability of the country to master 'frontier' technologies such as, electronic, informatics, new materials, biotechnology, etc.). These measures are useful for indicating weaknesses in specifically defined areas and determining the need for new policies in specific sectors, but they have shortcomings in reflecting the differences in the degree of technological intensity, or of the efficiency of technological inputs. A broader indicator for a multi-dimensional analysis of technological transformation includes the rate of growth of GDP, per capita GDP and productivity that also reflect changes in the structure of production and trade; domestic production of machinery; availability of advanced education; literacy rate, etc. (Patel, 1995).

Table 2.9 Technology indicators in the Gulf countries compared to World countries (1990–2002)

	Population access (per 1,000 people)[a]										
	Internet users		Telephone mainlines		Cellular subscribers		Spending on R&D as % of GDP[a, b]	Scientists and engineers in R&D (per million people)[a]	Patents[a, c]	High technology exports as % of manufactures exports[a]	
Country	1990	2002	1990	2002	1990	2002	1996–2002	1990–2001	1991–1999	1990	2002
Bahrain	0.0	245	191	261	10	579	0.06[b, d]	n/a	2[c, f]	n/a	n/a
Kuwait	0.0	105.8	188	204	12	519	0.22[b, d]	212	27[c, f]	3	n/a
Oman	0.0	70.0	60	92	2	183	0.07[b, d]	4	3[c, f]	2	2
Qatar	0.0	113.4	220	286	9	433	0.06[b, d]	591	0[c, f]	n/a	0
KSA	0.0	64.6	77	151	1	228	0.14[b, d]	n/a	103[c, f]	n/a	n/a
UAE	0.0	313.2	224	291	19	647	0.02[b, d]	n/a	15[c, f]	n/a	2
Average Gulf	0.0	152	160	214	8.83	432	0.095[b. d]	269	25[c, f]	2.5	2
Norway	7.1	502.6	502	734	46	844	1.6[a, e]	4,377	88[a, g]	12	22
Sweden	5.8	573.1	681	736	54	889	4.6[a, e]	5,186	235[a, g]	13	16
USA	8.0	551.4	547	646	39	906	2.8[a, e]	4,099	298[a, g]	33	32
UK	0.9	423.1	441	591	19	814	1.9[a, e]	2,666	71[a, g]	24	31
Japan	0.2	448.9	441	558	7	637	3.1[a, e]	5,321	884[a, g]	24	24
Korea	0.2	551.9	306	489	2	679	3[a, e]	2,880	490[a, g]	18	32
Singapore	0.0	504.4	346	463	17	796	2.1[a, e]	4,052	27[a, g]	40	60
Mexico	0.0	98.5	65	147	1	255	0.4[a, e]	225	1[a, g]	8	21
Brazil	0.0	82.2	65	223	n/a	201	1.1[a, e]	323	0[a, g]	7	19

Patent data for Norway, Sweden, UK, US, Korea and Singapore, Japan, Mexico and Brazil obtained from UNDP (2003) and refers to patents granted to residents per million people in 1999. For all Gulf countries patent data obtained from US patent office during 1991–1999, it refers to the number of registered US patents (in which the inventor of the patent is a resident) that originated from the selected Gulf countries. One limitation of the comparison in our analysis is that we use patent data from two different sources; the scarcity of data and information covering all countries limited our attempt to use a unified source.

[a]UNDP Human Development Report (2004)

[b]Calculated from Qasem (1998a, b) and GOIC (2000a)

[c]US Patent and Trademark office web site: www.uspto.govt

[d]Data refers to 1996

[e]Data refers to 1996–2002

[f]Data refers to 1991–1999

[g]Data refers to 2000

Table 2.10 Distribution of R&D institutional units and full– time equivalent (FTE) researchers by type of R&D Institution in the Gulf countries 1996

	Number of R&D institutions				Number of FTE researchers			
Country/area	Public	University	Private	Total	Public	University	Private	Total
Bahrain	3	1	0	4	27	59	0	86
Kuwait	11	0	4	15	334	83	23	440
Oman	6	0	0	6	56	26	0	82
Qatar	0	6	0	6	4	30	0	34
Saudi Arabia	19	28	2	49	308	538	0	846
UAE	3	2	0	5	56	51	0	107
Total	42	37	6	85	785	787	23	1,595
% Distribution	49.41	43.53	7.06	100	49.22	49.34	1.44	100

Source: Adapted from ESCWA–UNESCO (1998), Research and Development System in the Arab States: Development of Science and Technology Indicators 1998 (E/ESCWA/TECH/1998/3)

and mobile.[14] We observe that, due to the high GDP per capita income in the Gulf countries, both spending and use of ICT/access to Internet, telephone and mobile increased rapidly during the period 1990–2002. Moreover, technology indicators vary enormously across the Gulf countries, for instance, ICT indicators –access to Internet, telephone and mobile – are higher in the UAE than in Kuwait, Saudi Arabia and the other Gulf countries (cf. Nour, 2002a, b), whereas the percentage share of spending on R&D in GDP, the number of scientists and engineers in R&D and patent are higher in both Saudi Arabia and Kuwait compared to the UAE and other Gulf countries.

Poor technological performance is closely related to low R&D spending. More recently the UNESCO-UIS (2004a) indicates a remarkably serious weaknesses of investment in R&D in the Arab (including the Gulf) countries when compared to the New Industrialized Economies of South East Asia, such as China and India, and also compared to Latin America. "Despite efforts to increase investment in R&D, expenditures remain very low in developing countries. In 2000, developing countries spent 0.9 % of their GDP on R&D, still falling short of the target of 1 % mentioned in various S&T policy documents and international declarations for over 30 years.[15] Nevertheless, there is considerable variation across countries...... both sub-Saharan African countries and the Arab states showed much lower levels of R&D expenditures.... To complete the picture, the Arab states show a very low level (0.15 %) of research intensity." (UNESCO-UIS, p. 3).

Furthermore, the distribution of R&D institutions indicates that most of the R&D activities are carried out within the public (49.4 %) and university (43.5 %)

[14] As in most other developing countries, the Gulf countries show poor technological performance. In view of their high GDP per capita income, which is comparable to high-income countries, one would have expected a better performance in the Gulf.

[15] For early references to R&D expenditure target setting, cf. United Nations (1970)"United Nations Science and Technology for Development, Proposals for the Second United Nations Development Decade," New York, 1970.

Table 2.11 Technological structure of manufactured exports in the Gulf and developing countries (1985–1997) (% of total manufactured exports)

	Primary products[a]		Resources based manufactures[a, b]		Low technology manufactures[a, b]		Medium technology manufactures[a, b]		High technology manufactures[a, b]	
Countries	1985	1997	1985	1997	1985	1997	1985	1997	1985	1997
Bahrain[a]	54.4	56.1	10.9	12.5	11.8	13.1	22.0	16.7	0.6	1.5
Kuwait[a]	n/a	n/a	n/a	n/a	n/a	n/a	n/a	n/a	n/a	n/a
Oman[a]	93.8	76.9	0.7	5.7	0.4	2.6	3.3	11.8	1.2	1.6
Qatar[a]	72.2	67.4	11.0	10.5	5.2	7.9	11.4	13.9	0.1	0.3
KSA[a]	82.7	74.5	13.6	18.0	0.6	1.6	2.9	5.7	0.1	0.2
UAE[a]	22.3	35.6	15.0	14.9	16.1	33.4	33.0	15.7	5.6	0.3
Average Gulf[a]	65.08	62.1	10.24	12.32	6.82	11.72	14.52	12.76	1.52	0.78
World[b, c]	n/a	n/a	n/a	13.7	n/a	21.3	n/a	37.2	n/a	27.7
Singapore[b, c]	n/a	n/a	n/a	12.7	n/a	7.9	n/a	14.0	n/a	65.4
Malaysia[b, c]	n/a	n/a	n/a	17.8	n/a	13.1	n/a	8.7	n/a	60.4
Korea[b, c]	n/a	n/a	n/a	9.4	n/a	28.4	n/a	26.6	n/a	35.7
Mexico[b, c]	n/a	n/a	n/a	7.1	n/a	20.9	n/a	35.2	n/a	36.9
Brazil[b, c]	n/a	n/a	n/a	25.6	n/a	31.8	n/a	34.0	n/a	8.6

[a]Haddad (2001)
[b]Lall (1999) computations based on UNCOMTRADE data 2000 and 1996 respectively
[c]Data refers to 1996

sectors, while the private sector has only a minor contribution and accounts solely for 7 % of total R&D institutions in the Gulf countries – see Table 2.10 below. That also holds for the distribution of human resources available to R&D institutions – defined by the number of full-time equivalent (FTE)[16] researchers. For instance, Table 2.10 illustrates that the majority of FTE researchers are employed by public (49.2 %) and university (49.3 %) sectors, while the private sector absorbs only about 1.4 % of total FTE researchers in the Gulf countries (cf. Nour, 2005a, b). Therefore, these results imply that the private sector, and hence industry, makes only a minor contribution in both human resources (FTE researchers) and total R&D activities, and lags behind most of the industrialized countries, in which more than half of R&D expenditures are financed by industry.[17]

In addition, the large technological gap between the Gulf countries and the world's rapidly advanced countries like Singapore, Malaysia and Korea is also apparent from the technological structure of manufactured exports, in particular the share of high technology exports as a percentage of total manufactured exports. For instance, in contrast to Singapore, Malaysia and Korea, both medium and high technology exports lag behind and constitute only a minor share in total Gulf

[16] The concept of full – time equivalent researcher is adopted by UNESCO statistics on R&D personnel.

[17] See the OECD Second European Report on S&T (1997).

manufacturing exports. In addition, the Gulf countries show heavy concentration on primary and resources based manufactured exports, but serious negligence of medium and high technology exports. The average for Gulf countries also shows a worsening status or declining share of high and medium technologies over the periods 1985–1997 – see Table 2.11 below. Furthermore, the levels of net capital inflows and foreign direct investment indicate a large gap and weak competence of the Gulf countries to attract foreign investment for developing local technologies. For instance, the levels of net capital inflows and foreign direct investment in the Gulf countries fall below those of the rapidly advanced countries, namely Singapore, Malaysia and Korea (cf. UNDP, 2004).[18]

As a result of the poor technological performance and technological distance, the Gulf countries are facing the problem of strong dependence on foreign technologies, which is apparent from the trade balance in technological products.[19] Muysken and Nour (2006) measure the dependence on foreign technology by the share of chemical, machinery, equipment and manufactured products in total imports (Lall, 1999; Patel, 1995). They observe that despite the significant contribution of oil to GDP, government revenues and total exports, the share of chemical, machinery, equipment and manufactured products in total imports remains high in most of the Gulf countries. The high share of crude oil and mineral fuel in total exports together with the strong dependence on foreign technologies indicates a failure to manufacture oil domestically within the Gulf countries. They find that the heavy dependence on foreign technologies varies across the Gulf countries; however, in general, the average for all Gulf countries throughout the period 1989–1998 did not show a considerable change and remained above 70 % (Gulf Organization for Industrial Consulting [GOIC], 2000a, b). They attribute that to a lack of R&D efforts, skills and scientific cooperation and to a poor technology infrastructure (Rasiah, 2002; Zahlan, 1999a, b). Furthermore, the status of the Gulf countries according to the UNDP (2001) classification of world countries according to the technology achievement index (TAI[20])

[18] FDI stimulates the development and dispersion of technology as foreign investors transfer techniques and skills to their local affiliates. These skills then generally spill-over to other companies and institutions in the local markets, and are often the missing resource that countries need to expand their access to international markets and to develop areas in which they have a comparative advantage. FDI also leads to the transfer of important capital goods and intermediate inputs. It can help a country develop new comparative advantages, as was the case with the electronic industry in Southeast Asia. In addition it also contributes to increasing output and/or productivity (Hafasi, 2001, p. 41).

[19] This phenomenon of dependence on foreign technologies is similar to most other developing countries. The Gulf countries, however, are also highly dependent on the import of technical skills to operate them.

[20] According to the UNDP (2001), the technology achievement index (TAI) focuses on four dimensions of technological capacity that are important for reaping the benefits of the network age. TAI includes: (1) Creation of technology as measured by the number of patents granted per capita and receipt of royalty and licenses fees from abroad; (2) Diffusion of recent innovations as measured by diffusion of Internet and export of high and medium technology products as a share of all exports; (3) Diffusion of old innovations as measured by diffusion of telephone and electricity;

Table 2.12 Demand for and supply of technologies in the Gulf countries (1989–1998) (%)

Country/items		1989	1990	1991	1992	1993	1994	1995	1996	1997	1998
Bahrain	Demand[a]	48.7	39.4	45.6	52.4	51.2	50.8	45.2	39.7	44.6	53.2
	Supply[b]	n/a	n/a	n/a.	n/a	n/a	n/a	n/a	n/a	n/a	n/a
Kuwait	Demand[a]	76.5	79.1	87.4	84.5	82.5	80.4	82	81.5	80.7	81
	Supply[b]	28	23	15	63	53	53	34	36	40	48
Oman	Demand[a]	73.8	70.3	75.6	74.7	72.4	73.4	71.7	74.2	76.8	79
	Supply[b]	n/a	n/a	n/a	n/a	8	13	14	16	24	24
Qatar	Demand[a]	78	78.6	79.2	81.8	82.2	80.9	87.7	86.2	86.8	86.6
	Supply[b]	n/a	n/a	n/a	n/a	n/a	n/a	n/a	n/a	n/a	n/a
Saudi Arabia	Demand[a]	78	77.5	80.1	83	84	81.4	77.7	76.4	73.1	75.7
	Supply[b]	32	n/a	n/a	n/a	n/a	n/a	n/a	n/a	n/a	n/a
UAE	Demand[a]	78.5	79.5	66.6	85.3	85.1	85.3	85	86.4	86.4	86.4
	Supply[b]	n/a	n/a	n/a	n/a	n/a	n/a	n/a	n/a	n/a	n/a
Average Gulf	Demand[a]	75.6	74.7	74.3	81.4	81.5	80.2	78.8	78.3	78	79.8
	Supply[b]	30	23	15	63	31	33	24	26	32	36

Notes: The demand side refers to demand for imported technologies (or dependence on foreign technologies) and measured by the share of chemical, machinery, equipment and manufactured products in total imports. The supply side refers to technological specialization and is measured by the share of value added in machinery and transport equipment/GDP

[a]GOIC (1998, 2000a)

[b]World Development Indicators database and GOIC (1998, 2000a)

shows that none of the Gulf countries are classified as leaders, potential leaders or dynamic adopters of technologies in the world.

Since Muysken and Nour (2006) discuss only the demand side, using the demand for imported technology or dependence on foreign technologies, it may be interesting to complement their analysis by also examining the supply side. We measure the supply side by multiplying the manufactures/GDP ratio taken from Fig. 2.3 above by value added in machinery and transport equipment as % of value added in total manufactures using WDI data, the result is value added in machinery and transport equipment/GDP, which we use as a measure of specialization in production related to technology. When using this measure, our results show a low technological specialization in the Gulf countries – see Tables 2.12 and 2.13 below.[21]

and (4) Human skills as measured by mean years of schooling and gross enrolment ratio of tertiary students enrolled in science, mathematics and engineering (UNDP, 2001).

[21] Since the recent data from the WDI is available only for Kuwait and Oman, we therefore use an alternative set of indicators from GOIC in Table 2.13. Alternatively, we multiply the manufactures/GDP ratio from Fig. 2.3 above by investment in fabricated metal, machinery and equipment/manufactures and we get investment in fabricated metal, machinery and equipment/ GDP. This measure may have the advantage of increasing the consistency between supply and demand measures. However, it has a limitation and may also be inaccurate for our analysis since it does not reflect machinery and transport/GDP separately. Rather, it tends to somewhat overestimate the actual value as the figures include fabricated metal in addition to machinery and equipment, which are combined together in one category. This is most probably because the only available data is based on the International Standard Industrial Classification of all economic activities according to ISIC 1968 rather than ISIC Rev 3.

Table 2.13 Demand for and supply of technologies in the Gulf countries (1996–1998) (%)

Items	Supply		Demand	
Country/years	1996	1998	1996	1998
Bahrain	61	71	39.7	53.3
Kuwait	22	11	81.5	81
Oman	24	32	74.2	79
Qatar	11	15	86.2	86.6
Saudi Arabia	71	88	76.4	75.7
United Arab Emirates	64	73	86.4	86.4
Average Gulf	42.17	48.33	78.3	79.8

Notes: The demand for imported technologies is measured by the share of chemical, machinery, equipment and manufactured products in total imports, the supply is measured by the share of investment in fabricated metal, machinery and equipment in GDP
Source: Calculated from GOIC (2000a)

Hence, the Gulf countries need to upgrade skills (enhancing education and training), in order to develop local technologies, reduce dependence on foreign technologies, narrow the technological gap, adapt appropriate foreign technologies and enhance economic development. Although the development of local technologies is indeed a costly process, this can be funded from the oil revenues and by offering further incentives to motivate private investment in skill, technology and technical education.

2.2.6 The Declining Productivity of Labour and Economic Growth in the Gulf Countries

In recent times, the Gulf countries are facing serious additional problems due to the declining productivity of labour, value added and economic growth. Table 2.1 above, indicates that the average real GDP growth rate in the Gulf declined from 5.1 % in 2000 to 2.5 % in 2001. In addition, the declining productivity of labour and value added can be interpreted as implications of low skill levels amongst both domestic and foreign workers. For instance, the UAE Reports (UAE Ministry of Labour Report, 1999; UAE Ministry of Planning Report, 1998) indicate that the UAE migrant population shows a quantitative increase rather than a qualitative improvement, which hinders the improvement of skill structure and the average productivity of labour. The reports also indicate that between 1985 and 1995 an increase in the UAE total labour force at 8.1 %, the GDP at constant prices at average annual rate of 7.0 % and private sector employment at average annual rate of 3.2 % during 1990–1995 resulted in an annual decrease in average productivity of labour by 3.8 %. This implies that the UAE was importing an excess supply of unskilled workers, particularly in the private sector, while the marginal productivity was below zero.[22] Moreover, the UAE Ministry of Planning (2004) reported continuous annual decline in the productivity of labour in the period 1997–2002. In addition, Cohen (2000) provides evidence for the declining labour productivity and growth of labour productivity in the manufacturing sector in the UAE in the period 1993–1998. Further evidence of the declining growth rates and declining labour productivity in Kuwait and the UAE appear from the results of Wadi (2001) and Abdelkarim and Ibrahim (2001) respectively.

2.3 Conclusions

This chapter presents an introduction and background to motivate the research and explains some stylized facts, the research problem along with other strategic problems confronting economic development in the Gulf countries. We explain that oil has contributed to economic development in the Gulf countries. However, the heavy dependence on oil leads to serious challenges since oil is an exhaustible resource and also, because of the instability of oil prices, the revenue from oil is uncertain and volatile. Hence, economic growth and the sustainable development strategy in the Gulf depend on economic diversification, which is contingent upon availability of adequate and appropriate skills and technologies. Moreover, we present other serious structural problems in the Gulf countries that are related to the Dutch disease, structural imbalances in the labour market, duality between public and private sectors, growing unemployment, slowdown in economic growth, declining labour productivity and lack of incentives. We illustrate the low skill and technology indicators and the gap the Gulf countries exhibit when compared to rapidly advanced countries.

Hence, we show that the Gulf countries need to upgrade skill levels and motivate development of local technologies to narrow the technological gap and enhance economic development in the region. In our view, the upskilling of workers through enhancing the system of education and training will encourage R&D activities and the adoption of appropriate foreign technologies and so motivate both the development of local technologies and the bridging of the technological gap. Moreover, skill upgrading will facilitate economic diversification, restructuring of the labour market, enhancing productivity of labour, and reducing dependence on foreign workers, duality and unemployment.

Therefore, our findings in this chapter confirm our first hypothesis in Scheme 1.1 Chap. 1 above: the Gulf countries need to promote the local skill and local technologies to face the challenges created by the depletion of oil resources. They also need to implement the three strategies of diversification, building local technological capacity and restructuring the labour market. Our results confirm part of

[22] See the UAE Ministry of Planning Report (1998, p. 31) and the UAE Ministry of Labour Report (1999, p. 14) respectively.

the second hypothesis in Scheme 1.1 Chap. 1 above: in the short and medium term, the Gulf countries will be unable to rely on local skill and local technologies and remain heavily dependent on both foreign skills and foreign technologies at the macro level.

References

Abdelkarim, A., & Ibrahim, S. (2001, December). Productivity problems in the UAE: The role of productivity organization (Policy Research Series, No. 4). Dubai, UAE: Centre for Labour Market Research and Information.

Al-Tony, M. N. (2002, April). *Employment policies and human development in the Arab countries: Analysis of the experience of Kuwait* (Arab Planning Institute working paper series, Vol. 0204). Kuwait: Arab Planning Institute, Kuwait (in Arabic).

Arab Fund for Social and Economic Development. (2001). *The joint (unified) Arab economic report*. Abu-Dhabi, UAE: A joint publication by the Arab Fund for Economic and Social Development, The Arab Monetary Fund, The Arab Organization for Petroleum Exporting Countries, and the League of Arab States.

Askari, H., Nowshirvani, V., & Jaber, M. (1997). *Economic development in the GCC: The blessing and the curse of oil*. Greenwich, CT: JAI Press. In Datta, S. K., Nugent J. B., & Samman, H. (2000, October 26–29). *Labor market and private sector development policies in a labor scare, oil exporting country: A theoretical exploration* (p. 16). Conference Paper, The Seventh Annual Conference of the Economic Research Forum (ERF), Jordan.

Barro, R. J., & Lee. W. (2000, September). International data on educational attainment updates and implications. *NBER working paper series*, No. 7911. Cambridge, MA: National Bureau of Economic Research. http://www.nber.org/papers/w7911.pdf

Cohen, S. I. (2000, September). Employment imbalances in the private sector: Problems, solution and policies (Specialist Rep. No. 9). Dubai, UAE: The Ministry of Labour and Social Affairs: National Strategy for Labour Force Development and Employment Project, Unpublished Report.

Corden, W. M. (1984). Booming sector and Dutch disease economics: Survey and consolidation. *Oxford Economic Papers, 36*(3), 359–380.

Datta, S. K., Nugent J. B., & Samman, H. (2000, October 26–29). *Labor market and private sector development policies in a labor scare, oil exporting country: A theoretical exploration*. Conference Paper, The Seventh Annual Conference of the Economic Research Forum (ERF), Jordan.

Devlin, J. (Ed.). (1998). *Gulf economies: Strategies for growth in the 21st century* (ECSSR international studies, Vol. 20). Washington, DC: Center for Contemporary Arab Studies.

Economic Research Forum for the Arab Countries, Iran and Turkey (ERF). (2002a). Chapter three: Export competitiveness: Where the region stands? In *Economic trends in MENA region 2002* (p. 53). Dokki, Egypt: The ERF and the American University in Cairo.

Economic Research Forum for the Arab Countries, Iran and Turkey (ERF). (2002b). Chapter five: Labor market and human resource development: The GCC labor market: Private vs public. In *Economic trends in MENA region 2002*. Dokki, Egypt: The ERF and the American University in Cairo.

Economic Research Forum for the Arab Countries, Iran and Turkey [ERF]. (2000). Chapter five: Labor market and human resource development: Overview of the labor market in the GCC region, In *Economic trends in MENA region 2000*. http://www.erf.org.eg

Enos, J.L. (1991). The creation of technological capability in developing countries. In *A study prepared for the international labour office within the framework of the world employment programme*. London and New York: Pinter Publishers.

ESCWA- UNESCO. (1998, January). Research and development system in the Arab States: Development of science and technology indicators (*E/ESCWA/TECH/1998/3*). In ESCWA. (1999). *Review of science and technology in ESCWA member countries.* Issue No. 1. 1999 (*E/ ESCWA/TECH/1999/Rev. 1*) (pp. 3–4).

Fasano, G. (2002, October 21). *With open economy and sound policies, U.A.E. Has turned oil "curse" into a blessing, IMF Survey* (pp. 330–332). Washington, DC: International Monetary Fund.

Fasano, G., & Iqbal, Z. (2003, September). *GCC countries: From oil dependence to diversification, IMF publication.* Washington, DC: International Monetary Fund.

Fransman, M., & King, K. (Eds.). (1987). *Technological capability in the third world.* Houndmills, UK: Macmillan Press.

Gameldin, A. I. (1994). *Labour markets in the GCC countries: A survey.* Washington, DC: World Bank.

Girgis, M. (2000). Chapter five: Labor market and human resource development: Overview of the labor market in the GCC region. In *Economic research forum: Economic trends in MENA region 2000.* http://www.erf.org.eg

Goyal, R. (2003, March). Non-oil growth, competitiveness, and the labor market. In *United Arab Emirates: Selected issues and statistical appendix* (IMF Country Rep. No. 03/67) (pp. 41–58). Washington: International Monetary Fund.

Gray, L. (1999, April). *Private sector training and employment: Evaluation and intervention strategies* (Specialist Rep. No.4). Dubai, UAE: The Ministry of Labour and Social Affairs National Strategy for Labour Force Development and Employment Project.

Gulf Organization for Industrial Consulting [GOIC]. (1998). *Gulf statistical profile 1998: GOIC industrial data bank (1998).* Doha, Qatar: GOIC.

Gulf Organization for Industrial Consulting [GOIC]. (2000a). *Gulf statistical profile 2000: Industrial data bank (2000).* Doha, Qatar: GOIC.

Gulf Organization for Industrial Consulting [GOIC]. (2000b). *Features of industrial economy in the Gulf cooperation council countries GCC countries: Gulf industrial base: Industrial data bank.* Doha, Qatar: GOIC.

Haan, H. (1999, January/March). *The UAE: Assessment of technology use in some selected sectors- towards introduction and explaining capital and skill intensive technologies* (Specialist Rep. No. 6). Dubai/Amsterdam: National Human Resources Development and Employment Strategy Project.

Haddad, M. (2001). *Export competitiveness: Where does the Middle East and North Africa region stand? Background paper to economic trends in the MENA region.* Cairo: Economic Research Forum (ERF). In ERF. (2002). ERF economic trends in MENA region 2002: Chap. 2: financial and capital markets, privatization and FDI. Cairo, Egypt: AUC.

Hafsi, T. (2001). Foreign direct investment in the Middle East and North Africa regions: An overview. In *Background note for Economic Trends in the MENA Region.* Cairo: Economic Research Forum. In ERF *(ERF Economic Trends in MENA Region 2002,* ERF (2002): p. 41 (Box 2.2). Cairo, Egypt: AUC.

Hillebrand, W., Messner, D., & Meyer-Stamer, J. (1994). *Strengthening technological capability in developing countries: Lessons from German technical cooperation* (German development institute reports and working papers, Vol. 12/94). Berlin, Germany: German Development Institute.

World Development Indicators in Datta, S. K., Nugent J. B., & Samman, H. (2000, October 26–29). *Labor market and private sector development policies in a labor scare, oil exporting country: A theoretical exploration* (p. 16). Conference paper, the seventh annual conference of the Economic Research Forum (ERF), Jordan.

Issawi, C. (1982). *An economic history of the Middle East and North Africa.* New York: Columbia University Press. pp. 1, 8, 79, 204.

Khorshid, M. (1997). *Analysis of labour markets using economy wide simulation models– theoretical consideration and practical applications*. Finance and Industry- The Industrial Bank of Kuwait No. 15. p. 47.

Khorshid, M. (2000, October 26–29). *A prototype labour market economic interaction modle for a Gulf cooperation council country: Impact of structural imbalances and policy measures on medium term performance*. Paper presented at the seventh annual conference of the Economic Research Forum (ERF), Jordan.

Lall, S. (1987). *Learning to industrialize: The acquisition of technological capability by India*. Houndmills, UK: Macmillan Press.

Lall, S. (1999). *Competing with labour: Skills and competitiveness in developing countries* (Issues in development discussion paper, Vol. 31, p. 17). Geneva, Switzerland: Development Policies Department, ILO.

Muysken, J., & Nour, S. (2006, August). Deficiencies in education and poor prospects for economic growth in the Gulf countries: The case of the UAE. *The Journal of Development Studies, 42*(6), 957–980. Routledge: Taylor and Francis Group Ltd., UK.

Nour, S. (2002a). ICT opportunities and challenges for development in the Arab World, *UNU-WIDER Discussion Paper DP2002/83*. Helsinki. In A. P. D'Costa (Ed.), *The new economy in development: ICT challenges and opportunities* (Series of technology, globalization, and development, Vol. 2, pp. 161–187). Houndmills, Basingstoke: Palgrave Macmillan's.

Nour, S. (2002b, October 26–28). *The impact of ICT on economic development in the Arab World: A comparative study of Egypt and the Gulf countries*. ERF working paper series WP number: 200237. Paper prepared for the ninth annual conference of ERF, Sharjah, UAE.

Nour, S. (2005a, September). Science and Technology (S&T) development indicators in the Arab region: A comparative study of Arab Gulf and Mediterranean countries. *The Journal of Science, Technology and Society (SAGE Publications), 10*(2), 249–274.

Nour, S. (2005b, August). Science and Technology (S&T) development indicators in the Arab region: A comparative study of Arab Gulf and Mediterranean countries. UNU-INTECH discussion paper series UNU-INTECHDPS2005–3, Maastricht, The Netherlands.

OECD. (1997). *The second European report on science and technology indicators (1997)* (pp. 37, 90–91). Paris: OECD.

OPEC. (2002). *OPEC annual statistical bulletin 2002*. Vienna: OPEC.

Palma, G. (2003). *Four sources of de-industrialisation and a new concept of the Dutch disease* (p. 21). Unpublished paper presented at *UNU-INTECH research seminar series 2004–2*, Maastricht, 19 May 2004.

Patel, S. (1995). *Technological transformation: The historic process*, Vol. V. UK: The United Nations University, Avebury Publishing Ltd., p. 98.

Qasem, S. (1998a). *Research and development in the Arab states: Development of science and technology indicators* (Review of science and technology in ESCWA member countries, ESCWA (1999), Vol. 1). New York: United Nations.

Qasem, S. (1998b). Research and development systems in the Arab states: Development of science and technology indicators, Chapter 4. In *Economic trend in MENA region 2002*. Cairo, Egypt: Economic Research Forum and the American University in Cairo.

Rasiah, R. (2002, March). *TRIPs and capability building in developing economies* (UNU/INTECH discussion paper series, Vol. 2002-1). Maastricht: INTECH.

Richards, A., & Waterbury, J. (1998). *A political economy of the Middle East* (2nd ed.). Boulder, CO: Westview Press.

Romijn, H. (1999). *Acquisition of technological capability in small firms in developing countries*. Houndmills, UK: Macmillan Press.

Serageldin, I., Socknat, J. A., Birks, S., Li, B., Sinclair, C. A. (1983). *Manpower and international labour migration in the Middle East and North Africa* (MNS. Rep. No. 10139), Vol. 1.

Shiha, M. (2000, June 29–2). *Improving competitiveness of small and medium size enterprises in the GCC countries*. Paper presented in Arab Experts Meeting on "Improving the performance of Arab Enterprises in the Global Economy," Turin, Italy, pp. 20–22.

The International Monetary Fund. (2002, September). *World economic outlook: the Middle East and North Africa regional outlook*. Washington, DC: The International Monetary Fund.

The UAE Ministry of Economy. (1995). *The UAE population census data (1995)*. Abu Dhabi, UAE: UAE Ministry of Economy.

The UAE Ministry of Labour. (1999). *UAE ministry of labour unpublished labour report (1999)* (p. 14). Dubai, UAE: The UAE Ministry of Labour.

The UAE Ministry of Planning. (1998). *UAE ministry of planning labour report (1998)* (p. 31). Abu Dhabi, UAE: The UAE Ministry of Planning.

The UAE Ministry of Planning. (2004). *Annual report (2004)*. Abu Dhabi, UAE: The UAE Ministry of Planning.

The U.S. Patent and Trademark Office (USPTO). (2005). Annual reports – Various issues 1991–1999. U.S.: US Patent and Trade mark office: http://www.uspto.gov. Accessed April 10, 2005.

The World Bank, World Development Indicators Database (WDI). (2005). http://data.worldbank.org/data-catalog/world-development-indicators. Accessed April 10, 2005.

UNDP. (2001). *Summary human development report (2001): Making new technologies work for human development*. New York/Oxford: UNDP/Oxford University Press.

UNDP. (2002, July). *Human development report (2002): Deepening democracy in a fragmental world*. New York/Oxford: UNDP/Oxford University Press.

UNDP. (2003, July). *Human development report (2003): Millennium development goals: A compact among nations to end human poverty*. New York/Oxford: UNDP/Oxford University Press.

UNDP. (2004, July). *Human development report (2004): Cultural liberty in today's diverse world*. New York/Oxford: UNDP/Oxford University Press.

UNESCO Institute of Statistics Data and Statistics. (1996). *"UNESCO statistical yearbook": The world education indicators on school life expectancy 1992*. www.unesco.org

UNESCO-UIS. (2003). *The UNESCO education data and statistics indicators 1998–2001*. www.unesco.org

UNESCO-UIS. (2004a, May). *The UIS bulletin on science and technology statistics*. Number 1 UNESCO-UIS and Quebec's Institut National de la Recherche Scientifique (INRS).

UNESCO–UIS. (2004b). *Educational statistics (1998–2002)*. Paris: UNESCO.

United Nations. (1970). *United Nations science and technology for development, proposals for the second United Nations development decade*. New York: United Nations.

United Nations Conference on Trade and Development [UNCTAD]. (1996). *New technologies and technological capability-building at the enterprise level: Some policy implications* (Science and technology issues). New York: UN.

Wadi, M. A. (2001). *Education and labour market: The need for reform: The case of Kuwait* (Arab planning institute working paper series, Vol. 0104). Kuwait: Arab Planning Institute.

World Bank. (2004). *MENA development report (2004) "Unlocking the employment potential in the Middle East and North Africa: Toward a new social contract* (The World Bank (2004) Rep. No. 28815) (pp. 104, 222, 225, 228). Washington, DC: The World Bank.

Zahlan, A. B. (1999a). *The Arabs and the challenges of science and technology: Progress without change*. Beirut: The Centre for the Study of Arab Unity.

Zahlan, A. B. (1999b, March 10–12). Science policy for the twenty-first century: Mobilization and development (pp. 14–16). In *"ESCWA Proceedings of the Expert Group Meeting on Science and Technology Policies and Strategies for the Twenty-First Century*. Beirut: ESCWA.

Part II
Conceptual and Theoretical Framework

Chapter 3
Technological Change and Human Capital: Conceptual Framework, Theoretical and Empirical Literature

3.1 Introduction

Technical progress has been essential for the creation, determination, acceleration and improvement of both quantitative and qualitative aspects of economic growth and welfare in any society. Economic growth theories often emphasize the importance of science and technology and the role of technological change in increasing, improving and sustaining the marginal productivity of capital accumulation and the per capita growth rate of the economy. The crucial role of technological change in economic growth has long received particular recognition amongst economists of different schools of thought, from classical, neo-classical, Schumpeterian, evolutionary to new growth theories. However, despite this consonance, both classical and neo-classical economic growth theories view technical progress as an exogenous or unexplained variable. The new growth or endogenous growth theory endogenizes technological progress in economic growth model and explicitly mentions technological progress as the main endogenous factor behind economic growth. Ever since, economists highlight the endogenous role of technical progress in stimulating economic growth and human welfare and identify industrial innovation as the engine of growth (Freeman & Soete, 1997; Romer, 1990).

Moreover, economic growth literature equally recognizes human capital as an important element for economic growth, and many recent theoretical and empirical studies conducted across countries include some proxies for human capital and emphasize the role of investment in human capital, particularly in the form of education. A higher educational attainment implies more skilled and more productive workers, who in turn contribute to enhancing innovative activities and absorption of advanced technologies. Endogenous growth literature explicitly reveals human capital as one major source of economic growth and acknowledges the endogenous role of human capital accumulation in economic growth. More recent literature finds that various measures of schooling are important determinants of per capita growth: an increase in the quantity of human capital per person leads to higher rates of investment in human capital, and so to higher per capita growth.

S. Mohamed Nour, *Technological Change and Skill Development in Arab Gulf Countries*, Contributions to Economics, DOI 10.1007/978-3-319-01916-1_3,

In light of this background and the findings in Chap. 2 above, it is therefore reasonable to highlight the need for improvement of education, skill upgrading and technological progress for economic development in the Gulf countries. Before starting the empirical analysis, it is useful in this chapter to briefly explain the concepts, measures and theoretical and empirical literature in relation to human capital (education), technological change and economic growth. We provide a background for the empirical analysis in the following chapters by surveying the theoretical and empirical literature that emphasizes the positive endogenous growth effects of technical change and human capital in increasing and sustaining economic growth.

The rest of this chapter is organized as follows: in Sect. 3.2 we define the concepts of technological change and human capital; the theoretical and empirical literature on the relationship between technological change, human capital and economic growth are presented in Sect. 3.3. Section 3.4 describes the measures of technological change and human capital; Sect. 3.5 discusses the role of public policies in supporting endogenous growth, and finally, Sect. 3.6 concludes.

3.2 Conceptual Framework: Definition of Technological Change and Human Capital (Human Skills)

Before presenting the theoretical and empirical literature, it is useful to begin with the definition of the concepts of technological change and human capital.

Distinction has been made between the term technology, technological change and the effect of technological change. The term technology refers to the branch of knowledge concerned with applied sciences and means the systematic treatment, study, use and application of scientific knowledge for practical purposes, such as in industry. Freeman and Soete (1997) define technology as a body of knowledge about techniques, but frequently used to encompass both the knowledge itself and the tangible embodiment of that knowledge in an operating system using physical production equipment. They use the expression 'technical innovation' or simply 'innovation' to describe the introduction and spread of new and improved products and processes in the economy and 'technological innovation' to describe advances in knowledge.[1]

The rate of technological change is often defined by the rate of increase in the stock of knowledge and relates to the effect it introduces in shifting the production function, leading to either a new shift or an upward shift in the production function. Technological change can be neutral (unbiased) when it does not save any or leads to equal savings of all factors of production, but it can be biased when it results in increased using or saving of one factor rather than others. The classification of technical change into labour (capital) saving technical change implies that it

[1] See Freeman and Soete (1997, p. 24).

increases the marginal productivity of capital (labour) more than it increases the marginal productivity of labour (capital). Another interpretation indicates that technological change can be equally capital and labour augmenting if it leads to an increase in the production due to either unchanged or equal increases in capital and labour inputs. However, technological change can be purely labour (capital) augmenting, if it leads to increase in effective labour (capital), while effective capital (labour) is constant.

Schumpeter (1934) discusses technological change in the form of innovation including the introduction of new products, services or methods of production; improvement in the quality of existing product or service; development of new markets; exploitation of new sources of supply; and reorganization of methods of operation. Product innovation refers to a substantially new product or an essential improvement to an existing product, while process innovation refers to the introduction of a new or essentially improved method of production.

Human capital refers to health and education that measured by many indicators, for instance, the amount of human capital embodied in people and their respective influence on productivity on the job are determined by skills, ability, education and training (cf. Becker, 1962; Schultz, 1961). In particular, skill is a broad concept and represents one important form of human capital and tacit knowledge[2]: it refers to acquired and practiced ability or to qualifications needed to perform a job or certain tasks competently in the labour market. In addition, other indicators such as training, learning by doing and average years of experience are important components in the formation of skills and human capital.

3.3 Theoretical Framework: Technological Change, Human Capital and Economic Growth

Based on the above framework, in this section we show the theoretical and empirical literature on the relationship between technological change, human capital and economic growth. We explain that economic growth theories recognize and provide different perceptions and analytical frameworks for modelling the various effects of technical change, innovation and human capital on economic growth. The major differences arise because exogenous growth theories perceive and model technical progress and human capital as exogenous variables in growth accounting model,

[2] In distinguishing between codified and tacit knowledge Freeman and Soete (1997) argue: "the codified knowledge implies that knowledge is transformed into information which can either be embodied in new material goods (machines, new consumer goods) or easily transmitted through information infrastructure. While, the tacit knowledge refers to that which cannot easily transferred because it has not been stated or measured in an explicit form, one important kind of tacit knowledge is skill, which can be acquired through learning but often of a non-routine kind" (1997, pp. 404–405).

while, in contrast, the endogenous growth theory envisages and models technical progress and human capital as endogenous variables in determining growth process.

3.3.1 Economic Growth Theory and Exogenous Technical Change

The classical economists, starting with Adam Smith (1776), observe the importance of the variable of technical progress in the form of invention (discoveries of new goods and methods of production), innovations, increasing specialization of labour and market expansion in the capitalist system. Despite the apparent recognition of the importance of technical progress in the classical growth theory, technical progress is assumed to remain exogenous variable in growth process.

Next, the neo-classical economists place more emphasis on the significance of technological change. For instance, Solow (1957) attributed 90 % of the US growth rate during the period 1909–1949 to technical progress; Abramovitz (1956), Kendrick (1956) and Solow (1957) attributed almost all the change in output per hour worked in 1950s to technological change. Subsequent analysis by Jorgonson, Gallop, and Fraumeni (1987) showed the importance of technological change beside the increase in the effective labour force and the effective stock of capital in generating growth in output per worker. The neo-classical growth theory assumes an aggregate production function exhibiting constant returns in labour and capital; the only source of output growth being the increase of capital stock. While the rate of technological change is assumed exogenous variable, represented as a residual factor to measure the growth of TFP, thus in the absence of technological change diminishing returns will eventually cause all economic growth to cease (cf. Solow, 1956, 1957; Swan, 1956).[3] Therefore, in order to compensate the diminishing returns of capital in the neo-classical framework long run and sustainable growth rate of output per capita assume to equal the continuous advances in the exogenous rates of technological progress in the form of new goods, new markets or new processes. The major limitation of the neo-classical growth theory is that the long run per capita growth is exogenous and determined entirely by the exogenous technical change or residuals factor, which is determined outside the model. This also called the black box problem since the residuals factor includes technical progress beside the contributions of many other variables such as human capital (education), organization, management, knowledge, new machines, etc. Moreover,

[3] The neo-classical Solow – Swan model assumes a general production function $\boldsymbol{Y(t)}$, in which the flow of output produced at time $\boldsymbol{t}$ and there are only two inputs, physical capital $\boldsymbol{K(t)}$, and labour $\boldsymbol{L(t)}$, the production function takes the form:

$$Y(t) = F\ (K(t), L(t), t)$$

The growth rate of the production function depends on time $\boldsymbol{t}$, which reflects the effect of technological change. The long-run growth rate is determined entirely by exogenous elements such as the saving rate and the level of technology.

although, technical progress is included in the neo-classical model, it is not treated as a production factor like capital and labour, and the effect of technical progress is viewed only as a shift in the production function (cf. Solow, 1956, 1957).

3.3.2 Economic Growth Theory and Endogenous Technical Change

The neo-classical growth theory fails to explain persistent differences in growth rates across countries because it considers the rates of technological progress, which entirely determine the growth rate, as an exogenous variable and fails to deal with increasing returns in a dynamic general equilibrium framework.

The endogenous growth theory contributes to improving understanding of the interaction between technological change and economic growth and fills the gap in the neo-classical theory by recognizing the important endogenous effects of technological progress and innovation for creating and sustaining economic growth. In particular, the endogenous growth theory considers an endogenous technological change and innovation within a dynamic general equilibrium framework and avoids diminishing returns to capital. The endogenous growth theory assumes that technical change and human capital are the major sources of endogenous growth and the presence of increasing returns to scale and externalities prevent diminishing returns to accumulation of capital and so guarantee the steady state of growth in the long run.

An earlier attempt of the endogenous growth theory was made by Schumpeter (1934), who assumed that technological progress, innovation and their diffusion are driving forces and at the centre of the dynamics of the economic system. Schumpeter provides a pioneering theory of innovation that forms the basis for the subsequent thinking on the dynamic role of technological innovation in economic growth determination. Schumpeter considers innovation as an activity made by one or more workers (e.g. skilled workers), which produces an economic gain, growth and profit either by reducing costs or creating extra income.

A subsequent attempt by Arrow (1962) indicates that technology improvement and the growth of technical change become endogenous due to an unintended effect of learning by doing. Other earlier endogenous growth models represent the major sources of growth by technical progress, which is viewed as a by-product of production and investment in human capital (cf. Nelson & Phelps, 1966; Uzawa, 1965). Uzawa (1965) interprets technical progress as representing human capital per worker, assuming that its growth required the use of labour services in the form of educational inputs and analyzed optimal growth paths.[4]

Further efforts by Nelson and Winter (1977, 1982) attempt a search for a useful theory of innovation, and present an evolutionary theory of economic change that

[4] See Aghion and Howitt (1998, p. 24).

assumes economic change partially stems from innovation on the part of the firm. The ensuing attempt by Dosi, Freeman, Nelson, Silverberg, and Soete (1988) contributes to an evolutionary theory of endogenous technical change by investigating the interaction between technical change and economic theory.

Since the mid 1980s, starting with the work of Romer (1986, 1989, 1994), Lucas (1988) and Rebelo (1991), which are based on the work of Arrow (1962) and Uzawa (1965), the endogenous growth theory explicitly recognizes the endogenous role of technical change and distinguishes between labour and human capital. The endogenous growth theory avoids the diminishing returns to the accumulation of capital and highlights the role of increasing returns and assumes that growth may proceed indefinitely due to the presence of human capital and endogenous technical progress. The endogenous growth theory also predicts that, in the long run, economic growth at the aggregate level is determined by endogenous sources of human capital, technical change, learning by doing, spillovers of knowledge, external effect of human capital and R&D.

For instance, Romer (1986) and Lucas (1988) contributed to revitalizing the growth literature using Arrow's (1962) ideas to eliminate the tendency for diminishing returns by assuming that knowledge creation was a side product of investment and a positive effect of experience called learning by doing or learning by investing, but that the rate of technical change remains constant. Next, a major contribution by Romer (1990) presents a pioneering endogenous growth model where technical progress is defined by R&D; assumes that non-homogenous capital consists of a set of different intermediate goods; and new intermediate inputs are discovered when R&D resources are devoted to the search process. Romer (1990) identifies two major sources of increasing returns to capital due to specialization or product differentiation, as in Romer (1987), and research spillovers, in which growth will accelerate indefinitely. Romer (1990) assumes knowledge about technology is a nonrival input and induces spillover effects.

Different from Romer (1990), Aghion and Howitt (1992) present an endogenous growth model that defines technical progress by both R&D and accumulation of technological knowledge through the channel of industrial product and process innovations, which improve the quality of products. Aghion and Howitt's (1990, 1992, 1998) framework differs from earlier models of endogenous growth (Lucas, 1988; Romer, 1986, 1990) in assuming a model of growth based on Schumpeter's (1942) process of creative-destruction. Where growth results exclusively from technological progress, which has positive and normative implications for growth in creating losses as well as gains, by rendering obsolete skills, goods, markets and manufacturing processes. Innovation consists of 'creative-destructions' rather than just new additions to production, and individual innovations are sufficiently important to affect the entire economy. Aghion and Howitt (1990) follow Romer (1990) in endogenizing technical change in producing endogenous growth, and follow Arrow (1962), Romer (1986) and Lucas (1988) in introducing learning by doing as a second source of growth beside innovation. They assume that the accumulation of learning by doing in the intermediary industry will introduce an increase in productivity in the consumption goods sector, and, in particular, intermediate firms will experience a complete spillover of their learning by doing, which also spills over into the research sector. Different from Romer (1986), the spillover of learning by doing in Aghion and Howitt (1990) leads to private economy growth: they assume that an increase in learning by doing will have a positive direct external effect on the average growth rate. Aghion and Howitt (1992, 1998) assume that a stochastic economic growth is generated by random sequences of product innovations and quality-improving (or vertical) innovations that themselves result from (uncertain) research activities by firms. The average growth rate is determined by the interactions of spillovers or two externalities: positive effect, whereby the knowledge embedded in each innovation can be used by all future researchers to generate growth; and negative effects, namely the business stealing effects.

3.3.3 Human Capital and Economic Growth

Economists have long recognized the importance of human capital to the growth process. For instance, Adam Smith's writings at the beginning of the first industrial revolution recognized that human skills were already becoming more important than raw materials in the designed and manufactured machines. Endogenous growth theory fills the gap in earlier growth theories by assuming the accumulation of human capital is another source of endogenous growth. For instance, both Romer (1986) and Lucas (1988) present endogenous growth models where higher accumulation and an average level of human capital in a context of either increasing or constant returns lead to higher productivity of workers and a higher endogenous growth rate. The endogenous growth theory emphasizes the endogenous role of technology and human capital in economic growth, elaborates on the interaction between them and their central roles in determining the magnitude, speed and difference of growth rates across countries (cf. Abramovitz, 1986; Aghion & Howitt, 1992; Lucas, 1988; Romer, 1990). The literature discusses the relationship between human capital and economic growth following the pioneering approaches by Nelson and Phelps (1966) and Lucas (1988) and the contributions of Romer (1986, 1989, 1990) and Aghion and Howitt (1992).

An earlier attempt of the endogenous growth model is the AK model, which assumes a constant return to scale in a broad aggregate capital including physical and human components "K", an improvement in the level of technology, raises the marginal and average product of capital and the growth rate.[5] The AK model has the advantages of inclusion of physical and human capital, elimination of diminishing returns to accumulation of capital and creating endogenous growth; its limitations are the assumption of a fixed level of technology and the failure to explain long run balanced growth rate.

---

[5] The **AK** production function without diminishing returns and with a fixed level of technology A is defined by: $Y = AK$

An earlier pioneering approach refers to an important contribution by Nelson and Phelps (1966), which assumes growth rates as being driven by the stock of human capital, which in turn affects a country's ability to innovate or catch up with more advanced countries. Nelson and Phelps explain differences in growth across countries are primarily due to differences in human capital stocks and the abilities to generate technical progress. They assume that growth is primarily driven by the stock of human capital, but the effects of education and human capital are more important for producing technological change than for producing output under a given technology. Nelson and Phelps and, more recently, Benhabib and Spiegel (1994) assume that human capital[6] is necessary for innovations (capacity to innovate) and for adapting to new technologies and thereby speeding up technological diffusion throughout the economy. A first implication of the Nelson- Phelps approach is that productivity growth and the rate of innovations should increase with the level of educational attainment, particularly with the enrolment in secondary and higher education, which best reflects the numbers of potential R&D staff in a country. Recent empirical studies verify this result and show the significant impact of secondary and higher educational attainment level on the rate of productivity growth (cf. Barro & Sala–i–Martin, 1995; Benhabib & Spiegel, 1994). A second implication of Nelson and Phelps (1966) is that the marginal productivity of educational attainment is increasing in or with the rate of technological progress (including both innovation rate and speed of adapting to new technologies). Some studies verify this result and find that education induces a significant impact on productivity growth only when it is explicitly related to the rate of innovations and the speed of technological catch-up (cf. Bartel & Lichtenberg, 1987; Benhabib & Spiegel, 1994). A third interesting result of Nelson and Phelps (1966) is that education should permit the countries falling behind to learn more from advanced countries and thereby achieve a higher degree of productivity improvement when innovating. Recently, Benhabib and Spiegel (1994) support this result and indicate that the effect of past educational attainment levels on current growth rates is more obvious across countries that fall behind in terms of aggregate productivity, but growth is to be principally driven by technological catch-up. Thus, the inclusion of technical progress beside human capital substantiates the role of human capital in technological catch-up.[7]

A further interesting approach was introduced by Lucas (1988), based on Becker's (1964) theory of human capital, and on the idea that growth is primarily driven by the accumulation of human capital (education).[8] The Lucas (1988) approach is a pioneering contribution to the endogenous growth literature: it regards human capital accumulation as the engine of growth, as an alternative

---

[6] In Nelson and Phelps (1966) approach human capital is referring to education and the highly skilled workers.

[7] See Aghion and Howitt (1998), pp. 339–340.

[8] Lucas (1988) defines human capital as general human skills that are produced and acquired by education.

(to technological change) and as a complementary source of sustained growth.[9] Lucas adapts Uzawa (1965) and Rosen's (1976) formulation and assumes that growth rate is linearly related to human capital level and its accumulation over time. One implication of the Lucas model is that human capital accumulation is a social activity, involving groups of people, in a way that has no counterpart in the accumulation of physical capital. Another implication is that economies with high human capital stock can easily produce more and can thus sustain a high growth rate. On the other hand, an economy beginning with low levels of human and physical capital will remain permanently below an initially better endowed economy.

Hence, in the Lucas model, differences in growth rates across countries are mainly attributable to differences in the rate at which those countries accumulate human capital over time, assuming that the rate of technical progress remains fixed or exogenous, while Nelson and Phelps (1966) explain that differences in growth across countries are primarily due to differences in human capital stocks and the abilities to generate technical progress. Moreover, Lucas (1988) discusses the relationship between productivity growth and the rate of human capital accumulation, whereas Nelson and Phelps (1966) show that productivity growth and the rate of innovations should increase with the level of educational attainment and particularly so with the enrolment in secondary and higher education. Furthermore, Lucas (1988) assumes that the marginal productivity of education is determined and sustained only by the accumulation of human capital, while Nelson and Phelps (1966) assume the marginal productivity of educational attainment is increasing in the rate of technological progress (including both innovation rate and speed of adapting to new technologies).[10]

One feature of Lucas (1988) model is the assumption of constant returns to scale and the accumulation of human capital, which implies that a diminishing return can be avoided when the production function includes both physical and human capital and both these grow at the same rate. Thus, in the steady state, rates of return remain constant and the economy can grow at a constant and sustained rate mainly due to endogenous growth from human capital accumulation, and without the need for external 'engine of growth' or exogenous technological change. Barro and Sala–i–Martin's (1995) results indicate that the presence of human capital (as an alternative to improvements in technology as a mechanism to generate long-term growth) may relax the constraint of diminishing returns to a broad concept of capital and can lead thereby to long term per capita growth in the absence of exogenous technological progress.

Another interesting feature of Lucas (1988) model is the introduction of human capital with externalities or spillovers effects of education between individuals. Lucas distinguishes between the internal effects of human capital, i.e. the effects of an individual's human capital on his own productivity, and the external effects of

[9] See Aghion and Howitt (1998, p. 327).

[10] See Aghion and Howitt (1998, pp. 327, 339)

human capital that contributes to the productivity of all factors of production, including his or her own human capital. The external effects of human capital induce more rapid physical than human capital growth; the average skill level of a group of people is assumed to affect the productivity of each individual within the group. Both Lucas (1988) and Romer (1986) highlight the spillover effects or benefits from aggregate human capital, supposing that human capital can be passed down from generation to the next and can therefore grow without bound. Assuming that this special kind of knowledge is only produced as a side effect of other activities, investment in physical capital or investment in schooling respectively, while Romer (1989, 1990) allows this special kind of knowledge to be produced intentionally and not as a side effect. Azariadis and Drazen (1990) find that the existence of threshold externalities in education technology can lead to several steady state growth paths and explain existing continuous and perpetual differences in growth rates across countries due to unequal initial human capital endowments.[11]

Moreover, Lucas (1988) follows the theory of human capital and distinguishes between two main sources of human capital accumulation (or skill acquisition), namely education and learning by doing. Based on theory of human capital, Lucas assumes that the allocation of time over various activities in the current period affect productivity or affect the accumulation of human capital $h\ (t)$ level in future periods. Lucas identifies both the way the human capital level affects current production and the way the current time allocation affects the accumulation of human capital. Lucas assumes that a worker with skill level h devotes the fraction of $u\ (h)$ of his non-leisure time to current production and the remaining $1-u\ (h)$ to human capital accumulation. So, the human capital equation in the Lucas model is defined by: $\dot{h} = h(t)\delta\,(1-u(t)),\ \delta > 0$ which spells out how current schooling time $(1-u)$ affects the accumulation of human capital. If learning by doing rather than education is the primary source of human capital accumulation, the above equation should be replaced by the following equation: $\dot{h} = \delta hu$.[12]

The subsequent contribution by Romer (1990) presents a growth model of endogenous technical change assuming long run growth is increasing in and driven primarily by both technological change (the accumulation of knowledge) and the stock of human capital[13] rather than the total size of the labour force or the population. He emphasizes the central role of technological change, stock of human capital, externalities and increasing return associated with investments in human capital in the research sector and in determining the rate of growth. He finds that an economy with a larger stock of human capital will experience faster growth. Romer (1990) follows both Romer (1986) and Lucas (1988) in their assumption of external effects arising from knowledge spillover. Romer (1990) assumes that the final output is a function of physical labour, physical capital, human capital and an

[11] See Aghion and Howitt (1998, pp. 331–333)

[12] See Lucas (1988) and Aghion and Howitt (1998, pp. 327, 329).

[13] Romer's (1990) definition of human capital includes activities such as formal education and on the job training.

index of the level of technology. The application of more human capital to research leads to higher rate of production of new designs and stock of knowledge, which increases the productivity of engineers working in the research sector.[14] The output of the design is a linear function of human capital and technology when the other variables are held constant. The marginal productivity of human capital employed in the manufacturing sector grows in proportion to technology. Unlike Lucas (1988), Romer (1990) follows Schumpeter's (1942) assumption that technological change drives growth and provides the incentive for continued capital accumulation, the growth rate is increasing in the stock of human capital. So, both capital accumulation and technological change account for much of the increase in output per worker.

The endogenous growth model proposed by Aghion and Howitt (1992) assumes that capital accumulation includes both physical and human components. They assume that both the average and the variance of the growth rate are increasing functions of the size of innovations, size of skilled labour and the productivity of research, which is measured by the effect of research on the Poisson arrival rate of innovations. They distinguish between three categories of labour: unskilled labour, which can be used only in producing consumption goods; skilled labour, which can be used either in research or in intermediate sector; and specialized labour, which can be used only in research. They assume that skilled labour has two uses: in the manufacture of the latest generation of intermediate goods and research aimed at discovering the next generation of these goods. An expectation of more research in the next period must correspond to an expectation of higher demand for skilled labour in research in the next period. They assume that research produces a random sequence of innovations, and that the Poisson arrival rate of innovations in the economy at any instant is dependant on the current flow of skilled labour used in research. They assume that skilled labour is important factor in research, innovations and economic growth, and that an increase in the endowments of skilled labour increases both the marginal benefit and reduces the marginal costs of research by reducing the wage of skilled labour.

Moreover, several recent empirical studies conducted across countries use many measures of human capital and find that human capital is important determinant of long run economic growth or per capita growth.[15]

[14] One implication of Romer's (1990) argument is that, despite having the same amount of human capital, an engineer working at current time has higher productivity than one who worked in the previous century because he acquires the advantages of all additional improvements and accumulation in knowledge since then.

[15] For instance, Rebelo (1991), Barro (1991, 1996), Barro and Lee (1993, 1996, 2000a, b), Benhabib and Spiegel (1994), Barro and Sala–i–Martin (1995), Mankiw, Romer, and Weil (1992), and Kahn and Lim (1998) all find strong positive correlation between schooling and the growth rate or the subsequent growth rate of per capita GDP or TFP.

3.3.4 The Relationship Between Technological Progress, Human Capital (Skill) and Skill Upgrading

In this section, we show that the inclusion of technological change and human capital in growth accounting models motivates endogenous growth literature to postulate several explanations of the relationship between human capital and technical change. In particular, considerable debate arises around four issues regarding the complementary relationship between human capital and technical progress, skilled biased technical change, the role of technical progress in skill upgrading and the role of skill in skill upgrading.

The first hypothesis highlights the complementary relationship between technological progress and human capital. The interpretation of this hypothesis is that the high educated workers can adapt more and easier to changing technologies than the low educated workers. A large endowment of human capital facilitates the fast adaptation of technologies and induces positive impacts on economic growth, and faster technology driven growth in turn can induce more schooling by raising the rate of return on investment in schooling (cf. Benhabib & Spiegel, 1994; Nelson & Phelps, 1966). Moreover, human capital or skill is found to be more complementary with technology and capital (cf. Goldin & Katz, 1998; Mincer, 1989). Because the 'embodiment' of technical change in both physical and human capital indicates that the improvement in their quality implies their complementarity with technological change (Bartel & Lichtenberg, 1987). In addition, more innovation stimulates human and physical capital accumulation by raising the marginal product of capital, while more capital accumulation stimulates innovation by raising the profit accruing to innovation (Aghion & Howitt, 1998). Furthermore, a high proportion of skilled workers in the labour force implies a large market size for skill-complementary technologies and encourages faster upgrading of the productivity of skilled workers (cf. Acemoglu, 1998).

Several studies use many different indicators to examine the technological progress and human capital complementary hypothesis. For instance, the increasing utilization of higher educated workers shows positive correlation with TFP growth (cf. Kahn & Lim, 1998), with physical capital, capital equipment or capital intensity (cf. Bartel & Lichtenberg, 1987; Goldin & Katz, 1998; Griliches, 1969), with R&D (Acemoglu, 1998; Machin & Van Reenen, 1998) and with the use of new technologies (cf. Acemoglu, 1998), especially ICT (cf. Autor, Katz, & Krueger, 1998; Bresnahan, Brynjolfsson, & Hitt, 1999; Goldin & Katz, 1998).

The second hypothesis concerns the skill–biased nature of technical change. The rationale for this argument is that technical change has dual implications on employment and demand for skill, which is found biased against low skilled workers and lead to either unemployment/job mismatch (cf. Muysken et al., 2002a, b) or crowding out of low skilled workers (cf. Muysken & ter Weel, 1998).

Another interpretation is based on the argument that technical changes induce creative- destruction effects on growth and employment. While it enhances productivity growth, stimulates demand and the creation of new jobs, it also destroys jobs because it is primarily labour saving through automation and skill obsolescence (cf. Aghion & Howitt, 1992, 1998).

In the recent literature two features have received particular attention: the first issue is that economic debate has become focused on the significant change in the composition of labour demand, particularly the increase in the demand for skilled workers and sharp decline in the demand for low skilled workers. The second issue is focused on the distributional aspects of technical change, particularly the implications of skill-biased technical change (SBTC) on the structure of employment and wages that has shifted against the low skilled workers, leading to either an increase in unemployment of low skilled workers or increasing wages divergence between high skilled and low skilled workers, which leads to greater inequality (cf. Acemoglu, 1998; Autor et al., 1998; Bound & Johnson, 1992).

The skill-biased technical change (SBTC) hypothesis has been verified both at the macro level across both developed and developing countries (cf. Berman, Bound, & Machin, 1998) and at the micro level within industries (cf. Berman, Bound, & Griliches, 1994). SBTC is related to various measures of technical changes such as TFP growth (cf. Kahn & Lim, 1998), R&D (cf. Acemoglu, 1998; Berman et al., 1994; Machin & Van Reenen, 1998) and the use of IT or ICT (cf. Autor et al., 1998; Berman et al., 1994; Bound & Johnson, 1992; Freeman & Soete, 1994).

The third hypothesis explains the role of technical progress in skill upgrading. The interpretation of this hypothesis is that both the technology-human capital complementarity and skill-biased technical change hypotheses imply that a higher rate of technical progress should bring an increase or upgrading in skill level. Several studies in the literature use many indicators to show the role of technical progress (in the form of TFP, R&D, ICT, IT or computer use, etc.) in skill upgrading. For instance, skill upgrading, defined by the increasing incidence of training, increases with the rate of technological change (cf. Mincer, 1989; Bartel & Sicherman, 1995, 1999[16]), especially in sectors in which the Jorgenson measure of productivity growth was higher (cf. Lillard & Tan, 1986) or showing an increasing use of IT or computers (cf. Bresnahan et al., 1999). Skill upgrading, defined by the shift away from unskilled towards skilled employment or increase in the share of white-collar high skilled workers, is also positively correlated to variables related to technological change, such as R&D investment and growth in the number of patent (cf. Colecchia & Papaconstantinou, 1996[17]). In addition, skill upgrading, defined by the increase in the wage share of white-collar workers, is positively related to two measures of technology: the level of investment in R&D and computers

[16] Bartel and Sicherman (1995) find that on the job training will increase if technological change increases the productivity of human capital, reduces the costs of training or increases the value of time in training relative to work; and that the training gap between the highly educated and the less educated narrows, on average, as the rate of technological change increases.

[17] Colecchia and Papaconstantinou (1996) find that a one percentage point R&D intensity higher than average at the beginning of eighties has implied about 20 % higher than average upskilling per year.

(cf. Berman et al., 1994). Furthermore, skill upgrading, as defined by the change in the share of educated workers in employment and return to schooling or wage rate, is positively correlated with the increase of R&D intensity (cf. Machin & Van Reenen, 1998). Moreover, skill upgrading, as defined by the share of high skilled workers, is positively correlated with TFP (cf. Garcia Cervero, 1997) or the use of computers, IT, ICT or computer-intensive industries (cf. Autor et al., 1998; Bresnahan et al., 1999). Skill upgrading, decreasing motor skills and increasing cognitive skills accompany the diffusion of ICT, mainly through occupational change rather than educational improvement, and are also positively correlated with productivity growth (cf. Hwang, 2000).

The fourth hypothesis deals with the role of human capital or skill acquisition in skill upgrading. Along with the debate on the relation between technological change and human capital and the positive effects of human capital/education on productivity and economic growth, theoretical and empirical literature highlight the role of human capital/education in skill upgrading through externalities and learning by doing. Educational attainment is important because skills acquisition from formal schooling lead to improvement in training and learning abilities and increase the accumulation of human capital through experience or "learning by doing", which in turn interact together and lead to improvements in workers productivity (cf. Autor, 2000).[18] Theoretical literature highlights the role of human capital or skill in skill upgrading through externalities, spillover and learning by doing (cf. Lucas, 1988; Romer, 1986, 1989, 1990). In addition, the average human capital tends to grow over time as human capital investments have a positive external effect on the human capital of the later cohorts (Stokey, 1991). Moreover, recent empirical literature shows that in the developed countries, particularly across the OECD countries, human capital may accumulate at a faster rate with the past intensive use of high skilled workers (cf. Colecchia & Papaconstantinou, 1996). Furthermore, empirical literature from the developing countries shows that in Singapore and Korea investment in human capital via the expansion and improvement of education and training systems, particularly the development of tertiary, vocational and technical education, leads to an improvement in the overall skill content or skill upgrading of the working population. This appears from the improvement in the educational attainment – defined by highest qualification attained- and skill levels, the rise in the share of high skilled workers, scientists and engineers and the fall in the share of low skilled workers. In addition, upgrading of the occupational structure has resulted from the large/rising share of the supply of high educated, white-collar and non-production workers and the small/falling share of blue-collar workers.[19]

---

[18] Autor (2000) argues that: first, training is more productive and therefore valuable to high ability workers; second, workers have some prior information about their ability that is not initially visible to employers; and, third, firms are able to learn about ability through skills training.

[19] See Cheah (1997), Low (1998) and Cheon (1999). In Singapore, the transfer of foreign technology and foreign skills stimulates the acquisition of knowledge and skills from abroad and induces positive spillover in upgrading the skill of domestic workers. This has been

These findings emphasize the importance of the endogenous effects of technical progress and human capital for enhancing economic growth. In particular, these explanations imply that next to the important endogenous effects of technical progress and human capital in economic growth, the complementary relationships between them and between them and skill upgrading are also important for enhancing economic growth.

3.4 Measurement of Technological Change and Human Capital

While it is admitted that technological progress and human capital are difficult to measure, the theoretical and empirical literature use many indicators to approximate their effects. It will be useful to illustrate the advantages and weakness of these measures in order to select some relevant measures for the empirical analysis in the subsequent chapters.

3.4.1 Measurement of Technological Change

The literature uses several indicators to measure the role of technical progress in economic growth and particularly distinguishes between input indicators, which include variables such as R&D expenditures and human resources, and output indicators, which comprise variables such as patent, productivity growth, publication, etc. (cf. OECD, 1997). A comprehensive approach of technological progress should be based on integration of input and output indicators.

The traditional indicator used in the literature to measure the contribution of technical change in economic progress is represented by total factor productivity (TFP) (cf. Kahn & Lim, 1998). It is also known as Solow Residuals, as Solow (1956, 1957) was the one to find that the growth rate of technical progress emerges as the remaining unexplained variable or the residual parameter – defined as the factor of output that cannot explained by the input factors.[20] The use of TFP growth measure indicates the high significance of technical progress: for instance, Solow (1957) finds that around 90 % of the growth in US output per worker during the

accompanied with technological upgrading to promote mechanization, computerization, automation, etc. In the Republic of Korea, the integration into global economy or exposure to foreign competition leads to skill upgrading of domestic workers in the manufacturing sector. Skill upgrading of domestic skills facilitates the adoption of foreign technologies and technological catching-up with the advanced countries.

[20] Productivity growth is calculated as the differences between the rate of growth of output and (a weighted measure of) the rate of growth of the capital and labour inputs (Mincer, 1989), or the differences in growth rates of the social product and the capital and labour production factors.

period (1909–1949) was due to the effect of the residual factor, which measures the effect of technical progress. Moreover, Abramovitz (1956); Solow (1957); Kendrick (1956) and Dension (1962) find that about half of the growth of the US economy up to the 1950s was attributed to technical progress measured by TFP. However, the TFP indicator has several drawbacks such as the lack of relevant and adequate data and the inaccuracy and broadness of the concept of TFP, which includes factors other than technological progress such as human capital (education), organization, management, knowledge, new machines, etc. According to Mincer (1989), productivity growth indicates the consequences of technical change, but is not a measure of it; TFP is a useful measure of technological change only if other factors affecting productivity growth are either unimportant or considered in the statistical applications. In addition, TFP growth measure may imply some measurement errors due to business cycles and economies of scale (cf. Mincer, p. 4).

The major input indicator in measuring scientific and technological progress is often represented by the data relating to R&D expenditures, which have been widely used across the OECD countries due to their consistency and easier computation compared to output indicators in these countries. The R&D expenditure data can be utilized to analyze the comparative development and breakdown of R&D activities according to sector and source of finance. However, R&D expenditure data has several defects: for instance, that the data reflects only the recorded expenditures and the institutionalized aspects of technology aimed at increasing knowledge. It also does not include many activities that contribute to technological knowledge such as design, learning-by-doing, the indirect public spending on R&D, etc. Moreover, R&D data reflects only the effort put into research, and does not reflect the efficiency with which this effort leads to new knowledge, the quality of R&D work undertaken, the quality of the scientists performing the work, the cost of inputs of labour, equipment and materials, etc. Moreover, the definition of R&D expenditure varies substantially across countries and is difficult to measure for a large number of countries, and does not reflect the effects of the international spillover of S&T and variations across countries with respect to R&D performance. In addition, it does not produce immediate results, making it difficult to establish direct relation between R&D performance and indicators of economic growth, because R&D activities lead to knowledge creation, which may lead to improved performance only in the long run.[21]

The major output indicator is defined by the patent indicator, which is utilized in the literature to measure technological capacity and status of a country, sector or company. The literature uses patent data to measure the output of technological activities, to reflect the technological performance over time and across countries, to examine the technological specialization in key sectors of industry and to protect industrial property rights (cf. OECD, 1997). The patent indicator is often widely

[21] See OECD (1997) Second European Report on Science and Technology Indicators (1997, p. 37).

used in the measurement of technological change because it allows for international comparisons over a long period; it provides more accurate and specific analyses by sector and by technology; and allows for more focus on a company, institution and even single inventor or researcher. On the other hand, the patent indicator also has several limitations, such as: a lesser degree of reliability for countries or sectors with a small number of patents; and possible interruptions by reason of having to work with publication rather than priority dates.[22] Further limitations lie in the difficulty in interpreting average annual growth rates per period due to unstable patent numbers at the end of a period, lack of exact measurements and the potential inconsistency between the required and actual measurements, the latter problem admittedly also applicable to other indicators.[23]

Numerous empirical studies use innovation surveys such as the survey of resources (R&D) indicators, survey of direct progress (output) indicators and survey of indirect progress and impact indicators, which can be evaluated by questionnaires to measure technological change. A well-known example of this is the Community Innovation Survey (CIS). Distinction has been made between innovation surveys according to subject and object approaches. The subject approach focuses on the innovator or firm-level innovative activities, identifies both input and output indicators, includes small-scale incremental change, reflects economic indicators and permits for comparisons within industries or inter-firm comparison, but does not allow for comparison between different industries with different outputs. On the other hand, the object approach focuses on significant technological innovations (new product or process) or the objective output of the innovation process, on the technology itself. It allows for an external assessment of the importance of innovation independent of personal judgement and usually identified through expert appraisal or through new product announcement in trade journals or other literature. However, it has limitations as it is confined only to major innovations, neglects small incremental innovation and does not include an assessment of the economic significance of innovation.[24]

Some recent studies tend to measure technological change by using an index of use, investment or expenditures on ICT, IT, computers or computer equipment, which are also called the new general purposes technologies. These indicators are relatively easier to calculate and several studies provide strong results when using them to reflect the use and organization of technological innovation (cf. Autor et al., 1998; Bresnahan et al., 1999). However, the utilization of computer use as a measurement of technological progress and innovation may lead to endogenity and measurement problems (cf. Sanders & ter Weel, 2000, p. 26).

---

[22] The priority date of a patent refers to the date of first filing, whereas the publication date refers to the date on which the patent was published. This leads to a time lag between the priority and publication year. For example, in the European (EPO) system, patents are published 18 months after first application.

[23] See OECD's Second European Report on Science and Technology Indicators (1997, pp. 90–91).

[24] See Smith (2000).

For our macro–micro analysis we use R&D, patent and ICT as more relevant measures of technical change at the macro–micro levels. Moreover, at the micro/firm level we use the innovation survey following the subject approach, as it appears more relevant for assessing only small incremental innovation at firm level. Our analysis will not include the object approach since it focuses on big (radical) innovations and seems inappropriate for measuring the small incremental innovations in our case studies in the Gulf. Other measures, such as the TFP measure, are not very relevant for our analysis and will not be included in our study due to a lack of relevant data and information to estimate these at both macro and micro levels. In order to measure these indicators, we will use the available relevant secondary data and information at the macro level and use the firm survey data at the micro level, as we will explain in Chaps. 4 and 6 below.

3.4.2 Measurement of Human Capital (Human Skills)

The most widely used measures of skill in the literature is educational attainment, as measured by the average years of schooling, occupation measure, the share of non-production workers in total employment and the share of non- production workers wages to total wages. In addition, the literature uses other measures of human capital such as school enrolment ratios, adult literacy rates and school quality measures.

School gross and net enrolment ratios reflect current flows of education that accumulate to create the future stocks of human capital and have been used in several studies (cf. Barro, 1991; Barro & Lee, 1993, 1996).[25] However, they have several limitations: for instance, they only measure current flows of schooling and do not reflect the stock of human capital. In addition, they are susceptible to underestimation and overestimation measurement errors[26]: for instance, net enrolment ratios tend to underestimate the actual value of variables on both mortality and migration; gross enrolment ratios introduce errors related to repetition of grades and dropouts, which are widely observed in developing countries. Gross enrolment ratios overestimate the actual value because their calculation are based on annual surveys of educational institutions in each country and reflect registered number of

[25] The UNESCO definition distinguishes between gross and net enrolment ratios. "Gross enrolment ratio defines the ratio of all persons enrolled in a given level of schooling to the population of the age group that would be enrolled at that level. While, net enrolment ratio modifies the numerator of the gross enrolment ratio to count only the students enrolled within the designated age group i.e. the ratio of students at a given level of schooling in the designated age group to the total population of the same age group. The net enrolment ratios vary between zero and one, whereas the gross enrolment ratios can exceed one" (Barro & Lee, 1993, p. 4). For detailed definition, see also the UNESCO-UIS website: www.uis.unesco.org

[26] Lee and Barro (1997) use an adjusted enrolment ratio to overcome the problems of underestimation in net enrolment ratios and overestimation in gross enrolment ratios.

students at the beginning of each school year rather than computing the actual number in attendance. In general, the net enrolment ratio is relatively more appropriate for measuring the accumulation of human capital, however, the gross ratio has been widely used because it is more often available for developing countries.[27]

The adult literacy rates have been frequently used in several studies to estimate the relationship between human capital and economic growth (cf. Barro, 1991; Romer, 1989). They have an advantage over school enrolment ratios as they reflect the stock of human capital rather than the flow of investment. However, a major problem with adult literacy rates is that they measure only one component of the current stock of human capital or the first stage in the path of human capital formation, but do not reflect the skills that are obtained beyond the most elementary levels of schooling as well as many other important aspects of human capital and various types of technical knowledge, which are important for enhancing labour productivity and economic growth. The use of literacy to measure the stock of human capital implies that education beyond the most elementary level does not contribute significantly to productivity.[28]

The educational attainment or educational level is measured by average years of schooling to reflect the stock of human capital and allow for across countries or international comparison.[29] It has been widely used in the literature (cf. Barro & Lee, 1993, 1996) as an appropriate and accurate alternative measure to both school enrolment ratios and adult literacy rates. In recent literature, educational attainment is used to reflect the inflows of new school graduates to existing educational stocks across countries (cf. Barro & Lee, 2000a, b). The rapid growth in average years of schooling led to double growth in the stock of human capital in the USA (cf. Mulligan & Sala–i–Martin, 1995), educational attainment or the average years of schooling has a significant contribution to the growth of total factor productivity (cf. Kahn & Lim, 1998). Although the average years of schooling measure is often widely used as the most popular measure of human capital in the new growth literature and comparisons across countries, it has some drawbacks, such as the assumption of constant elasticity of substitution across workers of different group, which implies that always and everywhere workers of each education category are perfect substitutes for workers in

---

[27] See Barro and Lee (1993, pp. 4–6).

[28] See Barro and Lee (1993, p. 6). "The literacy rates have been used in the United Nations Development Programme UNDP, 1990, to construct an index of human capital. Moreover, Barro and Lee (1993) use adult literacy rates to proxy for the percentages of adult population who have no school attainment to fill the gap in the availability of census/survey data" (Barro and Lee, 1993, pp. 6–7). See also the UNESCO-UIS website: www.uis.unesco.org.

[29] The educational attainment is measured by the average years of schooling, which is computed by adding the product of the number of years of schooling times the number of people in each schooling category across school categories, "i.e. defined by the following formula:

Average Years of Schooling $= \Sigma_j YR_j. H S_j$

Where j is schooling level, YR_j is the number of years of schooling represented by the level j, and $H S_j$ is the fraction of the population for which the jth level is the highest value attained" Barro and Lee (1993, p. 7). For detailed definition, see also the UNESCO-UIS website: www.uis.unesco.org

other categories. It assumes that productivity differentials among workers with different levels of education are proportional to their years of schooling, that always and everywhere a year of education adds a constant quantity of human capital and delivers the same increase in skill, whether undertaken by a primary pupil or a college student. It implies that always and everywhere a worker with 16 years of schooling is 16 times as productive as worker with 1 year of schooling, irrespective of the wage rate differentials. It does not consider differences in the fields of study and quality of schooling (quality of teachers and education infrastructure) and wage rate across countries. Moreover, the educational attainment does not directly measure the human skills obtained at schools, namely quality of schooling across countries, and it does not reflect the skills and experience gained by individuals after their formal education.[30]

Some studies use schooling quality measure or the quality of educational output to measure the impacts on various dimensions of cognitive skills that affect an individual's productive behaviour, and thereby the quality of the future labour force (cf. Hanushek & Kim, 1995; Lee & Barro, 1997).[31, 32] Although both the quality and the quantity of schooling are important ingredients of human capital, schooling quality measure has several disadvantages as it varies substantially across countries and is difficult to measure for a large number of countries (Lee & Barro, p. 1).

The occupation measure or classification is based on the definition of employment structure and the relative shares of educated and non-educated workers in total employment. In particular, the ILO International Standards Classification of Occupations (ISCO)[33] is a widely used measure for measuring skill composition in the literature (cf. Colecchia & Papaconstantinou, 1996; Hwang, 2000[34]).

---

[30] See Mulligan and Sala–i–Martin (1995, p. 2) and Barro and Lee (2000a, p. 12).

[31] The definition of this measure includes the pupils/teacher ratios, spending per pupil at primary and secondary schools as a percentage of GDP, and also estimates average salaries of primary school teachers to per capita GDP.

[32] Hanushek and Kim (1995) find that cognitive skills are an important component of relevant variations in human capital, reinforcing the attention to school quality found in many countries today. Their results indicate that quality of labour force has a consistent, stable and strong influence on economic growth, the impact of quality indicates that one standard deviation in mathematics and science skills translates into 1 % point in average annual real growth. This growth effect is larger than would be obtained from over 8 years in average schooling.

[33] The ILO International Standards Classification of Occupations (ISCO) are aggregated in the following way:

White-Collar high-skilled (WCHS) includes legislators, senior officials, managers, professionals, technicians and associate professionals.

White-Collar low-skilled (WCLS) includes clerks, services workers, shop and market sales workers.

Blue-Collar high-skilled (BCHS) includes skilled agricultural and fishery workers, craft and related trade workers.

Blue-Collar low-skilled (BCLS) includes plant and machine operators and assemblers and elementary occupations.

[34] Hwang (2000) finds that skill upgrading, decreasing motor skills and increasing cognitive skills are accompanying the diffusion of ICT, mainly through occupational change rather than educational improvement.

According to the ISCO classification, only WCHS is referred to as "high-skilled", with all other groups regarded as low skilled. The advantage of the occupation measure is that the change in occupational distribution of employment provides more information on the skills required and measures the change in skills structure. But it has the drawback that it does not necessarily take into accounts on-the-job learning and, in particular, skills associated with the use of new technologies.[35] It also fails to account for the changing nature of skills under an occupational title.[36]

The share of non-production workers to total employment measure is defined by the ratio of the non-production workers to total employment and has been usually used in the literature (cf. Cheon, 1999; Kahn & Lim, 1998). However, it has several limitations: for instance, it does not exactly reflect change in relative demand for non-production workers, and it may over-represent the shift in demand for non-production workers. Moreover, the definition of non-production workers includes a lot of low-skilled service jobs such as janitors, cleaners or simple clerical jobs, and various liberal occupations, while excluding production supervisors, foremen and skilled workers that are of considerable importance in manufacturing sector of developing countries (Cheon, pp. 12–13).[37]

The share of non-production workers' wages in total wages is measured by the ratio of non-production workers wages to total wages, and has been used in several empirical studies (cf. Kahn & Lim, 1998). Its advantage is that the changes in the non-production share in the wage bill provide a better measure of the demand shift toward non-production workers, provided that the elasticity of substitution between production and non-production workers is above one (cf. Berman et al., 1994; Cheon, 1999). However, it has several limitations: for instance, the measure is originally based on the definition of non-production and production workers for skill and unskilled workers and may suffer the same measurement errors related to the definition of non-production and production workers as we explained above. Moreover, the wage measure is applicable only when the elasticity of substitution between production and non-production worker is above one. Furthermore, it may be inaccurate to reflect the movement in the stock of human capital when the relative wages change for reasons other than changes in human capital and technological stocks (e.g. due to price change). So, the wage measures may induce some measurement errors (cf. Cheon; Goldin & Katz, 1998; Machin & Van Reenen, 1998).[38]

For our analysis at the macro level we use the measures of school enrolment ratios, literacy rates, educational attainment, school quality measures and occupational classification to assess skill levels, based on information and data from many relevant sources (e.g. the UNESCO, UNDP, etc.). In addition, in our analysis at the micro/firm level, we use two more relevant measures of skill, namely, educational

[35] See Colecchia and Papaconstantinou (1996, p. 8).

[36] See ILO (1998) World Employment Report (1998/1999, p. 35).

[37] See Kahn and Lim (1998) and Cheon (1999, pp. 12–13).

[38] See Cheon (1999, pp. 12–13), Goldin and Katz (1998) and Machin and Van Reenen (1998).

attainment and occupational classification, based on data obtained from the firm survey as we will explain in Chaps. 4, 5 and 6. Our analysis will not include other indicators such as the share of non-production workers in total employment and the share of non-production workers wages in total wages due to a lack of relevant data to estimate these. Instead, we use the share of high-skilled in total employment and the share of high-skilled wages to low-skilled wages according to education and occupation definitions.

3.5 Endogenous Growth and Public Policy

We mentioned in Sect. 3.3 that endogenous growth literature revealed several robust facts and interesting implications that paved the way for growth, it is convenient in this section to explain that it also provided some insights for a possible role for government policy. We explain below the literature and arguments for government intervention to promote the accumulation of technology, human capital and hence growth rate.

The most popular view in the literature is that the rationale for government intervention is basically related to the idea that knowledge (in the form of technical progress or accumulation of human capital) is a public good, which is non-rival and partially excludable. As in Romer (1990) and Barro and Sala–i–Martin (1995), these two features imply an unbounded growth and incomplete appropriability of knowledge and raise the possibility of knowledge spillovers across firms and hence the whole economy. While the feature of spillovers of knowledge supports endogenous growth, it also creates a form of externality and implies that private investments generate a positive external effect and the private returns from investment tend to be lower than the social returns. The outcomes tend not to be Pareto optimal but sub optimal and require government intervention to correct the distortion. The social optimum can be achieved by many instruments such as providing subsidies (which can be financed by taxation) to improve the accumulation of technology and human capital, incentives and returns from investment for private investors.

In the endogenous growth literature some studies explicitly model the importance of technology and human capital for endogenous growth, but only implicitly indicate a role for public policy. For instance, while the Lucas (1988) model emphasizes investment in human capital, it only implicitly allows for a role for public policy through subsidies (Haslinger & Ziesemer, 1996, p. 230). Moreover, the Arrow (1962) learning-by-doing and Romer (1986) models imply an indirect intervention: an investment tax credit that increased the accumulation of capital necessarily also increased the accumulation of technology (Romer, 1990, p. S94).

According to Ziesemer's (1987) interpretation, T.W. Schultz (1964) presents a pioneering theoretical justification for a central role for government interference to promote public investment and emphasis their long-run effects on growth and development. Schultz's theory reveals that the provision of public factors, such as basic education and basic scientific research, is necessary for human capital formation and this would drive technical progress. Therefore, technical progress depends on human capital, and the production of human capital in turn requires public factors such as basic education and basic scientific research. It is assumed that the public goods are financed through a linear income tax rate: the lower the level of public goods and tax rate, the higher is the price of human capital and less human capital is supplied. If the rate of technical progress depends upon human capital, then technological progress is dependent upon taxation and public goods. The contribution by Shell (1967) involves public investment and assumes a public, non-rivalrous stock of technology; a flat-rate income tax is raised to finance the change in the stock of knowledge. Tax has two effects: it increases growth, but also decreases the returns from investment and negatively affects private capital formation.[39]

Ziesemer (1990, 1991, 1995) formulates Schultz's (1964) ideas that public factors – basic education and basic scientific research – are held as necessary for the formation of human capital and the development process. Ziesemer (1990) argues for an essential role of public factors, which are provided by the government and in turn financed by a simple flat-rate income tax to introduce an outstanding role of economic policy in economic development. Ziesemer (1991) assumes that, in a growth model with endogenous technical progress, if an externality arises at the firm's level, government intervention is needed to obtain the optimum and perfectly competitive market structure. Hence, a tax subsidy system is introduced to influence the rate of technical progress and brings it to the optimal level of growth. Ziesemer's (1995) model indicates that public factors are used in the formation of human capital and human capital, in turn, is necessary for the production of technical progress. If public factors are financed by a flat-rate income tax, then a higher rate of taxation or shares of public expenditure on education in the GDP will lead to a higher level of public factors, a higher rate of technical progress and will also lead to a higher growth if steady states are stable. In Ziesemer's (1991) model the optimal policy is a technology stock subsidy to reward firms and to provide an incentive for the spillovers of technology formation to the human capital schooling process. In Ziesemer's (1990, 1995) models the optimal policy is a tax financed by government spending on the provision or creation of public knowledge (basic education and basic scientific research). The share of GDP raised and spent on the provision of public factors has an impact on the level of GDP per capita or its growth rate respectively.[40]

---

[39] See Ziesemer (1987, pp. 107–108, 112, 115) and Haslinger and Ziesemer (1996, pp. 230, 232). Ziesemer (1987) summarises T.W. Schultz's (1964) view and indicates that the latter uses Nelson (1959) idea that both basic education and basic scientific research should be viewed as a public good.

[40] See Ziesemer (1990, pp. 268–280, 1991, pp. 47–68, 1995, pp. 1–19).

One assumption in Romer's (1990) model of endogenous technological change is that technological change arises in response to market incentives, and the latter play an essential role in the model. Romer assumes that in a growth model with spillover effects, the social optimum can be achieved by subsidizing the accumulation of technology. A subsidy to R&D works to compensate R&D firms for the learning-by-doing and the positive external effects they spillover to other R&D firms; in the absence of R&D, a subsidy creates further incentives for firms to gain entry. Although all the research is embodied in capital goods, a subsidy to physical capital accumulation may be a very poor substitute for direct subsidies that increase the incentives to undertake research. In the absence of feasible policies that can remove the divergence between the social and private returns to research, a second-best policy for a government would be to subsidize the accumulation of human capital. A subsidy to employment in research sector that is financed through lump-sum taxes has the same effects on growth as an increase in the productivity parameter: in the long run, a subsidy will cause an increase in the growth rate (Romer, pp. S72, S74, S93, S98–S99).

Barro and Sala-i- Martin (1992) allow for the effects of fiscal policy on long-term growth and discuss the role of tax policy in various models of endogenous economic growth. In their view, in growth models with learning-by-doing and spillover effects, the social optimum can be attained by financing government consumption purchases with an income tax, and monopoly pricing of new types of capital goods. The tax policies that encourage investment can raise the growth rate and thereby increase the utility of the representative household. In growth models that incorporate public services, the optimal tax policy depends on the characteristics of services. If the public services are publicly provided private goods, which are rival and excludable, or publicly provided public goods, which are non-rival and excludable, then lump-sum taxation is superior to income taxation (Barro & Sala-i- Martin, pp. 645, 660).

In many models of endogenous growth (e.g. Grossman & Helpman, 1991; Romer, 1987, 1990), technological progress corresponds to an expansion in the number of types of capital goods, inventions require active R&D, and firms are compensated through the retention of monopoly power over the use of their inventions. Therefore, the models involve elements of imperfect competition as the excess of the monopoly price over the competitive one implies that the private rate of return on investment falls short of the social return, and, hence, that the steady-state growth rate is below the socially optimal rate. A common feature in all three types of models – learning-by-doing with spillovers, taxation of income from capital (in models where government services are not subject to congestion) and varieties of capital goods under imperfect competition – is the shortfall of the private rate of return on investment from the social one. This implies that the Pareto optimum can be attained in each model if the government raises the private rate of return on investment to the social one without introducing other distortions. This outcome can be achieved either by subsidizing the purchase of capital goods or by subsidizing the income on capital. Another measure is to subsidize research to raise the private rate of return to the social rate and to provide further incentive to private producers to create new types of capital goods.[41]

Barro and Sala–i–Martin (1995) combine the Arrow (1962) and Romer (1986) assumptions of learning-by-doing and knowledge spillovers. In their model, the social optimum can be attained in a decentralized economy by providing various forms of subsidies that work to raise the private rate of return to investment and thereby tend to eliminate the excess of social over private returns. For instance, the government could induce the private sector to attain the social optimum if it provided subsidies to the purchases of capital goods (an investment-tax credit), financing it through a lump-sum tax. Further options open to the government are: providing subsidies to the purchase of intermediate goods, incentive to expand over time using a lump-sum tax to finance a subsidy, subsidies to final output so that producers receive units of revenue for each unit of good produced, or a direct subsidy to R&D spending to raise the private rate of return on R&D and provide a sufficient incentive for research. Therefore, two policy instruments are needed: one that encourages production of the monopolized intermediates and another that stimulates R&D.[42]

Aghion and Howitt (1998) argue for a role for public intervention to support innovative activities either through the design and use of subsidies (direct targeted or untargeted subsidies) or the design of property rights and patent legislation. They suggest that the R&D investments should be subsidized whenever positive external effects dominate and as a result growth under laissez-faire is suboptimal, but that R&D investment should be taxed if too much "business-stealing" or creative destruction takes place under laissez-faire. They distinguish between targeted and untargeted subsidies, the choice between them depends essentially on availability of information to the government. Targeted R&D subsidies are direct government subsidies that are deliberately aimed at particular sectors (e.g. defence), industries or firms. It may take the forms of public investments in state owned laboratories, research grants, participation in R&D funds, subsidies to enterprises (e.g., input subsidies), credit guarantees, and public investment in high-technology industries. Untargeted subsidies is another important instrument of direct policy intervention in the R&D sector, offered on a non-discriminatory basis according to market decision, without targeting particular firms, industries or projects; untargeted subsidies take the form of research tax credits, tax deductions, credit guarantees, subsidized insurance for risky capital investments, etc. Aghion and Howitt indicate other forms of government intervention to increase incentives/subsidies for R&D efforts: through the government's buying up or reducing of the outside investors' share or equity in independent research units and turning it over to R&D firms. Finally, they show that the government has a vital role in enforcing property rights by allowing firms involved to earn monopoly rents as a reward for innovation.[43]

[41] See Barro and Sala-i- Martin (1992, pp. 651–652, 654–655).

[42] See Barro and Sala–i–Martin (1995, pp. 146, 147, 150–151, 222, 223, 226, 229–230).

[43] See Aghion and Howitt (1998, pp. 474, 489).

Jones (1998) indicates that many models in the endogenous growth literature have the implication that changes in government policies, such as subsidies to research or taxes on investment, have level effects but no long-run growth effects. For instance, a government subsidy that increases the share of labour in research will typically increase the growth rate of the economy, but only temporarily, as the economy transits to a higher level of income.[44]

Several studies emphasize a role for government intervention and the positive impact of public provision of education and training. For instance, Azariadis and Drazen (1990) suggest a role for government intervention in the education sector (through education subsidies) to avoid low-development traps and thereby promote high sustained growth. Otani and Villanueva (1990) and Barro and Sala–i–Martin (1995) illustrate, for a cross section of countries, a positive impact of government interventions on growth rates coming from the expenditure side (i.e. the share of public expenditure on education of the GDP). Barro and Sala–i–Martin find that public spending on education has a significant positive effect on growth: a 1.5 % increase of the ratio of public education spending to GDP during the period 1965–1975 would have raised the average growth during the same period by 0.3 % per year. Aghion and Howitt (1998) indicate that centralized funding of education will always favor human capital accumulation and therefore growth in the long run, even though local funding may sometimes be growth-enhancing in the short run.[45] Trostel (2002) suggests that public provision of education through subsidy has the potential to be the most efficient educational policy because it provides incentives and stimulates investment in and accumulation of human capital. A recent report by the UNESCO–UIS/OECD (2003) stresses the role of public finance in enhancing investments and returns from education in a number of selected countries. Chatterji (1995) presents a growth model based on Lucas (1988) model to explore a potential role for government intervention by subsidizing training to compensate private sector for the positive externalities they generate and to provide more incentives for more investment in the accumulation of skills. The model assumes two possible sources of growth: exogenous technical progress and endogenously produced skills growth. The optimal subsidy on training rises with the rise/strength of the externality generated by the average skill level in output production; it also depends on macroeconomic variables such as the extent of productivity growth from other sources in the economy.[46]

One interesting observation by Aghion and Howitt (1998) indicates that the finding with respect to the complementarity between educational attainment and R&D activities has in turn many interesting policy implications. First, it suggests that "macroeconomic policies which affect rates of innovation and investment will

[44] See Jones (1998, pp. 147, 112).

[45] Otani and Villanueva (1990) is cited in Haslinger and Ziesemer (1996, p. 236). Azariadis and Drazen (1990) and Barro and Sala–i–Martin (1995) respectively are cited in Aghion and Howitt (1998, pp. 333, 328). See also Aghion and Howitt, p. 338).

[46] See Chatterji (1995, pp. 274–282).

affect the relative demand for workers classified by education, and hence the aggregate skill distribution of employment and earning. (Bartel & Lichtenberg, 1987)". In other words, governments will increase the average level of education not only directly through education policy, but also indirectly by actively supporting R&D activities. Conversely, government subsidies to education will increase the profitability of research and development activities, and thereby speed up technological progress (Aghion & Howitt, 1998, pp. 339–340).

Few studies examine the practical relevance of the models of growth enhancing policies, particularly for the developing countries. For instance, Haslinger and Ziesemer (1996) indicate that most of the models of publicly financed investment in human capital are basically intended for industrialized and not for developing countries. In their view, in the developing countries, raising the publicly financed investment is hampered by the lack of a well-developed institutional setup to use the instruments of taxation, mainly because of substantial engagement in non-monetised activities, a large informal sector, extreme poverty and different effects from the prevalent regressive trade tax (Haslinger & Ziesemer, pp. 240–241).[47]

Apart from these practical limitations for the developing countries, in the recent years there is a growing body of literature on the role of public policies and government intervention to promote human capital and technological capabilities in the developing countries. For instance, Lall (1999) discusses strategies to develop skills and capabilities in developing countries and argues that there is a valid case for policies to coordinate, guide and subsidize learning; and to develop such factors as skills and technology where externalities and information failures are particularly pervasive. He identifies two broad successful strategies in the developing world to promote skills and learning for competitiveness. First, autonomous strategies to accelerate and guide learning by domestic firms by promoting infant industries, coordinating investments in related activities, overcoming externalities, directing credit, and developing specific skills and institutions. Second, foreign direct investment (FDI) dependent strategies that rely on Transnational Corporations (TNCs) to lead export growth and upgrading, which has two subsets of strategies: those based on targeting TNCs and using industrial policy to guide them in more technology intensive activities; and more passive strategies that rely on market forces to attract and upgrade activities. Korea and Taiwan are leading example of national-led strategy, Singapore and Malaysia of the FDI-led targeted strategy, and Mexico and Thailand of the FDI-led market-led strategy (Lall, pp. 9–10).

[47] In the case of the Gulf countries, the extent of both the 'non-monetised' activities and informal sector is less clear. However, different from other developing countries, in the Gulf countries both the prevalence of the welfare states- absence of extreme poverty (cf. UNDP, 2004)- and the recent structural reform of fiscal and monetary policies and labour market (cf. Fasano & Iqbal, 2003) may imply a promising role for government intervention.

3.6 Conclusions

In this chapter we provide a background for the empirical analysis in the following chapters by surveying the theoretical and empirical literature that emphasize the positive growth effects of human capital and technological progress in increasing and sustaining economic growth. We explain that economic growth theories recognized and provided different perceptions and analytical frameworks for modelling the various effects of technical change, innovation and human capital on economic growth. The major differences arise because the exogenous growth theories perceive and model technical progress and human capital as exogenous variables in growth accounting model, whereas the endogenous growth theory envisages and models technical progress and human capital as endogenous variables determining the rates and differences of economic growth across countries. The endogenous growth theory contributes to improve understanding of the interaction between technological change, human capital and economic growth and fills the gap in earlier growth theories by considering the important endogenous effects of human capital, technological progress and innovation. The endogenous growth theory predicts that in the long run economic growth at the aggregate level is determined by endogenous sources of technological change, human capital, learning by doing, spillovers of knowledge and external effects of human capital. The presence of increasing returns to scale and externalities prevent diminishing returns to accumulation of capital, and so ensure the long run steady state of growth within a dynamic general equilibrium framework. We illustrate that the inclusion of human capital and technological change in growth accounting models motivate endogenous growth literature to provide several interesting explanations of the relationship between human capital and technical change. In particular, it stimulates considerable debate about the complementary relationship between human capital and technical progress, skilled biased technical change, the role of technical progress in skill upgrading and the role of skill and improvement in the accumulation of human capital in skill upgrading. These explanations imply that next to the important endogenous effects of technical progress and human capital for economic growth, the complementary relationships between them and between them and skill upgrading are also important for enhancing economic growth. Finally, we show the advantages and limitations of several measures of technological change and human capital that have been used in theoretical and empirical literature, some of these measures are relevant for the empirical analysis in the next chapters according to availability of data.

References

Abramovitz, M. (1956). Resource and output trends in the United States since 1870. *American Economic Review, Papers and Proceedings, 46*, 5–23.

Abramovitz, M. (1986). Catching up, forging ahead and falling behind. *Journal of Economic History, 46*, 385–406.

Acemoglu, D. (1998). Why do new technologies complement skills? Directed technical change and wage inequality. *Quarterly Journal of Economics, 113*(4), 1055–1089.

Aghion, P., & Howitt, P. (1990). *A model of growth through creative destruction* (NBER working paper series, Vol. 3223). Cambridge, MA: National Bureau of Economic Research, Jan 1990. http://www.nber.org/papers/w3223.pd

Aghion, P., & Howitt, P. (1992). A model of growth through creative destruction. *Econometrica, 60*(2), 323–351.

Aghion, P., & Howitt, P. (1998). *Endogenous growth theory*. Cambridge, MA: MIT Press.

Arrow, K. J. (1962). The economic implication of learning by doing. *Review of Economic Studies, 29*, 155–173.

Autor, D. H. (2000). *Why do temporary help firm provide free general skills training?* (NBER working paper series, Vol. 7637, p. 37). Cambridge, MA: National Bureau of Economic Research, Apr 2000. http://www.nber.org/papers/w7637.pdf?new_window=1

Autor, D. H., Katz, L. F., & Krueger, A. B. (1998). Computing inequality: Have computers changed the labour market? *Quarterly Journal of Economics, 113*(4), 1169–1213.

Azariadis, C., & Drazen, A. (1990). Threshold externalities in economic development. *Quarterly Journal of Economics, 105*(2), 501–526.

Barro, R. (1991). Economic growth in a cross section of countries. *Quarterly Journal of Economics CVI, 106*(2), 407–443.

Barro, R. (1996). *Determinants of economic growth: A cross- country empirical study* (NBER working paper series, Vol. 5698). Cambridge, MA: National Bureau of Economic Research, Aug 1996. http://www.nber.org/papers/w5698.pdf

Barro, R. J., & Lee, W. (1993). International comparison of educational attainment. *Journal of Monetary Economics, 32*(3), 363–394.

Barro, R. J., & Lee, W. (1996). International measures of schooling years and schooling quality. *American Economic Review, Paper and Proceedings, 86*(2), 218–223.

Barro, R. J., & Lee, W. (2000a). *International data on educational attainment updates and implications* (NBER working paper series, Vol. 7911). Cambridge, MA: National Bureau of Economic Research, Sept 2000. http://www.nber.org/papers/w7911.pdf

Barro, R., & Lee, W.-J. (2000b). *International data on educational attainment: Updates and implications*. Cambridge, MA: Department of Economics, Harvard University. Data set at International Development at Harvard University (CID), Apr 2000. http://www.cid.harvard.edu/cidwp/pdf/042.pdf

Barro, R. J., & Sala-i- Martin, X. (1992). Public finance in models of economic growth. *The Review of Economic Studies, 59*(4), 645–661.

Barro, R. J., & Sala–i–Martin, X. (1995). *Economic growth*. New York: McGraw Hill.

Bartel, A. P., & Lichtenberg, F. (1987). The comparative advantage of educated workers in implementing new technology. *The Review of Economics and Statistics, LXIX 69*, 1–11.

Bartel, A. P., & Sicherman, N. (1995). *Technological change and the skill acquisition of young workers* (Graduate School of Business Paper series, Vol. 95–10). New York: Columbia University.

Bartel, A. P., & Sicherman, N. (1999, August). *Technological change and the skill acquisition of young workers* (NBER working paper series, Vol. 5107). Cambridge, MA: National Bureau of Economic Research. http://www.nber.org/papers/w5107.pdf.

Becker, G. S. (1962). Investment in human capital: A theoretical analysis. *Journal of Political Economy, 70*(1), 9–49.

Becker, G. (1964). *Human capital*. Chicago: The University of Chicago press.

Benhabib, J., & Spiegel, M. M. (1994). The role of human capital in economic development: Evidence from aggregate cross-country data. *Journal of Monetary Economics, 34*, 143–173.

Berman, E., Bound J., & Griliches, Z. (1994). Change in the demand for skilled labour within U.S. manufacturing industries: Evidence from the Annual Survey of manufacturing. *Quarterly Journal of Economics*, *CIX*(2), 367–397 (*109* May, 367–398).

Berman, E., Bound, J., & Machin, S. (1998). Implications of skill-biased technological change: International evidence. *Quarterly Journal of Economics, 113*(4), 1245–1279.

Bound, J., & Johnson, G. (1992). Change in the structure of wages in the 1980s: An evaluation of alternative explanations. *American Economic Review, (LXXXII) 82*(3), 371–392.

Bresnahan, T. F., Brynjolfsson, E., & Hitt, L. M. (1999). *Information technology, workplace organization, and the demand for skilled labour: Firm- level evidence* (NBER working paper series, Vol. 7136). Cambridge, MA: National Bureau of Economic Research, May 1999. http://www.nber.org/papers/w7136.pdf?new_window=1

Chatterji, M. (1995, September). Training subsidies, technical progress and economic growth. *The Manchester School, LXIII*(3), 274–282. Blackwell, The Victoria University of Manchester.

Cheah, B. H. (1997). Can government engineer the transition from cheap labour to skill- based competitiveness? The case of Singapore – (Chap. 4). In M. Godfrey (Ed.), *Skill development for international competitiveness*. Cheltenham, Brookfield: Edward Elgar.

Cheon, B-Y. (1999). Employment, occupations and skills in increased international exposure: The Republic of Korea 1970–1990. *Employment and Training Papers, 39* – ILO, 2–3, 12–15, 18, 246–268.

Colecchia, A., & Papaconstantinou, G. (1996). *The evaluation of skills in OECD countries and the role of technology* (STI working paper, Vol. 1996/6). Paris: OECD – OECD/GD (96) 183.

Dension, E. F. (1962). *Sources of growth in the United States and the alternatives before us* (Supplement paper, Vol. 13). New York: Committee for Economic Development.

Dosi, G., Freeman, C., Nelson, R. R., Silverberg, G., & Soete, L. (Eds.). (1988). *Technical change and economic theory*. London/New York: Printer.

Fasano, G., & Iqbal, Z. (2003, September). *GCC countries: From oil dependence to diversification*. Washington, DC: International Monetary Fund.

Freeman, C., & Soete, L. (1994). *Work for all or mass unemployment? Computerised technical change into the twenty – first century*. London: Printer.

Freeman, C. & Soete, L. (1997). *The economic of industrial innovation* (3rd ed., pp. 2, 24, 404–405). London: Cassell.

Garcia Cervero, S. (1997). *Growth technology, and inequality: An industrial approach* (EUI working paper, ECO, Vol. EC 471/97/26). Florence: European University Institute. https://catalogue.lse.ac.uk/Author/Home?author=European%20University%20Institute.%20Economics%20Department."https://catalogue.lse.ac.uk/Record/517760

Goldin, C., & Katz, L. F. (1998). The origin of technology skill complementarity. *The Quarterly Journal of Economics, 113*(3), 693–732.

Griliches, Z. (1969). Capital– Skill complementarity. *The Review of Economic and Statistics, LI, 69*, 465–468.

Grossman, G. M., & Helpman, E. (1991). *Innovation and growth in the global economy*. Cambridge, MA: MIT Press.

Hanushek, E. A., & Kim, D. (1995). *Schooling, labour force quality and economic growth* (NBER working paper series, Vol. 5399). Cambridge, MA: National Bureau of Economic Research, Dec 1995. http://www.nber.org/papers/w5399.pdf?new_window=1

Haslinger, F., & Ziesemer, T. (1996). Endogenous growth and distributional conflict. In C. Gore, G. Köhler, U. Peter Reich, & T. Ziesemer (Eds.), *Questioning development* (pp. 223–240). Marburg: Metroplis Verlag.

Hwang, Gyu-heui (2000). *Diffusion of information and communication technologies and changes in skills* (Electronic working paper series, Vol. 48). Brighton, Sussex, UK: Science and Technology Policy Research (SPRU), University of Sussex, 3 Oct 2000. http://www.sussex.ac.uk/Units/spru/publications/imprint/sewps/sewp48/sewp48.pdf

ILO. (1998). World employment report 1998/1999: Employability in the global economy how training matters, Chap. 2. In *Globalization, technological change and demand for skilled labour* (p. 35). Geneva: ILO.

Jones, C. (1998). *Introduction to economic growth*. New York/London: W.W. Norton and Company.

Jorgonson, D. W., Gallop, F. M., & Fraumeni, B. M. (1987). *Productivity and U.S. economic growth*. Cambridge, MA: Harvard University Press.

Kahn, J. A., & Lim, J. S. (1998). Skilled labor-augmenting technical progress in U.-S. manufacturing. *The Quarterly Journal of Economics., 113*(4), 1281–1308.

Kendrick, J. W. (1956). Productivity trends: Capital and labour. *Review of Economic and Statistics, 38*(3), 248–257.

Lall, S. (1999). *Competing with labour: Skills and competitiveness in developing countries* (Issues in development discussion paper, Vol. 31, p. 17). Geneva: Development Policies Department, ILO.

Lee, W., & Barro, R. J. (1997). *Schooling quality in a cross section of countries* (NBER working paper). Cambridge, MA: National Bureau of Economic Research.

Lillard, L. A., & Tan, H. W. (1986). *Private sector training: Who gets it and what are its effects?* (Santa Monica RAND Corporation Report, R-3331, DOL-RC). Santa Monica, CA: Rand Corporation.

Low, L. (1998). *Jobs, technology and skills requirements in a globalized economy: Country study on Singapore* (Employment and training paper, Vol. 13). Geneva: Employment and Training Department-ILO.

Lucas, R. E. (1988). On the mechanics of economic development. *Journal of Monetary Economics, 22*, 3–42. North Holland.

Machin, S., & Van Reenen, J. (1998). Technology and changes in skill structure: Evidence from seven OECD countries. *Quarterly Journal of Economics, 113*(4), 1215–1244.

Mankiw, N. G., Romer, D., & Weil, D. (1992). A contribution to the empirics of economic growth. *The Quarterly Journal of Economics, 107*(2), 407–437.

Mincer, J. (1989). *Human capital response to technological change in the labor market* (NBER working paper series, Vol. 3207). Cambridge, MA: National Bureau of Economic Research, Dec 1989. http://www.nber.org/papers/w3207.pdf?new_window=1

Mulligan, C. B., & Sala–i–Martin, X. (1995). *Measuring aggregate human capital* (NBER working paper series, Vol. 5016, p. 2). Cambridge, MA: National Bureau of Economic Research, Feb 1995. http://www.nber.org/papers/w5016.pdf?new_window=1

Muysken, J., Hoppe, M., & Rieder, H. (2002a). *The impact of education and mismatch on wages: Germany, 1984-2000* (MERIT research memoranda, Vol. 2002–031). Maastricht: Maastricht University.

Muysken, J., Weissbrich, A., & von Restorff, C. H. (2002b). *The impact of education and mismatch on wages: The USA, 1986-1996* (MERIT research memoranda, Vol. 2002–015). Maastricht: Maastricht University.

Muysken, J., & ter Weel, B. (1998). *Overeducation and crowding out of low skilled workers* (MERIT research memorandum, Vol. 98–023). Maastricht: Maastricht University.

Nelson, R. R. (1959). The simple economics of basic scientific research. *Journal of Political Economy, 67*, 297–306.

Nelson, R., & Phelps, E. (1966). Investment in humans, technological diffusion and economic growth. *American Economic Review: Papers and Proceedings, LVI, 61*, 69–75.

Nelson, R. R., & Winter, S. G. (1977). In search of useful theory of innovation. *Research Policy, 6* (1), 36–76.

Nelson, R. R., & Winter, S. G. (1982). *An evolutionary theory of economic change*. Cambridge, MA: Harvard University Press.

OECD (Organisation for Economic Co-operation and Development). (1997). *The Second European Report on science and technology indicators (1997)* (pp. 37, 90–91). Paris: OECD.

Otani, I., & Villanueva, D. (1990). Long-term growth in developing countries and its determinants: An empirical analysis. *World Development, 18*(6), 769–783.
Rebelo, S. (1991). Long – run policy analysis and long – run growth. *Journal of Political Economy, 99*(3), 500–521.
Romer, P. M. (1986). Increasing returns and long run growth. *Journal of Political Economy, 94*(5), 1002–1037.
Romer, P. M. (1987). Growth based on increasing returns due to specialization. *American Economic Review, 77*(2), 56–62.
Romer, P. (1989). *Increasing returns and new development in the theory of growth* (NBER working paper series, Vol. 3098, p. 22). Cambridge, MA: National Bureau of Economic Research.
Romer, P. M. (1990). Endogenous technological change. *Journal of Political Economy, 98*(5, Part 2), 71–102.
Romer, P. M. (1994). The origin of endogenous growth. *Journal of Economic Perspectives, 8*, 3–22.
Rosen, S. (1976). A theory of life earnings. *Journal of Political Economy, 84*(4), S45–S67.
Sanders, M., & ter Weel, B. (2000). *Skilled biased technical change: Theoretical concept, empirical problems and a survey of the evidence* (MERIT research memorandum, Vol. 2000–12). Maastricht: Maastricht University.
Schultz, T. W. (1961). Investment in human capital. *American Economic Review, 51*(1), 1–17.
Schultz, T. W. (1964). *Transforming traditional agriculture*. New Haven, CT: Yale University Press.
Schumpeter, J. (1934). *The theory of economic development* (p. 66). Cambridge, MA: Harvard University Press.
Schumpeter, J. (1942). *A capitalism, socilaism and democracy*. New York: Harper and Brothers.
Shell, K. (1967). A model of inventive activity and capital accumulation. In K. Shell (Ed.), *Essay on the theory of optimal economic growth* (pp. 67–85). Cambridge, MA: MIT Press.
Smith, A. (1776). *An inquiry into the nature and causes of the wealth of nations*, Everyman Edition (1910), London, New York: J.M. Dent, Random House, 1937.
Smith, K. (2000, Aug 23–24). *Measurement of innovation in Europe: Concepts, experience and results, STEP Group*. Paper presented to Conference on the Measurement of Industrial, Technological Competitiveness for Knowledge – Based Economy, Taipei.
Solow, R. (1956). A contribution to the theory of economic growth. *Quarterly Journal of Economics, 70*, 65–94.
Solow, R. (1957). Technical progress and the aggregate production function. *Review of Economics and Statistics, 39*, 312–320.
Stokey, N. L. (1991). Human capital, product quality and growth. *Quarterly Journal of Economics, 106*(2), 587–616.
Swan, T. W. (1956). Economic growth and capital accumulation. *Economic Record, 32*, 334–361.
Trostel, P. A. (2002). Should education be publicly provided? *Bulletin-of-Economic-Research, 54* (4), 373–391.
UNDP. (2004, July). *Human development report (2004): Cultural liberty in today's diverse world*. New York/Oxford: UNDP/Oxford University Press.
Uzawa, H. (1965). Optimum technical change in an aggregative model of economic growth. *International Economic Review, 6*(1), 18–31.
Ziesemer, T. (1987). *Economic theory of underdevelopment*. Regensburg: Transfer Verlag.
Ziesemer, T. (1990). Public factors and democracy in poverty analysis, *Oxford economic papers* (Special issue on public economics, Vol. 42, pp. 268–280). Reprinted in P.J.N. Sinclair, & M.D.E. Slater (Eds.), *Taxation, private information and capital*. Oxford: Clarendon Press.
Ziesemer, T. (1991). Human capital, market structure and taxation in a growth model with endogenous technical progress. *Journal of Macroeconomics, 13*(1), 47–68.
Ziesemer, T. (1995). Endogenous growth with public factors and heterogeneous human capital producers. *Finanzarchiv*, Neue Folge, Band 52, Heft 1, 1–20.

Part III
Empirical Application

Chapter 4
Research Methodology and Method of Data Collection

4.1 Introduction

The previous chapter discussed the theoretical and empirical endogenous growth literature on the relationship between technical progress, human capital (education) and economic growth, which we considered as a useful background for the empirical investigation that follows in the next chapters. Before we go into the empirical analysis, it is appropriate to define the methods of data collection and illustrate the composition and operation of the surveys in this chapter. In Sect. 4.2 we explain the motives for performing the macro and firm surveys (2002) and selection of a case study. Next, we show the selection of the sample and composition of the surveys in Sect. 4.3; and explain the structure and design of the questionnaire in Sect. 4.4. Section 4.5 provides the conclusions, advantages and limitations of the surveys.

4.2 Motivation and Selection of a Case Study

The empirical investigation in this research uses a combination of primary and secondary data covering both the macro and micro levels. We collected our primary data using both macro and firm surveys (2002) and interviews. We explain the reasons for undertaking two surveys below, after which we spell out the selection of the case study, the sample, design and composition of the surveys.

The basic objective of conducting the macro and firm surveys (2002) was to obtain specific information to provide insights into the factors influencing or the causes and consequences of low skill and technology indicators and to help generate policies to enhance skill and technology. The macro survey (2002) examines the causes and consequences of the deficiency of the educational

S. Mohamed Nour, *Technological Change and Skill Development in Arab Gulf Countries*, Contributions to Economics, DOI 10.1007/978-3-319-01916-1_4,

system and the firm survey (2002) discusses the implications of the excessive use of unskilled foreign workers.[1]

We held the macro survey (2002) due to a lack of enough materials needed to investigate the research problem, assess upskilling efforts, examine the causes and consequences of deficient educational systems, training provision, skills mismatch and transfer of knowledge at the macro level. The survey also aimed to explore, from the perspectives of policy makers and experts, relevant short and long run plans and policies for the enhancement of skill levels, education, training, transfer of knowledge and technological upgrading.

The main reason for conducting the firm survey (2002) was to fill the information gap due to a lack of relevant, reliable and up-to-date information to allow a more comprehensive analysis and a deeper understanding of the status of skill and technology at the micro level. The survey requested quantitative data to assess technology indicators measured by R&D, patent and ICT and to evaluate skill indicators measured by educational attainment, average years of schooling and experience and occupational level. In addition, additional information was sought to assess the use, level, transfer and dependence on foreign technology, to determine the important factors hindering, and those contributing toward enhancing the provision of training, mechanisms and plans for skill upgrading across firms.

The field research to collect our primary data was held in the period from February to April, 2002 in the UAE as a case study of the Gulf countries. The selection and focus of our analysis on the UAE was related to the easy accessibility to data and information and facilities for the fulfilment of the fieldwork/surveys, which were offered by the Centre for Labour Market Research and Information affiliated to TANMIA – UAE Ministry of Labour and Social Affairs. Moreover, in recent times, the UAE ranks first amongst the Gulf countries in terms of ICT diffusion: for instance, the World Bank (2003) indicates that the share of the UAE population accessing the Internet represents 52.8 % and 42.3 % of total Gulf population accessing the Internet in 2000 and 2001 respectively. In addition, the UAE has the highest per capita manufacturing product in the Gulf region.[2] "The UAE business-friendly environment and good infrastructure have also been key sources to maintain competitiveness and growth in the non-oil sectors. These factors have made the UAE an attractive place to invest in, particularly in the free zones, for companies seeking to serve the growing markets of the Middle East, North Africa, India and Pakistan." (cf. Goyal, 2003, p. 49).

The main limitation of our selection was that the UAE does not report the highest performance within the Gulf region with respect to both skill and technology indicators. Our analysis in Chap. 2 above illustrates that the UAE is falling behind Saudi Arabia and Bahrain in terms of technological performance (patent and R&D indicators) and educational performance (educational enrolment, average years of schooling and the

[1] In the appendices, we list the set of questions that were sent out to the sample of firms, policy makers and experts included in the surveys. In addition, we present a brief definition of some of the terms used in the various questions that were provided as a guide to help the respondents.

[2] See for instance the UAE Ministry of planning, Annual report (2004).

percentage of students enrolled in S&T disciplines) respectively. Despite the possible advantages of considering the case of Saudi Arabia and Bahrain, due to some practical difficulties concerning accessibility to data and information, we will be focusing only on the UAE as an in-depth case study to represent the Gulf countries.

We observe a lack of coherence, insufficient performance and wide differences across the Gulf countries that are most noticeable in terms of skill and technology indicators – cf. Tables 2.8 and 2.9 above respectively. For instance, regarding skill indices – measured by the Harbison Myers index, technical enrolment index and engineering enrolment index – Kuwait shows high performance, followed by Saudi Arabia, UAE and Oman respectively. With respect to gross enrolment ratio in tertiary education, Qatar shows high performance followed by Saudi Arabia, Kuwait and Bahrain respectively, while UAE and Oman respectively show poor performance. Concerning the share of tertiary students in science, math and engineering, Oman shows high performance followed by UAE and Kuwait respectively, while Saudi Arabia shows poor performance. With regards to school life expectancy, Bahrain shows high performance followed by Qatar, the UAE shows medium performance, whereas Kuwait, Oman and Saudi Arabia respectively show poor performance. In terms of the technology indicator, as measured by expenditures on R&D as a percentage of GDP over the period 1996–2002, Kuwait shows high performance followed by Saudi Arabia, while Oman, Bahrain and Qatar respectively show medium performance, and the UAE only shows poor performance. In terms of technology indicator, as measured by application to patents over the period 1991–1999, Saudi Arabia shows high performance, Kuwait and the UAE respectively show medium performance, whereas Qatar and Bahrain respectively show poor performance– cf. Table 2.9. Probably, the only exception to the lack of coherence appears from the use of ICT in relation to income level. For instance, the high income Gulf countries (UAE, Kuwait, Bahrain and Qatar) achieve growth in the use of ICT that is higher than medium income Gulf countries (Oman and Saudi Arabia) – cf. Table 2.9 above. In terms of Internet users in the Gulf countries in 2000 and 2001, the UAE (53 % and 42 %), Kuwait (15 % and 13 %) and Bahrain (12 % and 28 %) had high shares; Qatar (10 % and 9 %) and Oman (9 % and 6 %) each had a medium share, whereas Saudi Arabia (2 % and 2 %) only had a low share.

The firm survey (2002) covers medium and large size firms engaged in two industries in the manufacturing sector: the chemical and metal industries.[3] The selection of both industries was based on the following reasons: First, the argument in favour of both upskilling and technological upgrading is promising in both sectors

[3] In the firm survey (2002), the chemical sector includes manufactures of basic industrial chemicals, fertilizers and pesticides, synthetics, resin and related materials, paints, varnishes and lacquers. In addition, petrochemicals, pharmaceuticals, drugs and medicines, soap and cleaning preparations, chemical products, petroleum refineries, miscellaneous petroleum and coal products, tyre and tube industries, rubber products and plastics product are also included in this sector. The metal sector includes basic metal products, fabricated metal products, machinery and equipment; however, the firm survey covers only the fabricated metal industries represented by aluminium and iron-steel because of their significant share in employment, capital and number of industrial establishments, as explained in this section.

and can be used to reduce the dependence on foreign workers. Second, both sectors have strategic importance in creating forward and backward linkages and spin-off effects to other sectors/industries. Third, both sectors have the potential to produce energy-intensive use products benefiting from the comparative advantage of the cheapest energy sources, particularly petroleum and natural gases available in the UAE and the Gulf region. Fourth, the potential for product diversification in both sectors is promising. Fifth, the important contribution of both sectors in the manufacturing sector, for instance, in the year 2000, the contribution of both sectors together was around 29.8 % of total labour force, 18.7 % of capital investment and 33.3 % of the total number of industrial establishments in the manufacturing sector. In particular, the shares of the chemical sector accounted for 10.7 %, 10.7 % and 16.59 %, while that for the metal sector accounted for 19.17 %, 7.98 % and 16.67 % respectively.[4] This implies that the contribution and distribution of both sectors enable us to compare between the chemical as a capital-intensive sector and the metal as a labour-intensive sector. Table 4.1 illustrates the distribution of both chemical and metal industrial establishments according to the size/share of employment in the UAE and the Gulf countries. Sixth, both basic metal and chemical industries have approached high levels in terms of both technological intensification and full automation in the UAE in the period 1991–1995 (cf. Cohen, 2000).

Other important reasons for the selection of the chemical industry are the strategic importance of this industry in the international market, and the diversified nature of the chemical sector in the Gulf. For instance, data and statistics from GOIC (1996) and the UAE Ministry of Industry (1998) indicate that, in the years 1995 and 1998, with the inclusion of the manufacture of refined petroleum products to the petrochemical, chemical and plastic sector, the whole sector tended to be capital-intensive. In the years 1998 and 1999, with the exclusion of the manufacture of refined petroleum products, the petrochemical, chemical and plastic sector alone show more intensity in terms of labour than capital. In the year 2000 the petrochemical, chemical and plastic sector shows similar/equal intensity of both labour and capital, which may indicate similar capital/labour and output/capital ratios. Further strategic importance of this industry is the significant contribution of oil in oil and related industries in the Gulf economy.

Other reasons for the selection of the fabricated metal (aluminium, iron and steel) industry are the significant contribution of both aluminium and iron-steel as sub sectors in the fabricated metal products sector. For instance, in the year 1995, both sub-sectors together accounted for 52.2 % of total employment, 61.4 % of total capital investment, and 54.2 % of total number of industrial establishments in the fabricated metal products sector.[5] In addition, aluminium is a significant industry in the UAE: for instance, Dubai Aluminium company is the largest single site aluminium smelter in the western world.[6] Furthermore, the aluminium industry could have

[4] See for instance the GOIC (1996) Data and Statistics.

[5] See the GOIC (1996) Data and Statistics (1996, p. 123).

[6] See Dubai Aluminium Company (DUABL). (2000). DUBAL achievement report. Unpublished report, http:// www.dubal.ae, Dubai, UAE. Accessed April 20, 2002.

Table 4.1 The distribution of chemical and metal industries defined by employment size in the UAE and the Gulf countries (1998–2000)

Industry	Chemical		Metal		Total manufacturing industries	
Employment size: N	UAE[a]	Total Gulf countries[b]	UAE[a]	Total Gulf countries[b]	UAE[a]	Total Gulf countries[b]
Small: N < 50	283 (74 %)	521 (40 %)	374 (63 %)	749 (38 %)	1,298 (60 %)	2,766 (38 %)
Medium: 50 ≤ N ≤ 100	57 (15 %)	327 (25 %)	120 (20 %)	472 (24 %)	382 (18 %)	1,659 (24 %)
Large: N > 100	43 (11 %)	466 (35 %)	104 (17 %)	763 (38 %)	473 (22 %)	2,663 (38 %)
Total	383	1,314	598	1,984	2,153	7,088

[a]UAE Ministry of Industry and Finance (2000) "Industrial Statistical Book. (2000)," Abu Dhabi, UAE, 2000
[b]GOIC Industrial Data Bank (1998)

a wider utility in the region, given the potential increase in the demand for aluminium products due to the possible wider use of aluminium, owing to the natural characteristics of aluminium as a metal with thin weight and high degree of purification and flexibility, to replace/substitute other metals (such as iron) in industry (GOIC, 2000, p. 99).

4.3 The Selection of the Sample and Composition of the Surveys

The sample in the firm survey (2002) was drawn from the medium and large size firms active in the chemical and metal industries, which are located in three emirates of Abu Dhabi, Dubai and Sharjah.[7] The selection of these emirates was based on their significant average share in total employment (87 %), capital investment (86.4 %) and total number of factories (82.6 %) in the chemical and fabricated metal industries in the UAE – cf. Table 4.2 below.[8] Moreover, the selection of medium and large size firms was based on their share in total employment, which accounted for 23.62 % of medium and large size enterprises working in the manufacturing sector (28.53 % of medium size and 19.66 % of large scale

[7] For the purpose of this study, firm size is defined by employment size N. The small size firms are firms with N <50, the medium size firms those with 49 < N < 100, and the large size firms those with N ≥ 100 workers.

[8] These emirates also have strategic importance in the UAE: for instance, Abu Dhabi accounts for more than half of the country's total GDP, close to 40 % of the population, and 90 % of oil and natural gas resources. Dubai contributes one-fourth of the country's total GDP and has been at the forefront of developing non-oil activities. Sharjah currently accounts for 45 % of UAE manufacturing (cf. Fasano, 2002, p. 330).

Table 4.2 The average percentage share of emirates of Abu Dhabi, Dubai and Sharjah in total number of factories, labour, capital and medium and large size firms in the chemical and metal industries (2000)

Industry	Number of factories	Share of capital (%)	Share of labour (%)	Employment size: % of employment in medium and large size establishments in the manufacturing sector		Total employment in medium and large size establishments in the manufacturing sector	
				Medium	Large	Medium	Large
Chemical products	80.75 %	83.30 %	83.25 %	11.25 %	7.40 %	43	35
Metal products	84.5 %	89.5 %	90.8 %	17.28 %	12.26 %	66	58
Average total	82.6 %	86.4 %	87 %	28.53 %	19.66 %	109	93

Source: UAE Ministry of Industry and Finance (2000) "Industrial Statistical Book. (2000)," Abu Dhabi, UAE, 2000

enterprises) in these three emirates. Our sample drawn from these three emirates is quite representative, since the coverage of firms in the sample and survey represents 81 % and 35 % of the chemical and metal industries respectively and 62 % and 44 % of the large and medium size firms respectively.[9] We employed the recent secondary data published by the UAE Ministry of finance and industry "The Industrial Statistics Book (2000)" in selecting a sample of the firms in the survey.

The questionnaire on "Technological Change and Skill Development" was circulated amongst 106 of the chemical and metal medium and large size enterprises in the UAE. It aimed at collecting micro qualitative and quantitative data, and covered the medium and large size firms engaged in both the chemical and metal industries in the UAE. Table 4.3 below presents the composition of the firm survey. The response rate varied according to firm size and industrial activity: for the chemical industry the total response rate was 40 %, and the weighted response rates by employment size was 44 % and 37 % for medium and large size firms respectively. For the metal industry the total response rate was 44 %, and the weighted response rates by employment size were 47 % and 41 % for medium and large size firms respectively.[10]

[9] The distribution of firms in the sample is based on two facts: the great diversity of the chemical compared to metal industries and the potential for upgrading skill and technologies in the large compared to medium size firms.

[10] For the implementation of the firm survey (2002), a team of part-time researchers from the National Human Resources Development and Employment Authority (TANMIA) – UAE Ministry of Labour and Social Affairs were hired to make direct personal contact, determine the contact address, then handle, distribute and collect the survey from firms. On request from some of the approached firms, an additional copy of the survey was sent by fax to accelerate and increase the response rates.

Table 4.3 Composition of the firm survey (2002) in the UAE, 2002

Industry	Employment size	Share of employment in sample	Share of capital in sample	Share of firms in sample	Number of firms in the sample	Number of the respondent firms[a]	Response rate
Chemical	Medium	57 %	87 %	26 %	25	11	44 %
	Large	59 %	17 %	33 %	38	14	37 %
	Total	59 %	20 %	59 %	63	25	40 %
Metal	Medium	42 %	14 %	22 %	19	9	47 %
	Large	40 %	83 %	19 %	24	10	41 %
	Total	41 %	80 %	41 %	43	19	44 %
Grand total		100 %	100 %	100 %	106	44	42 %

[a]The term respondent firms in Table 4.3 refers to all firms that returned the questionnaire, including the firms who did not answer/respond to some questions. This implies that response rates vary enormously across firms as some firms did not respond to all questions – see Table 4.5 below. This may constitute further limitations, as we explain below

The macro survey (2002) on "Skill Creation, Human Resources Development and Policy Intervention" provides primary macro qualitative data. The questionnaire was sent to 40 policy makers in government and experts in 14 public, university and educational institutions in the UAE. It aimed to collect macro qualitative data to reflect the opinions of policy makers and experts with respect to assessment of skill upgrading efforts and the causes and consequences of deficient educational system, provision of training, transfer of knowledge and technological upgrading. It was also intended to provide insights to help to generate policies to enhance them by implementation of short and long terms plans at the macro level. The selection of both institutions and policy makers and experts was based on their experience and potential contribution to enhance upskilling process. The advantage of the macro survey (2002) is that it examines these problems after integrating two different perspectives of policy makers and experts. Moreover, due to their close association to educational and training institutions, the approached policy makers and experts provided some useful information from both the analytical and policy perspectives. Table 4.4 below presents the composition of the macro survey (2002), and indicates a total response rate of 75 %; the shares of universities, ministries and other public institutions are quite representative and yield different response rate.[11]

The data from the surveys is supported by ten face-to-face interviews with firm managers and five interviews with policy makers and experts. The purpose of these interviews was to obtain more information to support the findings from the macro survey concerning the failure of upskilling efforts, the deficiency in educational and

[11] For the implementation of the macro survey (2002), we established direct personal contact to handle and accelerate the distribution and collection of the survey. On request from some of the approached officials, an additional copy of the survey was sent by fax to accelerate and increase the response rates. The translated Arabic version of the macro survey was distributed along with the English version.

Table 4.4 Composition of the macro survey (2002) in the UAE, 2002

	Institutions			Individuals		
Representation	Number in sample	Total response	Response rate (%)	Number in sample	Total response	Response rate (%)
Universities	5	2	40	12	6	50
Ministries	5	5	100	15	11	73
Other public centres and authorities	4	4	100	13	13	100
Total	14	11	79	40	30	75

training systems, and the implications on skills mismatch, transfer of knowledge, R&D efforts and development of the local technologies, as well as the policies and plans of government and private sector to enhance the upgrading of local skills and local technology, the R&D efforts, networks and transfer of knowledge.

4.4 Structure and Design of the Questionnaire

We present the general structure and design of the questionnaire of the macro and firm surveys (2002) in Table 4.5. The questionnaire in the macro survey (2002) was composed of six sections, and the average response rate ranked in a descending (downward) way, i.e. generally higher for the first four sections, moderate for the fifth section and low for the sixth section.[12] Each of the six sections in the macro survey was designed to request specific information. Section 1 requested general assessment of upskilling efforts from the perspectives of policy makers and experts. Section 2 inquired the relevant policies and important factors contributing to enhance skill upgrading, education, training and the transfer of knowledge. Section 3 investigated the causes of low skill, deficient education, training, external effects of schooling, transfer of knowledge and skills mismatch. Section 4 examined both currently implemented plans and suggested future short and long run plans and policies for skill upgrading and determined the role of skill upgrading and technological upgrading in fulfilling the socio-economic development objectives. Section 5 sought information to check the incidence of external effects of schooling/the transfer of knowledge and the important factors hindering and those contributing toward enhancing the external effects and the transfer of knowledge. Finally, section 6 requested further recommendations for skill upgrading in the UAE.

The questionnaire in the firm survey (2002) was composed of five sections; the average response rate was higher for the first section, moderate for the second and

[12] The design of the questionnaire in the macro survey (2002) includes three types of questions: nominal (Yes/No), scalar or categories, and open questions. The distribution of question types and their corresponding average response rate are identical, for instance, majority of questions are of scalar type, which also receives higher average response rate, followed by nominal and open questions respectively.

Table 4.5 Structure, aims and average response rate of the questionnaire in the firm and macro surveys (2002) in the UAE, 2002

	Macro survey (2002)		Firm survey (2002)	
Section No	Aim of the section	Average Response Rate (%)	Aim of the section	Average response rate (%)
1	Request general assessment of upskilling efforts	99	Request general background information about the structure, identification and characteristics of the firms	82
2	Investigate the relevant policies to enhance skill upgrading, education, training and transfer of knowledge	97	Investigate the use, level, transfer and dependence on foreign technology, value and trend of ICT expenditures. Technology indicators, patent, R&D, ICT and product/process innovations	60
3	Examine the causes of low skill, deficient educational system and the consequences on training provision, external schooling effect/transfer of knowledge and skills mismatch	94	Measure human capital (skill) indicators: distribution of workers by skill levels, educational attainment/ average schooling years, occupational level, average years of experience, required qualifications and average wages. Assess the effect of skilled workers and their shortage on firm product, the factors hindering and other enhancing the incidence and transfer of knowledge/ external effects of schooling and firm upskilling plan	45
4	Examine the short and long-term mechanisms for skill upgrading, their effect on technological upgrading and fulfilling socio-economic aims	93	Examine the use of technology and the implications on upgrading skill level and the past and future demand for skilled and unskilled workers. The effect of upskilling on technological upgrading and self-reliance on local skills	67
5	Investigate the incidence of external effects of schooling and transfer of knowledge, their hindering and promoting factors	74	Examine the relative importance of firm training and short and long run skill upgrading mechanisms. The information,	54

(continued)

Table 4.5 (continued)

	Macro survey (2002)		Firm survey (2002)	
Section No	Aim of the section	Average Response Rate (%)	Aim of the section	Average response rate (%)
			coverage, resources and support to firm training, the factors hindering and other promoting the provision of training	
6	Conclusions	43		

fourth sections and low for the third and fifth sections.[13] Each of the five sections in the firm survey aimed to request particular information. Section 1 requested general background information about the structure, identification and characteristics of the firms, it also requested (interval) economic quantitative data on the value and trend of firm production and performance indicators, including: employment, net worth (capital), profit, sale, output and product diversification by sale and employment. Section 2 examined the use of technology, level, transfer and dependence on foreign technologies. It assessed technology indicators, patent applications, spending on R&D, and product and process innovations, the use of ICT, firm production and demand for high skilled and also requested quantitative data on the value and trend of ICT expenditure. Section 3 requested quantitative data to measure human capital/skill indicators, defined by the distribution of workers by skill level, educational attainment (average year of schooling), occupational levels, average years of experience, attained and required education and average wages. This section also examined the effect of skilled workers on firm production, the incidence of external effects of schooling, the factors hindering and others contributing toward enhancing the transfer of knowledge at the firm level, firm upskilling plans and their various effects. Section 4 inquired into the implication of technology use on both upgrading skill levels and on the past and future demand for skilled and unskilled workers, and also examined the effect of firm upskilling plans on technological upgrading and self-reliance on local skill. Section 5 investigated the relative importance of the effort of training, the short and long run skill development mechanisms, the coverage, resources and support offered to firm training, the factors hindering and other contribute toward promoting the success of training at the firm level.

[13] The design of the questionnaire in the firm survey (2002) includes four types of questions: nominal (Yes/No), scalar or categories, open and interval questions. The distribution of the questions and their corresponding average response rates vary. Most of the questions are of scalar type, followed by nominal, interval and open questions respectively; and the corresponding average response rate is higher for nominal questions, followed by scalar, open and interval questions respectively.

4.5 Conclusions

The data from the firm and macro surveys (2002) provides us with the required information, which is particularly useful for presenting a macro-micro comparative analysis to identify the causes and consequences of the skills problem, and the plans and policies for skill development from the macro-micro perspectives. The results of the macro survey (2002) seem quite representative, since the selection covers government, universities, and educational and training institutions. One advantage of the macro survey (2002) is that it examines the problem after integrating two different perspectives of policy makers and experts. Another advantage is that, due to their close association to educational and training institutions, the approached policy makers and experts provided some useful information, particularly from both the analytical and policy perspectives. Moreover, the data evaluates upskilling efforts, examines the causes and consequences of a deficient educational system, training provision, skills mismatch and transfer of knowledge; and also suggests relevant short and long run plans and policies for the enhancement of skill level, education, training, transfer of knowledge and technological upgrading. The main limitation of the macro survey (2002) is the low response rate from the university sector, probably because some of the academics lacked adequate information to enable them to contribute to a critical analysis of the causes and consequences of low skill levels.

The results of the firm survey are quite representative, since the selection and coverage of firms in the survey include a broad range of firms working in the chemical and metal industries, which provides us with relevant data and information that of considerable use in our analysis. Such coverage also has the advantage of enabling us to compare between firms according to two criteria, i.e. the size of employment and industrial activity. Moreover, the firm survey presents some background information, which is also quite useful for a further analysis of firms based on other characteristics such as the geographical location, sector (public-private), net worth (capital), ownership and nationality of owner (government, foreign, mixed) and foreign orientation or affiliation to multinational corporation (MNC/TNC). Another advantage of the firm survey is that it presents more specific but also quite comprehensive data and information that allow us to use a wide range of quantitative data and information for measuring skill and technology indicators and the link between them at the micro level/across firms. In addition, the survey data allows us to approximate and examine the importance of tacit knowledge, and enables us to compare between attained and required education and to measure the skills mismatch across firms. At the micro level, realizing the differences in both tacit knowledge and technologies used across chemical and metal industries when comparing their effects and interaction, we define tacit knowledge by the share of high skilled workers in total employment and technology by the share or total spending on ICT.

One major limitation with respect to firm survey (2002) is the low response rate for some questions, especially where the answers or data required quantitative measurement. Such problems arose because some of the respondents firms were unwilling to provide complete and reliable quantitative data or some of the respondents firms offered somewhat selective answers. For example, some firms seemed hesitant to provide information about training and skill upgrading efforts – see Table 4.5 above. An intensive follow-up with firms often improved the quality and quantity of the response rate. However, the hesitance of some firms compelled us to exclude them when their observations were incomplete, missing and unreliable. Therefore we used only completed and reliable observations in our estimation and analysis in the next chapters. Apart from this limitation, the data from the firm and macro surveys remains useful from both the analytical and policy perspectives and is suitable to use in the empirical investigation in Chaps. 5, 6 and 7 and also for the policy analysis and recommendations in Chap. 8.

References

Cohen, S. I. (2000, September). *Employment imbalances in the private sector: Problems, solution and policies* (Specialist Rep. No. 9). Dubai: The Ministry of Labour and Social Affairs: National Strategy for Labour Force Development and Employment Project. Unpublished Report.

Dubai Aluminium Company (DUABL). (2000). DUBAL achievement report. Unpublished report, http://www.dubal.ae, Dubai, UAE. Accessed April 20, 2002.

Fasano, G. (2002). *With open economy and sound policies, U.A.E. Has turned oil "curse" into a blessing, IMF Survey* (pp. 330–332). Washington: International Monetary Fund.

Firm Survey. (2002, April). *Technological change and skill development: A comparative study of chemical and metal medium and large scale enterprises in the UAE*. UAE: Firm Survey.

Goyal, R. (2003, March). Non-oil growth, competitiveness, and the labor market. In *United Arab Emirates: Selected issues and statistical appendix* (pp. 41–58) (IMF Country Rep. No. 03/67). Washington: International Monetary Fund.

Gulf Organization for Industrial Consulting (GOIC). (1996). *Features of industrial economy in the UAE*, Data and Statistics (1996) (p. 123). GOIC: Doha.

Gulf Organization for Industrial Consulting (GOIC). (1998). *Gulf statistical profile 1998: GOIC industrial data bank*. Doha: GOIC.

Gulf Organization for Industrial Consulting (GOIC). (2000). *Features of industrial economy in the Gulf cooperation council countries GCC countries: Gulf industrial base: Industrial data bank*. Doha: GOIC.

Macro Survey. (2002, April). *Skill creation, human resources development and policy intervention: Interviews with policy makers and experts in the UAE*. UAE: Macro Survey.

The UAE Ministry of Planning. (2004). Annual report (2004). Abu Dhabi.

The World Bank. (2003). World development indicators (2003). Washington, DC: The World Bank.

UAE Ministry of Industry and Finance. (2000). Industrial statistical book (2000). Abu Dhabi, UAE.

Chapter 5
Assessment of Skill and Technology Indicators

5.1 Introduction

In this chapter we use the data and results of the firm and macro surveys set out in Chap. 4 to examine the third hypothesis in Chap. 1 about the serious implications of the interaction between the deficient educational system and the high incidence of unskilled foreign workers. In particular, we use the results of the macro survey to show the causes of the deficient educational system and consequences on low skill levels, poor provision of training, skills mismatch and low transfer of knowledge at the macro level. In addition, we use the results of the firm survey to illustrate that the high incidence of unskilled foreign workers leads to low skill level, poor provision of training, skills mismatch, poor technology indicators and a heavy dependence on foreign technologies. The rest of this chapter is organized as follows: Sect. 5.2 shows the causes and consequences of the deficient educational system and the high incidence of unskilled foreign workers and their implications on low skill levels, poor provision of training, skills mismatch, lack of knowledge transfer, low level of local technology and heavy dependence on foreign technology. Section 5.3 presents the micro–macro views about the upgrading of skill and technology and their potential implications. Section 5.4 provides the conclusions. The main ideas discussed in this chapter are summarized in Scheme 5.1 below.

5.2 Causes and Consequences of Deficient Educational System

The results of the macro survey indicate that, at the aggregate level, the official efforts to promote and upgrade the levels of local skill have been relatively successful only in some sectors.[1] In general, there has been a serious failure and

[1] As reported by 63 % of the respondent policy makers and experts to the macro survey.

S. Mohamed Nour, *Technological Change and Skill Development in Arab Gulf Countries*, Contributions to Economics, DOI 10.1007/978-3-319-01916-1_5,

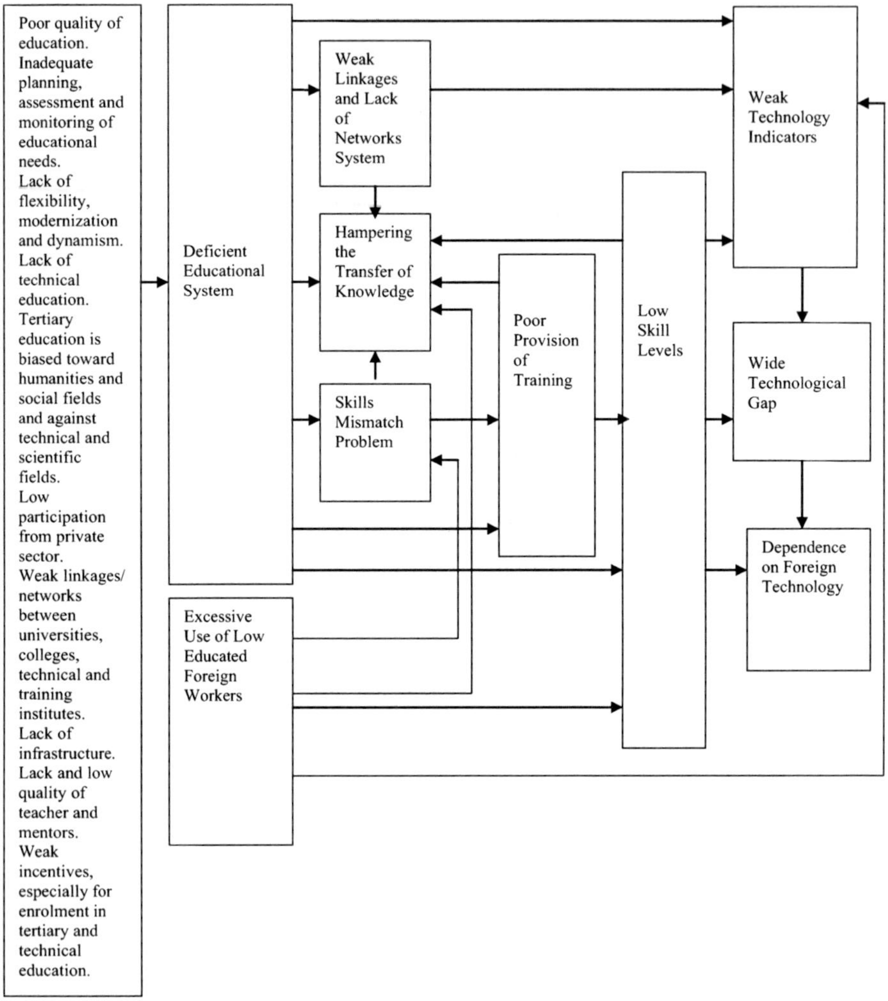

Scheme 5.1 The causes and consequences of the deficient educational system and the excessive use of low educated foreign workers

shortcoming of the upskilling process, which is mainly attributed to: (1) inadequate training provision; (2) the deficient educational system; (3) misallocation of resources; and (4) failure of educated and trained workers to transfer knowledge.[2]

We begin our discussion by the second reason i.e. the deficient educational system, because we want to argue that both inadequate training provision and the failure of educated and trained workers to transfer knowledge are direct

[2] As indicated by 97 %, 83 %, 70 % and 70 % of the respondent policy makers and experts respectively.

implications of deficient education, while the misallocation of resources is indicated as one cause of both deficient education and the poor provision of training.

5.2.1 Causes of Deficiency in the Educational System

With respect to the second cause, Table 5.1 shows that the deficiencies of the educational system appear in both the basic and tertiary educational systems. Major causes are the inadequate assessment and monitoring of educational needs, low quality and internal efficiency of the educational system, and inadequate planning. Other important factors are the weak linkages/networks between universities, colleges, technical and training institutes, the lack of flexibility of educational institutions, the weak incentives for enrolment in technical education and the lack of modernization and dynamism. Finally, the low involvement and spending by the private sector and the low spending in technical education are also mentioned, but are of somewhat less importance. That also holds good for the lack of infrastructure (due to inadequate investment/public spending on education) and the lack of teachers and mentors. For instance, the share of public spending on education in GDP in the UAE (1.9 %) is low compared to other Gulf countries like Saudi Arabia (9.5 %) and other advanced Asian countries such as Korea (3.6 %) and Malaysia (7.9 %) (The UNDP, 2004) – see our discussion of the supply side of educational policies in Chap. 8. Moreover, according to the twin-peaks analysis in Ziesemer (2004), which compares the distribution of public spending on education across countries, the UAE's less than 2 % public spending on education falls below the average 4.6 % of public spending on education to improve the accumulation of human capital in 1998.

We observe that, according to 82 % of the respondents to the macro survey, the low quality and efficiency of the educational system appears from the low quality at basic, secondary and tertiary education relative to international standards. Important causes are the low rates of accomplishments and motivation at higher secondary and tertiary education levels relative to international standards, but the problem is somewhat less at the basic education level. Another serious problem is the low quality of teachers and mentors,[3] while less important causes include, the high pupil/teacher ratios, the low public current expenditure per pupil, the low survival rates and high drop-out and the high repetition rates.[4, 5]

[3] As reported by 79 % of the respondent policy makers and experts to the macro survey.

[4] As indicated by about 61 %, 54 %, 50%and 50 % of the respondent policy makers and experts to the macro survey respectively.

[5] We observe that the presence of high drop-out levels in the transition from schooling education to university education, which implies the lack of social awareness of the importance of tertiary education or preference of more certain short term return to available jobs than long term investment in education and skills.

Table 5.1 The causes of deficient educational system in the UAE, 2002

Causes of deficiency	General educational system (basic + tertiary) (%)	Basic education (%)	Tertiary education (%)
Inadequate assessments and monitoring of educational needs	84.5	83	86
Low quality/efficiency of educational system	82.5	79	86
Inadequate planning for educational needs	82.5	79	86
Lack of flexibility of educational institutions	77.5	76	79
Weak incentives for enrolment in technical education	75.5	76	75
Lack of modernization and dynamism	73.5	76	71
Low involvement and spending by private sector	70	72	68
Low spending in technical education	68.5	69	68
Weak linkages [networks] between universities, colleges, technical and the training institutes	79	–	79
Lack of infrastructures due to Inadequate investment (public spending on education)	58	55	61
Lack of teachers and mentors	54.5	55	54

Source: Own calculation based on the Macro Survey (2002)

5.2.2 *Consequences of the Deficient Educational System*

5.2.2.1 Mismatch Between the Output of Education and the Market Needs

We find that both the deficient basic (primary and secondary) and tertiary educational systems together lead to serious mismatch between the output of education and the market needs. In particular, about 96 % of the respondents to the macro survey reported that the mismatch is mainly attributed to deficiency of both tertiary and basic education. Moreover, the follow-up interviews with policy makers and experts show that the mismatch is attributed to the deficient educational system,[6] the lack of coordination and planning to meet the critical skill needs and the cultural/social reasons: preference for white-collar jobs and biased against technical education and technical jobs. For instance, the deficiency of tertiary educational system is caused by the inconsistent structure: the share of students enrolled in the UAE between 1994 and 1997 in all social sciences, humanities and art faculties (73 %) was much higher than those of sciences, math and engineering (27 %).

[6] As in most other developing countries, the mismatch is attributed to deficiency in the educational system. Another interpretation in the Gulf countries attributes this to culture: i.e. preference for white-collar jobs.

The share of students enrolled in sciences, math and engineering in the UAE is also low compared to both Korea (34 %) and China (53 %) (The UNDP, 2002, 2003) – cf. our discussion on the demand for education in Chap. 8.[7]

5.2.2.2 Lowering Skill Levels

From the UAE Ministry of Economy (1985, 1995), (The UAE Population Census Data (1985, 1995)) and the educational matrix for the period 1985–1995 set out in Table 5.2, we observe the low skill levels – defined by educational level of total population. The share of low educated (71–66 %) is much higher than that of high educated (10–12 %) in total population. That also indicates a minimal skill upgrading, defined by the relative rise in the share of high educated population and the relative decline of the share of low educated population during the period 1985–1995.[8] In addition, the UAE Ministry of Planning Statistical data (1995–1997) on the distribution of economically active population by occupational classification (1985–1995) shows the low skill level defined by occupational levels, for instance, the share of unskilled population (86–81 %) is much higher than that of high skilled population (13–18 %). That also implies a slight improvement in skill

[7] These results are also consistent with the findings of both El Sabaa (1997) and Haan (1999) respectively. "Reviewing the numbers of student enrolled in the UAE University shows that the total number of enrolled students in engineering, science, agriculture and medicine faculties in 1994 was nearly 24 % of the total number of the enrolled students. While the number of other theoretical faculties, mainly, literature, economics, education, and law in the same year were accounting for 76 % of the total number of enrolled students. The other foreign and private faculties operating in the UAE are stressing on the theoretical branches of education. Similarly, the Higher Faculties of Technology are also allocated the larger part of its studies to business management at the expense of other technological and engineering branches. This leads to imbalanced distribution of graduates and the limited contribution of researchers, technologists and engineering to the local manpower: It is noticeable that the larger segment of local manpower tends to prefer managerial and commercial domains. Thus, the number of theoretical faculties graduates has been much more than the vacancies available in managerial careers and government services" (El Sabaa, pp. 20–21). "While the UAE has in recent years made progress in developing its human resource base, its educational system is still largely geared towards general education and most of the students in higher education are found in humanity and similar studies. Technical skills are lacking and technical education and training, which historically does not enjoy much status in society, are lagging far behind. For instance, from the HCTs, the first one of which only opened their doors in the late 1980s, have so far graduated only 264 engineers, some of these graduates still lack a great deal of field practice. Moreover, most of the qualified people with technical skills still end up working in the government and white collar work in general reflecting the bias against technical and manual work in particular, very, very few actually work in practical jobs in private firms and other jobs which would require them to work in the field" (Haan, p. 37).

[8] At the aggregate level, the educational matrix implies the distribution of population according to educational level: low level of education refers to illiterate, literate, primary and preparatory school; medium level of education includes secondary, post-secondary and below university; and high level of education includes university and postgraduate levels.

Table 5.2 The UAE educational matrix: the distribution of population by educational level (1985–1995)

1985		Low	Medium	High	Not stated	Total
Native	Male	0.079314	0.009192	0.005544	0.000012	0.094062
	Female	0.001677	0.002463	0.001705	0	0.005845
	Total	0.080991	0.011655	0.007249	0.000012	0.099907
Non-native	Male	0.585299	0.143734	0.081035	0.000209	0.810277
	Female	0.044652	0.02966	0.015462	0.000042	0.089815
	Total	0.629951	0.173394	0.096497	0.000252	0.900093
Total population		0.710942	0.185049	0.103746	0.000263	1
1995						
Native	Male	0.052143	0.017576	0.00929	0.00001	0.07902
	Female	0.001916	0.00433	0.005526	0.000001	0.011774
	Total	0.05406	0.021907	0.014816	0.000012	0.090794
Non-native	Male	0.557998	0.150259	0.093477	0.002628	0.804362
	Female	0.05228	0.032108	0.020365	0.000091	0.104844
	Total	0.610278	0.182367	0.113841	0.00272	0.909206
Total population		0.664338	0.204274	0.128657	0.002732	1

Source: Own calculation from the UAE Ministry of Economy (1985, 1995), "The UAE Population Census Data (1985, 1995)," UAE Ministry of Economy, Abu Dhabi, UAE, (1985, 1995).

upgrading defined by the increasing share of high skilled and a falling share of unskilled during the period (1985–1995). Furthermore, as we explain below, the low skill levels at the macro level is consistent with that at the micro level.

5.2.2.3 Hampering Transfer of Knowledge

Our results in Table 5.3 show that the low quality of education hindered the easy transfer of knowledge and external schooling effects. According to the macro survey, only 42 % of the respondent policy makers and experts reported that the incidence of knowledge transfer/external schooling effect is successful, while around 58 % reported that the transfer of knowledge/the external schooling effects are constrained by several factors. The major important factors include: the low quality of education, the low quality of training, prevailing conditions in the firm do not encourage external effects, failure of skilled workers to deliver knowledge to unskilled workers and failure of unskilled workers to acquire knowledge from skilled workers.[9]

[9] The transfer of knowledge and external schooling effects refers to knowledge transferred from knowledge holders (high skilled workers/people) to knowledge recipients (low skilled workers/people) – cf. Cowan, Soete and Tchervonnaya (2001, p. 9). Knowledge in this sense refers to know how or tacit knowledge embodied in people, and is different from the broad definition of technology, which refers to both embodied and disembodied knowledge.

Table 5.3 The factors constrained the transfer of knowledge/external schooling effect in the UAE, 2002

Factors constrained the transfer of knowledge/external effect of schooling	Officials (%)
Low quality/return from education	95
Low return form/quality of training compared to international standard	95
Prevailing conditions in the Firm conditions do not encourage the external effect	95
Failure of skilled workers to deliver their knowledge and experiences to benefit unskilled workers	90
Failure of unskilled workers to acquire the knowledge and experience from skilled workers	90

Source: Own calculation based on the Macro Survey (2002)

In strong contrast to this view, the results of the firm survey show that, at the micro/firm level, the incidence of knowledge transfer/external schooling effect is successful among 95 % of the respondents firms. It is only unsuccessful within two firms because of the following: the low quality of education, the low quality of training, the prevailing conditions in the firm do not encourage the external effects and the failure of unskilled workers to acquire knowledge from skilled workers.[10]

This contradicting optimistic-pessimistic views at the micro and macro levels regarding the incidence and success of knowledge transfer/external schooling effect implies that the transfer of knowledge/the external schooling effects is probably successful within firms but unsuccessful between firms and within society at large. This is consistent with our observations from the follow-up interviews that the transfer of knowledge is hindered by both the low quality of education and the lack of cooperation with university sector due to inadequate awareness and lack of social partnership between public sector, private sector, university sector and society. The weak linkages and lack of networks between universities, colleges, technical and training institutes and the productive sectors is mentioned by 79 % of the respondents to the macro survey as factor that constrains the efficiency of educational system – it probably also constrains the transfer of knowledge. An additional factor is that the transfer of knowledge within society at large is probably hindered by the imbalanced structure of population and labour market. Mainly due to the excessive share of foreign workers with different nationalities, cultures, languages, etc. that probably hindered their sufficient integration and interaction with local

[10] Another possible explanation for the low transfer of knowledge can be interpreted in relation to the prevailing conditions within private firms. Since within private firms most of the highly skilled posts as well as most of the low skilled posts are held by foreigners, there may be less incentives for the incidence of transfer of knowledge from high to low skilled workers.

workers and local population.[11] This is probably also due to a lack of incentives at the aggregate level.[12]

Finally, the macro survey indicates that the contribution of both educated and trained population to promote the local skills is constrained by several causes. Major causes are the lack of interaction to market needs (mismatch) and the lack of information on educational and training needs in the productive sectors and their demand for graduate students.[13] Other important causes are: risk aversion, i.e. the preference of more certain short term returns to available jobs than long term skill investments; the uncertainties about future skill needs; the lack of a system of certification of skilled acquired; and inadequate incentives for trainers.[14] Relatively less important causes include the uncertainties about the future value of investment in education and training and the high costs to finance education and training.[15] These factors probably also contribute to hinder the transfer of knowledge within society at large.

5.2.2.4 Poor Provision of Training

Both the deficient educational system and the excess supply of low skilled foreign workers lead to a low skill level and hinder the provision of training. Table 5.4 shows that both the policy makers and experts (officials) and firm managers mentioned the low educational qualifications of workers among the important factors constraining the provision of training. Other important factors are the lack of appreciation/information about training, inadequate assessment and planning for training programmes and the mismatch problem. Moreover, the results of the firm

---

[11] This result is consistent with the finding of El Sabaa (1997), who notes: "It is widely observed that industrial entrepreneurs in the technically advanced projects are strictly against leakage of their technologies outside their factories. Thus, they minimally contribute to developing the technology environment in the country. This adverse impact has been amplified by the unwillingness of foreign as well as local entrepreneurs to employ local manpower, to train them in their factories, either because they doubt their capabilities, or for fear to leaking their technology secret to other competitors. The limited supply of local industrial manpower, coincided with the unwillingness to employ them in both foreign and local industries applying advanced technologies, resulted in constricting the role supposed to be played by expatriate manpower in transferring technology to the industrial sector in the Gulf region. Moreover, the large scale industries despite using more sophisticated advanced technologies, however, they minimally contribute to elevate the technology transfer to the local industrial sector, as they strictly keep their operational and managerial techniques as top confidential secrete and prevent their leaking outside their units. To some extent, the chance of their flow to the rest of the operating factories seems better in the medium size factories" (El Sabaa, p. 22, pp. 24–25).

[12] The lack of transfer of knowledge can be interpreted as a lack of absorptive capacity, mainly related to deficiencies of education and continued dependence on imported technologies.

[13] As indicated by 82 % and 79 % of the respondent policy makers and experts respectively.

[14] As reported by 75 % of the respondent policy makers and experts.

[15] As indicated by 71 %, and 61 % of the respondent policy makers and experts respectively.

Table 5.4 The factors constrained the provision of training in the UAE, 2002

Factors constrained the provision of training	Official	All firms	Chemical	Metal	Medium	Large
Inadequate planning for training programme	93 %	42 %	43 %	40 %	50 %	25 %
Inadequate assessment of training needs	93 %	50 %	57 %	40 %	63 %	25 %
Mismatch between training programme and changing technical needs	96 %	33 %	29 %	40 %	38 %	25 %
Mismatch between training programmes and changing skill needs	96 %	33 %	29 %	40 %	38 %	25 %
Low quality of trainers and mentors	82 %	33 %	43 %	20 %	38 %	25 %
Low educational qualifications of workers	79 %	58 %	43 %	80 %	50 %	75 %
Lack of trainers and mentors	79 %	33 %	43 %	20 %	38 %	25 %
Lack of appreciation/information about training	75 %	50 %	57 %	40 %	63 %	25 %
Lack of specialized training institutions	79 %	33 %	29 %	40 %	50 %	
Lack of full appropriability of the return from training investment	71 %	33 %	29 %	40 %	50 %	
Lack of interactions between training institutions and firms	71 %	33 %	29 %	40 %	50 %	
Lack of finance to cover the cost of training	68 %	33 %	29 %	40 %	50 %	
Lack of training materials and equipment	68 %	33 %	29 %	40 %	38 %	25 %
High rate of mobility of trainers to move for better paid jobs after training	68 %	33 %	29 %	40 %	50 %	
Lack of a system of training certification of skills acquired	71 %	8 %	14 %		13 %	
Total response	28	12	7	5	8	4

Source: Own calculation based on the Macro Survey (2002), Firm Survey (2002)

survey illustrate that the low provision of training appears from the following: (1) The lack of an in house training unit – only 23 % of the respondent firms have an in house training unit; (2) The complete absence of public financial support: for instance, none of the respondent firms received any government subsidies to support training provision; (3) The selective training provision: in the year 2001, the priority for training among the respondent firms was mostly given to production workers, production engineering staff, management staff and services workers[16]; (4) The limited type of training: most of training provision is focused on the job training, and on the job and off the job combined, which are preferred by 87 % and 91 % of the respondent firms respectively. The other types of training such as: off the job within the firm (training centre), off the job outside the firm (outside the country) and (specialist training centre inside the country) are very limited.[17] (5) The limited sources of information about training opportunities, as most of

[16] As reported by 68 %, 54 %, 43 % and 35 % of the respondent firms respectively.

[17] As indicated by 55 %, 27 % and 27 % of the respondent firms respectively.

the information about training opportunities is provided by private trainers (local and foreign companies) and the chambers of commerce. Few firms find information from public educational institutions/universities, other firms working in the same sector, and government and semi government units.,[18, 19]

5.2.3 *Consequences of the Low Educational Qualifications of Foreign Workers at the Micro/Firm Level*

In Chap. 2 we explained that one well-known fact about the Gulf countries is the high share of foreign workers in total employment. In this section we show that next to the consequences of the deficient educational system at the macro level, the high incidence of unskilled foreign workers also causes several serious implications at the micro/firm level.

5.2.3.1 Low Skill Level and Skills Mismatch at the Micro/Firm Level

From the demand perspective, the results of the firm survey can be used to argue that firm demand for low skilled workers leads to an excessive share of low skilled

---

[18] As reported by 65 %, 42 %, 35 %, 29 % and 26 % of the respondent firms respectively.

[19] These results seem consistent with the findings of the earlier studies conducted by the UAE University (1994, 1997), Gray (1999) and Abdelkaraim and Haan (2002). For instance, the UAE Education Assessment Report (1994) shows that both technical and vocational education and training provision are unregulated, uncoordinated and unplanned, while the results of the UAE University (1997) show the limited contribution to private sector training provision by both the public and government sectors. Moreover, the findings of Gray (1999) show that only 30 % of the respondent firms provide systematic training. The provision of training is selective in most cases – focused on some occupational groups, but not others – and for two-thirds of the respondent firms, the provision of training was limited to on-the-job training. The study concluded that the UAE does not have a training-led employment culture. Employers have become used to bringing in their workers from outside the country with readymade skills and replacing them with similarly skilled workers. There has been little incentive to provide skill upgrading except in response to immediate needs such as the introduction of new technology. The local training industry has suffered from the uncoordinated nature of provision and the very limited contribution by public sector organisations and higher education institutions to this variety of provision. Most of training provision has been in low-investment, low-cost and quick-profit areas such as marketing, public relations, sales, computer awareness and management development. The private sector training is relatively undeveloped and un-coordinated, and has limited market due to both limited demand and limited supply. Moreover, the provision of public sector training is constrained by the inadequate involvement of public education institutions. For instance, the Higher Colleges of Technology (HCTs) had little involvement in the important area of adult technical education, including vocational training and retraining (Gray, p. 15, pp. 33–34, p. 43). Additionally, the findings of Abdelkaraim and Haan (2002) show that the UAE public sector training is still limited due to less attention, awareness and resources (Abdelkaraim & Haan, p. 15).

workers.[20] On the other hand, from the supply perspective, our findings from the firm survey show that the excessive share of low skilled foreign workers has direct implications in lowering skill levels at the micro/firm level. For instance, Table 5.5 below shows that across firms the average percentage share of low skilled workers (71 % and 75 %) is much higher than that of high-skilled workers (29 % and 25 %) defined by both educational and occupational classifications respectively. Moreover, Tables 5.4 and 5.5 show that the poor educational qualifications of foreign workers lead to poor provision of training – see our discussion above – and a serious skills mismatch across firms, as we will explain in detail in the next chapter.[21]

5.2.3.2 Weak Technology Indicators

From the demand perspective, the results of the firm survey can be used to argue that weak technology indicators lead firms to demand and rely heavily on low skilled workers. On the other hand, from the supply perspective, the excessive share of unskilled foreign workers leads to weak technology input–output indicators across firms. From Table 5.5 above, we observe that a weak R&D indicator appears from the following: (a) The limited R&D activities/efforts performed continuously or occasionally amongst only 37 % of all the respondents firms; (b) The limited R&D activities and expenditure particularly devoted/aimed at improving firm product and to produce a new product; (c) The low R&D expenditures and R&D expenditures as percentage of total output expenditures. For instance, amongst all the respondent firms, average R&D expenditure was around 0.9 million Dirhams,[22] while the average R&D expenditures as a percentage of total output (sales value) amongst all the respondents firms accounted for only 0.01 %; (d) The low number of both full time and part time R&D employees. For instance, a large majority

[20] It is convenient in this chapter to briefly indicate the consequences with respect to low skill and skills mismatch at the micro level and to discuss this more fully later in Chap. 6. That serves our aim in this chapter to compare and integrate the macro–micro consequences of low skill level – cf. Scheme 5.1. above. This brief discussion in this chapter also substantiates the third hypothesis in Chap. 1 above about the interaction between the deficient educational system at the macro level and the high incidence of unskilled foreign workers at the micro level and the serious implications on low skill levels and skills mismatch. It is appropriate to discuss the skills mismatch problem more extensively later in Chap. 6, where we provide a broader, more in-depth and coherent analysis of skill problem and the implications of the prevalence of low-skilled foreign workers at the micro/firm level.

[21] We define the mismatch as the differences between the required and actual education. Actual education refers to high (university and above), medium (secondary) and low (below secondary) levels of attained years of education that represent the supply of skills. We define the required education by the required qualifications for each of the occupational classes translated into average years of schooling that represent the demand for skills. We observe that the inconsistency between the required and actual education implies inconsistency between demand for and supply of skills, which we interpreted as skills mismatch – cf. the detailed discussion in Chap. 6 below.

[22] The value is measured in the UAE local currency: Dirham, which equalled 3.67 US Dollars when the survey was held (2002).

Table 5.5 Main technology and skill indicators defined by firm size and industry in the UAE, 2002

		Industry		Size	
Indicator	All firms	Chemical	Metal	Large	Medium
Skill and skills mismatch indicators					
Share of high skilled (education) (%)	29 %	35 %	23 %	33 %	27 %
Share of high skilled (occupation) (%)	25 %	28 %	21 %	21 %	28 %
Share of low skilled (education) (%)	71 %	65 %	77 %	67 %	73 %
Share of low skilled (occupation) (%)	75 %	72 %	79 %	79 %	72 %
Share of firm conducting R&D (%)	37 %	47.8 %	26.3 %	47.8 %	26.3 %
high skilled wages/low skilled wages	7.5	6.9	8.1	6.3	8.4
Share of firm with skills mismatch (%)					
The high skilled group(%)	29 %	28.6 %	30 %	35.7 %	20 %
The medium skilled group (%)	72 %	69.2 %	75 %	83.3 %	55.6 %
The low skilled group (%)	66 %	60 %	71.4 %	72.7 %	50 %
Technology indicators					
Share of R&D expenditure/ total output (sales value) (%)	0.01 %	0.0115 %	0.005 %	0.017 %	0.014 %
Average R&D expenditure (×1 million UAE Dirham)	0.9	1.5	0.2	1.4	0.5
Number of R&D employees (R)	$1 \leq R \geq 11$	$1 \leq R \geq 11$	$1 \leq R \leq 10$	$1 \leq R \geq 11$	$1 \leq R \leq 5$
Number of full time R&D employees	1–11	1–11	1–5	1–11	1–5
Number of part time R&D employees	$6 \leq R \geq 11$	$6 \leq R \geq 11$	6–10	$6 \leq R \geq 11$	0
Share of firm applying for patents (%)	13 %	13 %	0	12 %	0
Share of firm in total spending on ICT (%)	100 %	88 %	12 %	95 %	5 %
Share of firm in total spending on ICT training (%)	100 %	86 %	14 %	94 %	6 %
Share of firm in total spending on ICT (%)	69 %	67 %	72 %	73 %	65 %
Share of firm with spending on ICT training (%)	52 %	50 %	56 %	68 %	35 %
The degree of automation/ use of sophisticated technologies[a] (%)	40 %	54.5 %	26.3 %	45.5 %	36.8 %

(continued)

Table 5.5 (continued)

Indicator	All firms	Industry: Chemical	Industry: Metal	Size: Large	Size: Medium
Dependence on foreign technology[b] (%)	90 %	96 %	84 %	91 %	90 %
Share of firm providing training (%)	23 %	32 %	8 %	24 %	22 %
Incidence of external schooling effect (%)	95 %	95 %	94 %	94 %	95 %

Source: Own calculation based on the Firm Survey (2002)

[a]We measure the degree of automation/sophisticated technologies qualitatively, we asked firms about their own appreciation or evaluation of the level of technologies they are using in their production

[b]We measure the dependence on foreign technologies qualitatively, we asked firms if they have an adequate capacity/ability to produce and develop local technologies and if they have purchased equipment, machines and techniques from abroad. Our definition also include quantitative measurement of the value of imported capital equipment to total capital equipment, the percentage value of capital equipment to total capital equipment that has been build by foreign companies. Finally technology transfer is also an indicator of dependence on foreign technologies – see Table 5.7 below

(87.5 %) of the respondents firms with R&D activities have a low number (1–5) of full time research employees. Only two of the large chemical firms have more than 11 full and part-time research employees and only one large metal firm has 6–10 part time research employees. For instance, the contribution of research units in adapting the imported technologies is constrained by a shortage of skilled and qualified workers amongst 86 %, 82 %, 100 %, 80 % and 89 % of all firms, chemical, metal, medium and large firms respectively, see Table 5.8 below.[23] Moreover, the follow- up interviews with the officials and firms managers revealed that R&D activities are constrained by several factors such as high costs and low public and private spending, lack of information systems, and the absence of a R&D culture due to inadequate awareness and concern. Additional constraints relate to the poor coordination between the institutions engaging in R&D activities, either due to the absence of explicit government policy or the ineffective role of a central body (e.g. government) to coordinate and promote R&D efforts and motivate collaborative research efforts between the firms sector and university sector. In addition to weak network systems, R&D efforts, in particular, are limited across

[23] We measured the contribution of a research unit to adapt the imported technologies qualitatively, by asking firms how the research unit contributed to adapting imported technologies. In addition to a lack of qualified workers, there may also be other factors such as a lack of incentives or pressure to adapt or master imported technologies as firms can always opt to buy the required technologies or techniques.

firms because of weak contact and collaboration with the university sector, this is probably attributable to the fact that the university sector is lacking resources or concern and interest to conduct joint research with the firms sector.[24]

Moreover, Table 5.5 above shows the weak technology output indicator as measured by patent applications. For instance, in the year 2001, only 13 % of all respondent firms applied for a patent; the low degree of patenting may be attributable to low R&D efforts.

In addition, a lack of R&D efforts may hinder innovative activities across firms. The increasing uses of technology has encouraged the incidence of product and process innovations, in particular, the incidence of incremental product innovation, namely, improvement of product quality amongst 88 % of all respondent firms. It has also encouraged the incidence of new process, new method of production and new combination of old output and new product.[25] But it has only slight effect on reducing total costs and increasing total sales and total profits – see Table 5.6 below.[26]

5.2.3.3 Dependence on Foreign Technology

From the demand perspective, the results of the firm survey can be used to argue that the dependency on foreign technology leads firms to demand and rely heavily

[24] This can also be interpreted as a lack of demand-pull since firms can buy all technologies or techniques. Our findings are consistent in some respects with the findings of Haan (1999) "R&D capacity in the UAE is presently very limited. While some research is taking place at the University and other institutes of higher education, it is -as usual in such institutions- more geared towards pure science and tend to have only limited relevance for the productive sector. While the Higher Colleges of Technology place emphasis on more practical training, hardly any R&D takes place, only as a by-product of the training. Within the private sector in the UAE likewise very few R&D activities are going on. Most manufacturing and other firms tend to rely on imported technologies (both in terms of hardware and software), as well as imported materials and even expatriate manpower. There is very little interest in carrying out research, and the R&D activities are small-scale in nature and mostly only concern -minor- adaptations to the companies' own products. In all it is estimated that less than 1 % of turnover is used for this purpose. The parastatel sector, in which a number of large basic industries are operating, will do better. There is also some agricultural research ongoing. Without such R&D facilities and efforts, the UAE is almost completely dependent on imported technologies. And without the necessary adaptations to local conditions (e.g. temperatures, effects of dust and sand winds, special cultural aspects, the country's socio-political system, etc.), even these technologies cannot be optimally applied. Moreover, a genuine technology culture to motivate the involvement in R&D and promotion of local technology is now absent in the UAE. The UAE society is geared more predominantly to non-technical education, training and employment. Technical qualifications and occupations are not rated very high by its social values and cultural traditions. The UAE only has a limited industrial tradition (e.g. trade), and lacks explicit policies to stimulate and direct technological development" (Haan, pp. 37–38).

[25] As reported by 73 %, 69 %, 69 % and 62 % of all respondent firms respectively.

[26] The terms new product and new process refers to new products and processes intended even just for local firm or for local market and not necessarily for the international market.

Table 5.6 The effects of increasing use of technology product and process innovations across firms in the UAE, 1999–2001

		Firm industry		Firm size	
Product/process innovation (1999–2001)	All firms	Chemical	Metal	Medium	Large
Improvement of product quality	88 %	88 %	90 %	100	82 %
Production of a new method of production	69 %	63 %	80 %	78 %	65 %
Production of a new combination of old output	69 %	75 %	60 %	78 %	65 %
Production of a new process	73 %	75 %	70 %	67 %	76 %
Production of a new product	62 %	63 %	60 %	44 %	71 %
Production of new organizational method	58 %	50 %	70 %	44 %	65 %
Improvement of training within the firm	50 %	44 %	60 %	44 %	53 %
Improvement of communication within the firm	54 %	50 %	60 %	44 %	59 %
Production of more output with low cost	58 %	50 %	70 %	56 %	59 %
Production of the same output with low cost	38 %	38 %	40 %	56 %	29 %
Open of a new market	46 %	44 %	50 %	33 %	53 %
Reduction in per unit material costs	27 %	25 %	30 %	33 %	24 %
Reduction in per unit energy costs	27 %	25 %	30 %	33 %	24 %
Reduction in total cost	35 %	25 %	50 %	44 %	29 %
Increase in total sales	38 %	19 %	70 %	33 %	41 %
Increase in total profit	27 %	6 %	60 %	33 %	24 %
Total response	26	16	10	9	17

Source: Own calculation based on the Firm Survey (2002)

on low skilled workers. On the other hand, from the supply perspective, the deficient educational and training system and a high supply of low skilled foreign workers lead to low skill levels, lack of knowledge transfer and low capability to build and promote the local technology. The results of the firm survey show that this condition leads to weak technology indicators and dependence on imported technology that appears from the following: (1) The high dependence on the imported equipment, machines and techniques among 90 % of the respondent firms. (2) The high percentage value of capital equipment to total capital equipment that has been built by foreign companies (70 %) among the respondent firms. (3) The considerable percentage value of imported capital equipment to total capital (40 %) among the respondent firms in the year 2001. (4) The short run plan for 46 % of the respondent firms is based/depends on imported technology.[27] The main reasons for the dependence on foreign technology are the lack of local technology from local suppliers, better price and better quality of foreign technology in that order.[28] Due to the high dependency on imported technologies, it is not surprising that the level of technology used is similar to international standards amongst all the respondent firms. However, a high degree of automation through the use of sophisticated and advanced technology is limited only within 40 % of all the respondent firms- see

[27] Short, medium and long run refers to next 3 years, next 3–5 years and next 10 years respectively.

[28] As reported by 84 %, 37 % and 34 % of the respondent firms respectively.

Table 5.7 The channels of technology transfer and their effects on firm production and development of local technology across firms in the UAE, 2002

	All firms	Chemical	Metal	Medium	Large
(a) Channels of technology transfer (1999–2001)					
Strategic alliance	42 %	33 %	57 %	43 %	42 %
Hiring foreign skills/technologically advanced workers/consultants	32 %	42 %	14 %	43 %	25 %
Joint ventures	32 %	25 %	43 %	43 %	25 %
FDI	21 %	33 %	0	29 %	17 %
Licensing	16 %	8 %	29 %	14 %	17 %
Others (e.g. in house technology development by hiring technologically advanced persons)	8 %	8 %	0	0	8 %
Total response (1999–2001)	19	12	7	7	12
(b) The effects of technology transfer in (1999–2001)					
Enhancing firm production	87 %	72 %	47 %	77 %	50 %
Enhancing the capacity to develop the local technologies	48 %	44 %	20 %	38 %	30 %
Total response (1999–2001)	23	18	15	13	20
(c) The effects of technologically advanced workers in					
Enhancing firm production	47 %	63 %	29 %	50 %	45 %
Enhancing the capacity to develop the local technologies	33 %	26 %	41 %	25 %	40 %
Total response (1999–2001)	36	19	17	16	20

Source: Own calculation based on the Firm Survey (2002)

Table 5.5 above. The degree of automation/sophisticated use of advanced technologies is determined by both firm size and industry/activity.[29]

The dependence on foreign technologies also appears from the reported information on the transfer of foreign technology that is made through different channels. For instance, Table 5.7 below illustrates that strategic alliances, hiring foreign skills/technologically advanced workers/consultants and joint ventures are more common channels of technology transfer, while FDI and technology licensing are less preferred channels. The transfer of technology, mainly the transfer of technologically advanced workers/consultants, has induced important effects in enhancing firm production but has had only slight effects in enhancing the capacity to develop the local technologies.[30]

[29] These results are consistent with the findings of El Sabaa (1997) "The adoption of different approaches in transferring technology differs according to certain criteria, such as: the scale of industry and its activity. Large size and some specific sectors, namely chemical and petrochemicals industries have better use of sophisticated advanced technologies" (El Sabaa, pp. 21–22).

[30] These results are consistent in some respects but differ in others with the findings of El-Sabaa (1997) and Haan (1999) respectively. "The major channels of technology transfer are: joint ventures, and industrial foreign projects, the latter accounts for the first source of technology transfer. The turn-key

In the firm survey questionnaire the question on the channels of technology transfer allows for multiple answers, assuming that firms may choose more than one channel to transfer technology.[31] Our results indicate that chemical firms are less interested in transferring technologies through formal licenses. These may not be often requested, probably because of more liberalized and open market policies that led to considerable presence of foreign capital investment and allowed for foreign and mixed ownership – cf. Table 6.1 Chap. 6 below.[32]

These findings on weak technology indicators and dependence on foreign technologies at the micro level are consistent with those at the macro level and the interaction of these findings lead to a large technological gap – see also our earlier discussion in Chap. 2 above. Our results in this chapter and Chap. 2 above verify the second hypothesis in Scheme 1.1 in Chap. 1 above that, in the short and medium term, the Gulf countries are unable to rely on local technologies and remain heavily dependent on foreign technologies.

Our findings from the firm survey show that both skill and technology indicators, product and process innovations, the channels of technology transfer and their

---

projects are preferred channel of technology transfer in the Gulf region mainly because of the keenness to avoid defects of execution and to guarantee the maximum consistency of the project's design, lines of production, quality of the products, facilities of training, etc. But it has very limited role in transferring technology to local industry, because it is confined to their plants, with no minimum leakage allowed. Thus they contribute nothing to implant advanced technologies in the country. Technology transfer to the UAE has obviously contributed to accelerating industrial and economic growth, elevating the standard of national products both quality- wise and quantity-wise. In particular, the transfer of technology contributed to rapid growth of local industrial sector. However, a number of negative factors are still adversely affecting the transfer of technology, the technologies transferred could hardly approach its target of constituting an autonomously developing local technological base, similar to those in the Far East industrial countries. Because of: the inadequate awareness of the end target of technology transfer, the lack of a constitutional framework or comprehensive plan for transferring technology, the insufficient local base of technological data, the lack of qualified local manpower necessary for transferring technology and the contracts of technology transfer" (El Sabaa, pp. 23–26)."....... The UAE is almost completely dependent on imported technologies. And without the necessary adaptations to local conditions (e.g. temperatures, effects of dust and sand winds, special cultural aspects, the country's socio-political system, etc.), even these technologies cannot be optimally applied" (Haan, p. 38).

[31] Our assumption and respective findings are plausible and consistent with the results of El Sabaa (1997), which indicate numerous different channels of technology transfer to the UAE, such as: foreign industrial investments, offset programs, training missions, technological imports, industrialization licenses, patents, technological products, foreign manpower and industrial consulting offices (El Sabaa, p. 26).

[32] For instance, Fasano (2002) indicates that other than Abu Dhabi, the emirates have established free zones that allow 100 % foreign ownership of companies. These zones are particularly important in Dubai, where they have attracted a large number of foreign companies (Fasano, p. 331). El Sabaa (1997) finds that the adoption of open market philosophy, supported by the existence of nine free zones in the seven emirates and the advantage of 100 % foreign ownership and control, encourages foreign industrial investors to set up their projects and to promote technology transfer to the UAE (El Sabaa, p. 23).

respective effects vary enormously across firms and seem determined by both firm size and industry level. For instance, Table 5.5 above shows that skill levels, technology input–output indicators (R&D and patent), the provision of training (upskilling), the dependence on imported technology, the degree of automation and the use of sophisticated and advanced technology vary across firms and increase with firm size and industry level. Moreover, the use of ICT and provision of ICT training increase with firm size, while the transfer of knowledge/external effects of schooling increase with industry level.

5.2.3.4 Shortage of Skilled Workers and Weak Adaptation of Imported Technologies

From the demand perspective, the results of the firm survey can be used to argue that low supply of skilled workers lead firms to demand and rely heavily on low skilled workers. On the other hand, from the supply perspective, our findings show that the excessive share (supply) of low skilled foreign workers and low supply of high skilled workers lead to some shortage of skilled workers, since firms are experiencing increasing demand for skilled workers, see Fig. 5.1 below. We find that the increasing demand for high skilled workers is related to increasing use of new technologies, which has not only raised the demand for these workers in the past few years, but has also encouraged firms to predict a future/long run increase in this demand. For instance, Fig. 5.1 identifies and compares past and future trends of the demand for skilled workers, which vary enormously across firms according to size and industry level. According to 61 % of the respondent firms, the interpretations of the predicted long run increase in the demand for skilled workers are related to expansions of production, project plans, increasing R&D activities, implementation of new processes, output technologies, advanced control systems and purchases of new machines and equipment. Additional reasons for the rising demand are the increasing adoption of international standards and enhancement of production, product diversification, market share, turnover, sales, shortage of man-power, competition, increasing motivation to reduce costs, increasing production, achieving high standard precision work and improving productivity and quality of work and demand for more specialized skills in IT. On the other hand, the major explanations for the predicted long run stability in the demand for skilled workers across 39 % of all respondent firms is related to the stability in quantity of production, sales, business, demand and market; as well as to the lack of a plan for critical expansion of product operations, potential stability in substituting and replacing the outgoing skilled worker in any field, the use of automated technology and the dependence on the policy of parent company-MNC and its affiliated research group.

We observe that the expected future rise in the demand for high skilled workers across firms is reasonable since increased use of skilled workers in the past has had significant effects. In particular, there have been improvements in firm production, the level of competitiveness in the local market, faster adaptation of foreign

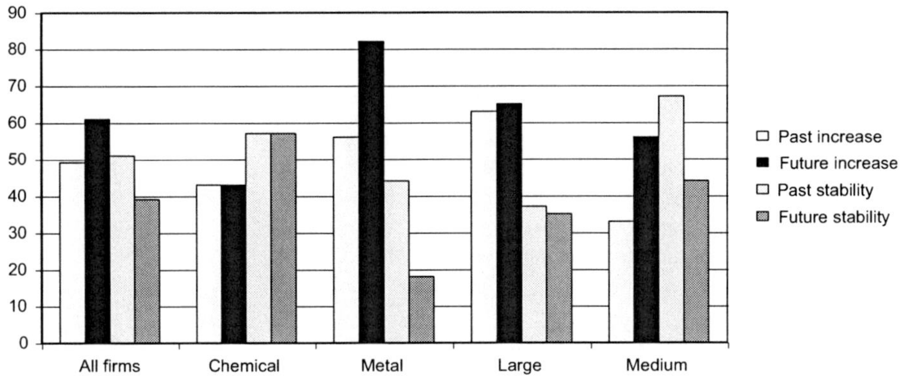

Fig. 5.1 Past and future trends (increase or stability) in the demand for skilled workers across firms (Source: Firm Survey (2002))

technology, utilization of technology and product quality.[33] On the other hand, our results from the firm survey indicate that the relative shortage of skilled workers amongst 32 % of the respondent firms leads to serious delay, slight abolishment/ cancellation of project implementation and constrains the R&D units in adapting imported technologies – see Table 5.8 below.[34]

Our analysis of the shortage in skilled workers is based on the economic interpretation and definition of 'skilled shortage' as scarcity or lack of sufficient skilled workers needed, mainly because the supply of skills (as shaped by systems of education and training) has not responded fully to the rising demand across firms. However, managers may have a different interpretation and understand this as a lack of sufficient skilled workers in conjunction with wages constraints, due to limitations on their ability to pay higher wages for the high skilled workers they demand. This may constitute a limitation and appropriate caution should be exercised in interpreting our results with respect to skilled shortage, mainly because the firms answered the questionnaires do not really make it very clear how they have perceived the shortage of skilled workers and their further consequences.

5.3 The Impacts of Skill Upgrading and Technological Upgrading: Micro–Macro Views

In view of the above findings and our results in Chap. 2 above on poor skill and technology indicators, it is therefore essential to recommend further incentives to upgrade both skill and technology levels at both micro and macro levels. From that

[33] As indicated by 90 %, 90 %, 80 %, 75 % and 60 % of the respondent firms respectively

[34] As indicated by 43 %, 15 % and 86 % of the respondent firms respectively.

Table 5.8 The shortage of skilled workers and effects across firms in the UAE, (1999–2001)

Shortage of skilled workers and effects on firm projects	All firms	Chemical	Metal	Medium	Large
Shortage of skilled workers	32 %	19 %	47 %	16 %	47 %
Effects of shortage of skilled workers on firm projects					
Serious delay of firm project	43 %	31 %	63 %	50 %	38 %
Abolishment/cancellation of firm project	15 %	16 %	13 %	0	23 %
Constrained the R&D units to adapt the imported technologies	86 %	82 %	100 %	80 %	89 %
Total response	21	13	8	8	13

Source: Own calculation based on the Firm Survey (2002)

Table 5.9 The effect of upskilling plan and technological upgrading across firms in the UAE, 2002: micro view

	All firms	Chemical	Metal	Medium	Large
(a) Upskilling plan and its impacts, self-reliance strategy					
General Upskilling plan	55 %	48 %	65 %	47 %	63 %
Upskilling plan specially for national workers	19 %	21 %	17 %	10 %	27 %
Self-reliance strategy: special training programs for upskilling national workers	52 %	59 %	42 %	40 %	64 %
Self- reliance on national skills	15 %	17 %	13 %	11 %	20 %
(b)The effect of general upskilling on					
Enhancing firm production	96 %	92 %	100 %	90 %	100 %
Facilitating effective utilization and upgrading of technologies	73 %	61 %	87 %	67 %	80 %
Hiring more skilled national workers	48 %	62 %	33 %	50 %	47 %
Upskilling national workers in the firm	48 %	54 %	42 %	50 %	47 %
Reducing future demand for foreign workers	52 %	58 %	44 %	40 %	64 %
Reinforcing the employment of national skill workers	36 %	33 %	40 %	33 %	40 %
(c) The effects of technological upgrading in					
Enhancing firm production	89 %	90 %	88 %	89 %	90 %
Raising skill level	79 %	81 %	76 %	78 %	80 %
Reinforcing firm ability to promote the local technology	68 %	62 %	76 %	61 %	75 %
Total response	38	21	17	18	20
Upskilling national workers in the firm	45 %	47 %	43 %	40 %	50 %
Hiring more national skill workers	48 %	58 %	36 %	33 %	61 %
Total response	25	13	12	10	15

Source: Own calculation based on the Firm Survey (2002)

perspective, our findings in Table 5.9 below show that at the micro level the upskilling plan amongst 55 % of the respondent firms induced significant effect in enhancing firm production and facilitating the effective utilization and upgrading of technologies. But it has only a slight effect on restructuring the imbalances of labour market via hiring more skilled national workers, upskilling national workers

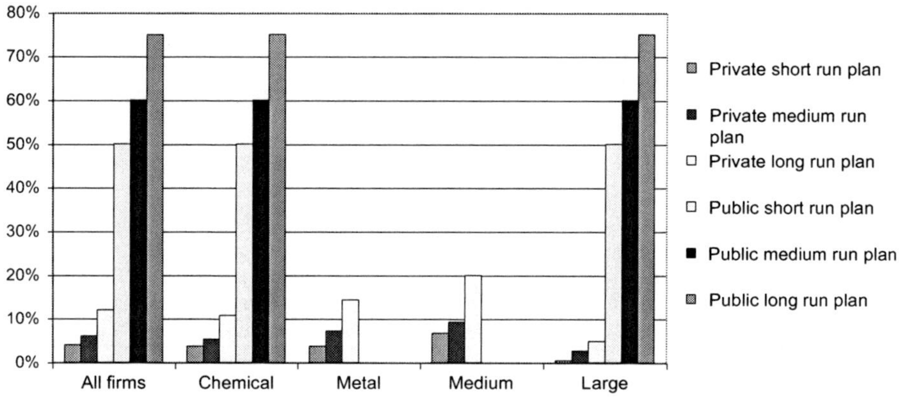

Fig. 5.2 Short, medium and long run plans of self- reliance on national skills across public and private firms (Source: Firm Survey (2002))

in the firm, reducing future demand for foreign workers and reinforcing the employment of national skills. Moreover, technological upgrading induced significant effects in enhancing firm production, raising skill levels and reinforcing firm ability to promote the local technology, but it has only a slight effect on both upskilling and hiring more skilled national workers.

At the micro level, Fig. 5.2 below compares the plans of public and private firms to depend on national skills. It predicts a great disparity between private and public firms that appears from the potential strong commitment to rely on national skills in the short, medium and long run plans in the large public firm. While our results from the firm survey and Fig. 5.2 below show that managers of private firms have a somewhat pessimistic view regarding the self-reliance on local skills and the potential role of both technological upgrading and upskilling in reinforcing the self- reliance strategy. For instance only 19 % of the respondent firms provide special training programmes for upskilling national workers and only 15 % of the respondent firms have plans to rely on national skilled workers even in restricted fields. Amongst all the respondent private firms the plan for depending on the national skills over the long run will not exceed 20 % of the total skilled workers.

In strong contrast to the above view, the macro survey shows that the respondent policy makers and experts are highly optimistic regarding the interactions between technological upgrading and upskilling and their roles in reinforcing economic growth, self-reliance on local skills and restructuring the labour market at the aggregate/macro level. For instance, Table 5.10 below shows that all the respondent policy makers and experts predict strong linkages between both upgrading of technology and upskilling of labour force to reinforce each other and to have a similar effect on reinforcing the self-reliance strategy and reducing unemployment rate. The official view predicts that the effect of upskilling is stronger than the effect of technological upgrading in both reinforcing economic growth and solving the imbalances in the labour market and so reducing the future demand for foreign skilled workers.

Table 5.10 The effects of technological upgrading, skill upgrading at the aggregate level in the UAE, 2002: macro view

The effects of technological upgrading	%	The effects of skill upgrading	%
Enhancing/accelerating upskilling	100	Enhancing/accelerating technological upgrading	100
Increasing/reinforcing economic growth	96	Increasing/reinforcing economic growth	100
Reinforcing self-reliance strategy	89	Reinforcing self-reliance strategy	89
Solving the imbalances in the labour market: reducing the future demand for foreign skilled workers	86	Solving the imbalances in the labour market: reducing the future demand for foreign skilled workers	93
Reducing unemployment rate	82	Reducing unemployment rate	82

Source: Own calculation based on the Macro Survey (2002)

This contradicting optimistic-pessimistic views at the macro and micro levels, regarding the self-reliance on local skills and the role of both technology and upskilling in reinforcing it, imply that the self-reliance strategy is probably a preferred government strategy, but not necessarily favoured by firms. This is consistent with the observation that 96 % of the respondent firms are private firms dominated by foreign workers and probably lack the incentives/interests to rely on national workers, mainly due to low skill and high salary requirements – see also our earlier discussion in Chap. 2 above. The respondent firms, which are costs minimizers/profits maximizers, are probably willing to continue hiring cheap readymade skilled foreign workers instead of hiring, training and upskilling expensive national workers.

5.4 Conclusions

This chapter uses the results of the macro and firm surveys to show the interaction between the deficient educational system and the high incidence of unskilled foreign workers and their implications.

Our results confirm a part of the second hypothesis in Scheme 1.1 Chap. 1 above: that in the short and medium term, the Gulf countries are unable to rely on local skills and local technologies and remain heavily dependent on both foreign skills and foreign technologies at the micro level. The major reasons are low levels of both skill and technology due to the deficient educational system and the high incidence of unskilled foreign workers and their implications.

On the one hand, from the demand perspective, the results of the firm survey can be used to argue that firm demand for low skilled workers, weak technology indicators and dependency on foreign technology led firms to demand and rely heavily on low skilled workers. On the other hand, from the supply perspective, our findings in Sect. 5.2 show that the deficient educational system – due to low quality of education – and the excessive share of unskilled foreign workers led to low skill levels, poor provision of training, serious skills mismatch, weak linkages, lack of a networks and hindered the transfer of knowledge. These factors interacted with each other and led to poor technology indicators, poor indigenous capability to build the local technology and a heavy dependence on foreign technology. These results prove hypotheses 3.a and 3.b in Scheme 1.1 in Chap. 1 above concerning the low skill and technology indicators at the micro–macro levels: the serious implications of the interaction between the causes and consequences of the deficient educational system and the high use of unskilled foreign workers. We confirm hypothesis 3.c. in Scheme 1.1 in Chap. 1 above that the major causes of low level of local technology are low/a lack of R&D activities due to a lack of skills, transfer of knowledge, networks and collaborations between universities and industry/firms.

Our findings show two surprising contradicting macro–micro views. The first contradicting optimistic – pessimistic micro and macro views regarding the incidence and success of knowledge transfer/external schooling effect implies that, probably, the transfer of knowledge/the external effects of schooling is successful within firms but is unsuccessful within society at large. This is probably because the transfer of knowledge is hindered by: low quality of education; the weak linkages and lack of networks between universities, colleges, technical and training institutes and the productive sectors; and the imbalanced structure of population and labour market. We show that the major cause behind the low transfer of knowledge/external schooling effect is low educational qualifications, and deficient educational and training systems. The major consequences are the lack of networks and collaboration between universities and firms, low R&D efforts and low technology indicators. These results prove part of the sixth hypothesis in Scheme 1.1 in Chap. 1 above with respect to the failure and the factors hindering the transfer of knowledge/external schooling effect at the macro level. But, on the other hand, our findings surprisingly reject a part of the sixth hypothesis in Scheme 1.1 in Chap. 1 above concerning the failure of the transfer of knowledge/external schooling effect at the micro level.

Our observation of the second contradicting optimistic-pessimistic macro and micro views concerning the self-reliance on local skills, and the role of both technological upgrading and upskilling in reinforcing it, implies that the self-reliance strategy is probably a preferred government strategy, but is not necessarily one followed by private firms. Driven by profit-maximizing considerations, private firms are likely to continue in hiring cheap readymade skilled foreign workers rather than hiring, training and upskilling expensive national workers. From these observations, our results reject hypothesis 8.c. in Scheme 1.1 in Chap. 1 above about the consistency of upskilling and transfer of knowledge at the macro–micro levels.

References

Abdelkarim, A. & Haan, H. (2002, January). *Skills and training in the UAE: The need for and the dimensions of institutional intervention* (Policy Research No. 5). Dubai: Centre for Labour Market Research and Information.

Cowan, R., Soete, L., & Tchervonnaya, O. (2001). Knowledge transfer and the services sector in the context of the new economy. *MERIT-INFONOMIC research memorandum* 2001–021 (p. 9). Maastricht: Maastricht University.

El Sabaa, S. (1997). Linking technology to industrial development in the United Arab Emirates. *Trade and Industry Magazine, 22*(263), 16–29. Dubai, UAE.

Fasano, G. (2002, October 21). *With open economy and sound policies, U.A.E. Has turned oil "curse" into a blessing* (IMF Survey) (pp. 330–332). Washington, DC: International Monetary Fund.

Firm Survey. (2002, April). *Technological change and skill development: A comparative study of chemical and metal medium and large scale enterprises in the UAE*. UAE: Firm Survey.

Gray, L. (1999, April). *Private sector training and employment: Evaluation and intervention strategies* (Specialist Rep. No.4- Dubai). Dubai: The Ministry of Labour and Social Affairs National Strategy for Labour Force Development and Employment Project.

Haan, H. (1999, January/March). *The UAE: Assessment of technology use in some selected sectors- towards introduction and explaining capital and skill intensive technologies* (Specialist Rep. No. 6). Dubai/Amsterdam: National Human Resources Development and Employment Strategy Project.

Macro Survey. (2002, April). *Skill creation, human resources development and policy intervention: Interviews with policy makers and experts in the UAE*. UAE: Macro Survey.

The UAE Ministry of Economy. (1985). *The UAE population census data (1985)*. Abu Dhabi, UAE: UAE Ministry of Economy.

The UAE Ministry of Economy. (1995). *The UAE population census data (1995)*. Abu Dhabi, UAE: UAE Ministry of Economy.

The UAE University. (1994). *The UAE Education Assessment Report*. Al-Ain: The UAE University.

The UAE University. (1997). *Private sector employment and labour market in the UAE*. Al-Ain: The UAE University.

UNDP. (2002). *Human Development Report (2002): Deepening democracy in a fragmental world*. New York/Oxford: UNDP/Oxford University Press.

UNDP. (2003). *Human Development Report (2003): Millennium development goals: A compact among nations to end human poverty*. New York/Oxford: UNDP/Oxford University Press.

UNDP. (2004). *Human Development Report (2004): Cultural liberty in today's diverse world*. New York/Oxford: UNDP/Oxford University Press.

Ziesemer, T. (2004). Multiple-steady-state growth models explaining twin-peak empirics? In G. Grözinger & A. van Aaken (Eds.), *Inequality: New analytical approaches* (pp. 145–168). Marburg: Metropolis- Verlag.

Chapter 6
Relationship Between Skill, Technology and Input–Output Indicators

6.1 Introduction

Earlier findings in Chap. 5 show the serious implications of the deficient educational system and excessive use of low educated workers, and illustrate two surprising contradicting macro–micro views regarding the transfer of knowledge/external schooling effects and upskilling plans. These surprising results from Chap. 5 motivate our research to attempt a more comprehensive analysis of skill problem and implications of unskilled foreign workers at the micro level/across private firms. Hence, the aim of this chapter is to broaden our earlier analysis in Chap. 5 by providing an in-depth analysis of skill and technology indicators and the relationship between them and the implications of the prevalence of low-skilled foreign workers at the micro level. In addition, we examine the relationships between: skill indicators (education/actual education and occupation/required education respectively and experience) and average wages; between skill, upskilling (spending on ICT training) and technology (spending on ICT); and between technology (spending on ICT) and input–output indicators across firms. We also compare the relevance of our results to the theoretical framework in Chap. 3 and the findings concerning these relationships in the new growth literature.

The rest of this chapter is organized as follows: Section 6.1 defines the variables used in our analysis and the general characteristics of firms. Section 6.2 presents our hypotheses and discusses differences in prevalent skill levels and requirements and the implications of low skill levels on skills mismatch, public-private duality and productivity decline across private firms. Section 6.3 examines the relationships between actual and required education, experience and wages. Section 6.4 shows the relationships between skill, technology (spending on ICT) and upskilling (spending on ICT training) and between technology (ICT) and input–output indicators. Section 6.5 concludes.

S. Mohamed Nour, *Technological Change and Skill Development in Arab Gulf Countries*, Contributions to Economics, DOI 10.1007/978-3-319-01916-1_6,

6.2 Data, Definition of Variables and General Characteristics of Firms

Before commencing with the empirical analysis, it will be useful to briefly explain the data used in our analysis and the general characteristics of firms.

6.2.1 Data and Definition of Variables

Our analysis in this chapter uses the data from the Firm Survey (2002), which provides us with three sets of micro variables[1]. The first set includes skill variables, while the second and third sets include both technology and input–output related variables respectively. We define skill variables by educational attainment, occupational level (measured by the required qualifications/schooling years) and average years of experience.[2] We use the total spending on ICT[3] to define "technology", the share of spending on ICT training as a percentage of total spending on ICT to define "upskilling", total sales value to define "output", total profit to define "performance", total employment and net worth to define "labour" and "capital" inputs, respectively.[4]

We use the first set of skill variables in Sect. 6.2 to discuss hypotheses 3.b and 4. a. in Scheme 1.1 Chap. 1 above regarding the implications of unskilled foreign workers across firms. We use input–output indicators to illustrate the decline in productivity, output/labour and capital/labour ratios. Next, in Sect. 6.3, we test

[1] All data, information and analysis in this chapter are based on the results covering 26 firms obtained from the Firm Survey (2002).

[2] We classify the educational qualifications of workers into three groups: high skilled (H) with postgraduate, university and diploma degree (more than twelve years of schooling), medium skilled (M) with secondary education (twelve years of schooling) and low skilled (L) with less than secondary education (less than twelve years of schooling). We define the occupational status according to five categories, including white-collar high (managers, professionals, management executives, scientists, technicians and engineers); white-collar low (clerical and administrative); blue collar high (skilled craftsmen); blue-collar low (plant machinery operators, assemblers and elementary occupation) and other workers. We define the required qualifications by required years of schooling including: postgraduate/ Ph.D. (19–20 years); professional, MSc./ postgraduate (18 years); university graduate (16 years); diploma (14 years); higher secondary schooling (12 years); and less than secondary schooling (less than 12 years). We measure the average wages by average monthly wages (in Dirhams, the UAE national currency), and average years of experience by both actual and required average years of experience for both educational and occupational definition respectively.

[3] ICT is the sum of total expenses on computers, telecommunications, training, maintenance and other related items.

[4] We measure output by the total sales value because the measurement units of sales value is unified (in local currency) across firms, while the measurement units of output in physical terms (tonne, litre, etc.) varies across firms.

hypothesis 4.b. in Scheme 1.1 Chap. 1 above about the relationships between actual and required education and experience and wages. In Sect. 6.4, we use the first and second sets of variables including skill, ICT and the share of spending on ICT training to test hypothesis 4.c. in Scheme 1.1 Chap. 1 above regarding the relationship between skill, technology (ICT) and upskilling. Next, we use the second and third sets of technology and input–output variables to test the fifth hypothesis in Scheme 1.1 Chap. 1 above about the relationship between technology (ICT) and input–output indicators.[5]

6.2.2 General Characteristics of Firms

Table 6.1 presents the main general characteristics of firms and economic indicators such as the share of firms in total employment, capital, profit and output (total sales value), and their differences defined by firm size and industry level. We observe that the market size or structure – defined by the share in total employment, capital, output (total sales value) and profit – seems biased toward large size and chemical firms. For instance, on average, the large size and chemical firms respectively employ 89 % and 75 % of total workers, absorb 92 % and 87 % of total capital, and constitute 93 % and 89 % of total output (total sales value) and 71 % and 56 % of total profit. These differences in market size leads to several implications, as we explain below and in the next sections.

From Table 6.1 we observe the limited contribution of public sector and high share of private sector in the chemical and metal industries. We also note the high share of local ownership and also a considerable share of foreign and mixed ownership, which implies the dependency on foreign capital and foreign workers. But despite the presence of foreign capital, there is limited contribution of multinational companies; however, such contribution is diversified as the sources of foreign capital of multinational companies originate from different countries and increases with industry level, but decreases with firm size. We also observe limited changes in the general structure of firms during the period 1999–2001, which may indicate a lack of dynamism, particularly with respect to the distribution of economic indicators, i.e. total employment, capital and output/sales value across firms. The reported change since establishment and in ownership, nationality of main owner and length of year in operation (age) vary across firms and generally are increase with firm size and industry level. In addition, the geographical distribution of firms indicates that most of firms are clustered in two main locations and only some have branches in cities other than the main location, though the probability of both clustering and having branches increases with firm size and industry. Moreover,

[5] We use few observations in the estimated equations, due to limited availability of reliable data covering these indicators, because some of the respondent firms were particularly reluctant to provide adequate reliable quantitative data covering these indicators.

Table 6.1 Main characteristics of firms in the UAE (1999–2001)

Main indicators (1999–2001)[a]		No. of respondent firms	Chemical	Metal	Large	Medium
Share in employment (%)	1999	28	74	26	89	11
	2000	28	75	25	89	11
	2001	30	75	25	89	11
	Average 1999–2001	28	75	25	89	11
Share in capital (%)	1999	20	85	15	92	8
	2000	19	88	12	92	8
	2001	19	89	11	92	8
	Average 1999–2001	19	87.3	12.7	92	8
Share in profit (%)	1999	23	39	61	79	21
	2000	22	60	40	68	32
	2001	22	68	32	66	34
	Average 1999–2001	22	56	44	71	29
Share in output (total sales value)(%)	1999	29	85	15	93	7
	2000	28	92	8	94	6
	2001	28	91	9	93	7
	Average 1999–2001	28	89.3	10.7	93.3	6.7
Share in spending on ICT (%)	Average 1999–2001	26	76	24	98	2
Share in spending on ICT training (%)	Average 1999–2001	14	94	6	98	2
Share of private firms (%)	2001	40	92	100	92	100
Share of ownership (%)[b]	Local – 2001	34	70	69	75.2	61.3
	Foreign – 2001	22	30	31	24.8	38.7
Share of main owners (%)	Local – 2001	19	48	37	58	25
	Foreign – 2001	13	32	26	25	35
	Mixed – 2001	12	20	37	17	40
Affiliation to multinational	2001	43	27	5	17	19
Change after establishment[c]	2001	23	35	16	29	24
Main location (%)	Abu Dhabi – 2001	3	4	11	13	0
	Dubai – 2001	20	46	42	38	52
	Sharjah – 2001	22	50	47	50	48
Branches other than main location (%)	2001	20	46	42	46	43
Average age/operation years	2001	43	17.7	15.6	18.9	14.4

(continued)

Table 6.1 (continued)

Main indicators (1999–2001)[a]		No. of respondent firms	Chemical	Metal	Large	Medium
Average rate of diversification	Sales – 2001	33	1.58	1.5	1.52	1.57
	Employment – 2001	27	1.35	1.3	1.2	1.5

Sources: Firm Survey (2002)
Notes: [a]All indicators are calculated from the Firm Survey (2002); some refer to observations over only 1 year (2001) and others use observations over 3 years (1999–2001). [b]Some of the respondent firms reported a mixed share of local and foreign ownership. [c]Change after establishment refers to changes in ownership, management and structure (e.g. expansion; opening new branches or merger with other firms)

we realize the limited scope for diversification as measured by sales and employment indices across firms.[6] The average diversification index increases with industry but decreases with firm size: this implies that large size firms have more interest in specialization/concentration, whereas medium size firms have more interest in diversification. As expected, chemical firms reported more interest in diversification than metal firms.

6.3 Differences in Skill Level and Requirements and the Implications Across Firms

Our earlier findings in Chap. 5 indicate that the share of high skilled workers in total employment, the number of full time equivalent researchers, R&D and ICT expenditure, patent, product and process innovations are higher within large size and chemical firms when compared to medium size and metal firms. Our result with respect to R&D and chemical sector is consistent with the standard classification developed by the OECD in the mid-1980s, which distinguishes between industries in terms of R&D intensity (cf. OECD, 1997). For instance, in the mid-1980s, the OECD classification distinguished between industries in terms of R&D intensity, considering pharmaceutical and ICT as high-technology, chemical and vehicle as medium-technology and food and textile as low technology (cf. OECD). Our findings with respect to firm size are consistent with the literature and the Schumpeterian hypothesis, which indicate that large size/market concentration is

[6] We use a modified definition of the diversification index developed by Utton (1979). We define the diversification index by output/ sales diversification Di = [P1 + 2P2 + 3P3 + 4P4] −1/ 2], where Pi refers to the percentage share of diversified sale product in total sale products within firms. Ranked from large to small, when Di = 1, Di =4 and 1 < Di < 4, it implies complete specialization, complete diversification and some degree of diversification respectively. We apply the same definition for employment diversification index (cf. Utton, pp. 15–16, 104–105).

conducive to R&D investment (cf. Braga & Willmore, 1991). For instance, Kumar and Saqib (1994) suggest that the probability of undertaking R&D increases with firm size only up to certain level, while R&D intensity increases with it linearly. However, one should also expect that these results could imply a possibility for reversed causality, mainly because R&D is a fixed cost that requires high financial capacity, which is most likely to be strong amongst large size firms.

In addition to earlier findings, we observe that skill levels and requirements (actual and required education and experience) and skills mismatch are not homogenous across firms and vary with industry and size. As we explained in Sect. 6.2, these findings can be used to test the first hypothesis that, irrespective of these differences, high skill requirements and low skill levels – due to high share of unskilled foreign workers – lead to skills mismatch, public-private duality and contribute to the productivity decline across private firms. In Sects. 6.3 and 6.4, we then examined the second hypothesis that an increase in skill levels and firm size lead to improved relationships between actual and required education and experience; between actual education, experience and wages; and between skill, upskilling and technology (ICT). Finally, in Sect. 6.4, we also investigated the third hypothesis concerning the relationships between technology (the use of ICT) and input–output indicators at the micro/firm level.

6.3.1 Differences in Skill Level and Requirements (Education and Experience) Across Firms

Prior to investigating the first hypothesis on the extended implications of low skill levels as presented above, it is convenient to begin with explaining differences in skill levels and requirements across firms because understanding why and how they vary with industry and firm size can help in investigating both the first and second hypotheses.

In Figs. 6.1, 6.2 and 6.3 below we explain differences in skill levels and requirements and low skill levels – defined by education and occupation groups – across firms defined by size and industry.[7] Figures 6.1 and 6.2 show the low share of high skilled – high educated and white-collar – workers, differences in skill levels according to education and occupation definitions and differences across firms. For instance, Fig. 6.1 indicates that for 50 % of all respondent firms, the share of high skilled (educated) represents 1–30 % of total employed workers. For a further 40 % of all respondent firms, the share of high skilled (educated) represents 31–50 % of total employed workers, but for the remaining 10 % the share is more than 50 % of

[7] In Figs. 6.1, 6.2, and 6.3, the horizontal axis defines firms, industry, size (chemical/metal, large/medium), and skill level (high (H), medium (M) and low (L)). The vertical axis defines the intensity/share of H, M and L across firms. The information in the right margin defines the distribution of workers in Figs. 6.1 and 6.2, and the average required years of education in Fig. 6.3.

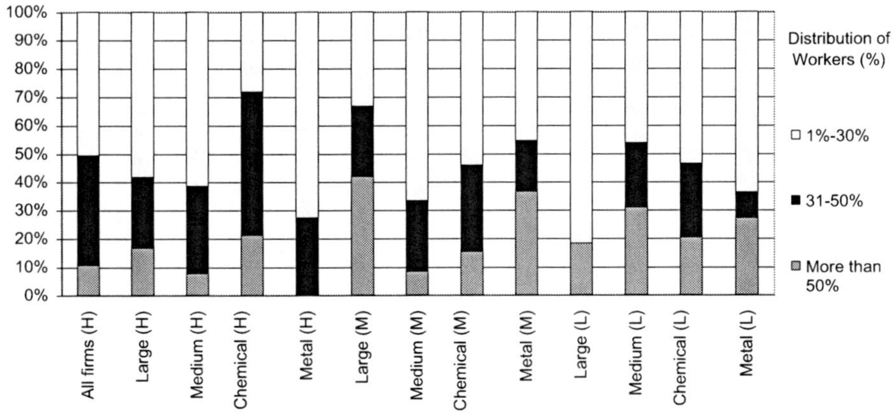

Fig. 6.1 Differences in the distribution of workers by educational level across firms (% share) 2001 (Source: Firm Survey (2002))

the workforce. Figure 6.2 shows, for example, that for 88 % of all respondent firms, the share of white collar (WC) represents 1–30 % of total employed workers; for 4 % of all respondent firms the WC share is 31–50 % and for 8 % the figure stands at 50 % of total employed workers. The results show that the incidence of high educated and white-collar workers constituting more than half of total employment is observed only within 10 % and 8 % of all respondent firms respectively. They also indicate that the share of high skilled – measured by education – is less than one third of total workers for 50 % of all firms and the share of high skilled – white-collar measured by occupational level – is less than one third of total workers for 88 % of all firms. That means that across all firms the share of high educated and white-collar respectively are less than one third and two thirds; therefore, the majority of employed workers are low and medium skilled.

Figures 6.3 and 6.4 show that skill requirements – average required years of schooling – vary and increase with occupational level across firms.[8] For instance, Fig. 6.3 indicates that for 12 % of all respondent firms the average required years of education for white collar (WC) is 12 and above; for 19 % it is 14 years and above; 52 % of all respondent firms require an average of 16 years; whilst 17 % of all respondent firms put this figure at 17 and above. Moreover, Fig. 6.4 indicates that for 20 % of all respondent firms the average required years of education for white collar high (WCH) is 14 years (diploma degree); for 50 % the requirement is 16 years (university degree); and for 30 % the requirement is 17–19 years (post graduate degree). The figures show that the university degree is the major preferred required qualification only within the first and second occupational groups, while

[8] White collar (WC) includes white collar high and low. Blue collar (BC) includes blue collar high and low.

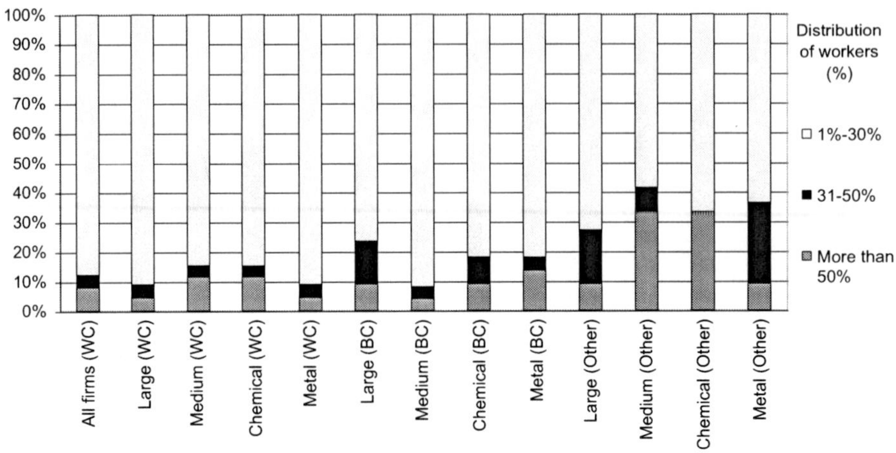

Fig. 6.2 Differences in the distribution of workers by occupational level across firms (% share) 2001 (Source: Firm Survey (2002))

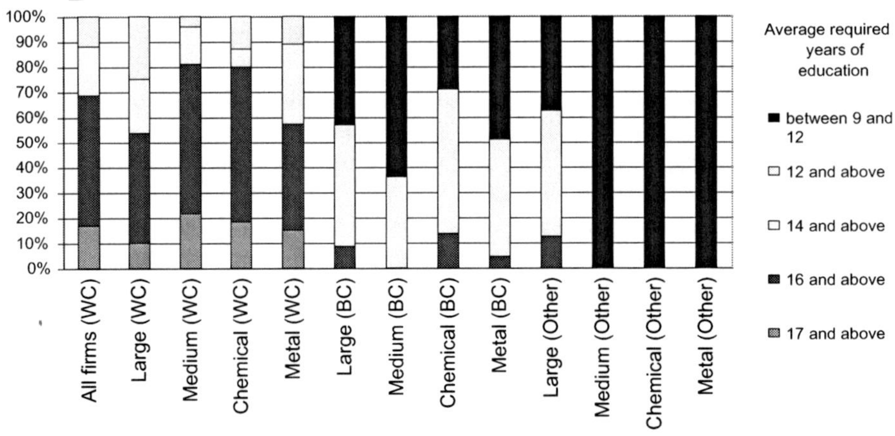

Fig. 6.3 Differences in the educational requirements by occupational level across firms (% share) 2001 (Source: Firm Survey (2002))

for the other occupational groups either a diploma or secondary or less than secondary schooling is required.

Figure 6.5 below indicates the variation in skill requirements (required years of experience), defined by educational and occupational levels. For instance, for 8 % of all respondents firms the average required years of experience for white collar high (WCH) is 5–10 years; for 64 % the experience requirement stands at 10–15 years; and for 28 % the figure is 15–20 years. Figure 6.5 illustrates that average years of experience are increasing in educational and occupational levels respectively. In the next section, we explain the relationships between required education/actual education; occupation/required education; and experience and wages across firms.

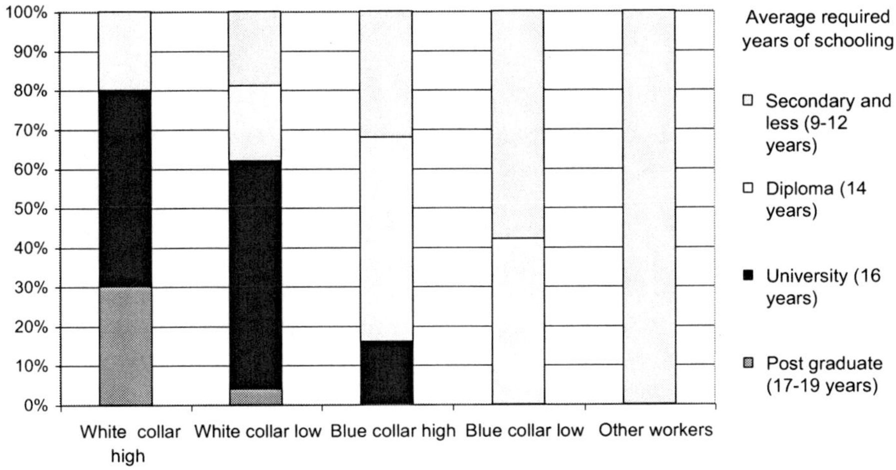

Fig. 6.4 Average required years of schooling defined by occupation classes across firms (2001) (Source: Firm Survey (2002))

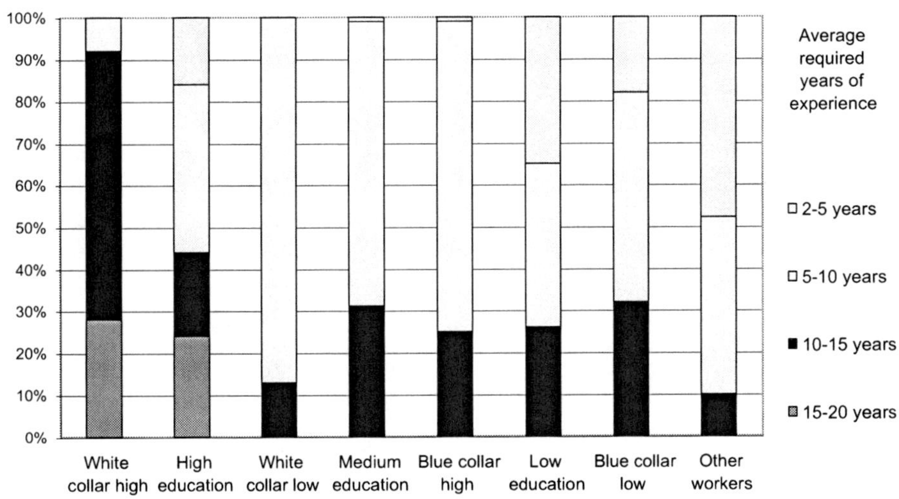

Fig. 6.5 Average years of experience defined by education and occupation classes across firms (2001) (Sources: Firm Survey (2002))

6.3.2 The Implications of Low Skill Levels Across Private Firms

In this section we examine the first hypothesis that, irrespective of the observed differences in skill levels and requirements and as we explained above, the low skill levels – due to high share of unskilled foreign workers – lead to skills mismatch, public-private duality and probably contribute to productivity decline across private firms.

6.3.2.1 Low Skill Levels and Skills Mismatch (Differences in Required and Attained Education)

When comparing the required schooling with the actual/attained schooling, we find that differences in schooling requirements across firms have caused considerable variations between the required and actual/attained schooling for high, medium and low skilled groups. When we interpret the required schooling as the demand for skills and the actual/attained schooling as the supply of skills, we observe that the inconsistency between the required and actual/attained schooling indicates an inconsistency between the demand for and supply of skills, which can be interpreted as skills mismatch.[9] For instance, Fig. 6.6 below illustrates the differences between the required and actual/attained schooling across firms defined by firm size and industry level and skill levels. We observe that the inconsistency between the demand for and supply of skills, or skills mismatch, is particularly higher/serious within both medium and low skilled groups respectively and across large and metal firms respectively. We find mismatch amongst all employment categories, especially within both medium and low skilled labour: for instance, we observe that for all firms, on average, the intensity of mismatch for high, medium and low skill groups accounts for 29 %, 72 % and 66 % respectively. This implies that the educational attainment amongst medium skilled labour does not match the required skills/educational level for medium skilled jobs across approximately more than 70 % of total respondents firms. The mismatch is highest for medium skills, probably because of both insufficient educational attainment and high

[9] Our definition of actual education refers to educational attainment classified under three groups: high (post secondary) educational attainment: university degree and above (16 years of schooling); medium educational attainment: secondary education (12 years of schooling); and low educational attainment: less than secondary education (9 years of schooling). We define the required education by the translated merged required qualifications for each occupation group defined by average years of schooling. The occupational classification includes the following five categories/ groups: (1) Managers, professional, management executive, scientific, technical and engineers; (2) Clerical and administrative; (3) Skilled craftsmen; (4) Plant machinery operators, assemblers and elementary occupation; and (5) Other workers. We translate the required qualifications associated with each occupational class into average years of schooling and group them in the following way: (1) PhD/postgraduate (19–20 years); (2) Professional, MSc./ postgraduates (18 years); (3) University graduate (16 years); (4) Diploma (14 years); (5) Higher/ Secondary Schooling (12 years) and (6) Less than Secondary Schooling (9 years). We then merge the required qualifications into three groups, assuming that the high occupation group includes both the first and second occupation categories, the medium occupation group includes both the third and fourth occupation categories and, finally, the low occupation group includes the fifth occupation category. We then use this definition to compare between the required education for each occupation class and actual/ attained education, and we assume that the difference between these indicates the presence of skills mismatch between jobs requirements and educational attainment.

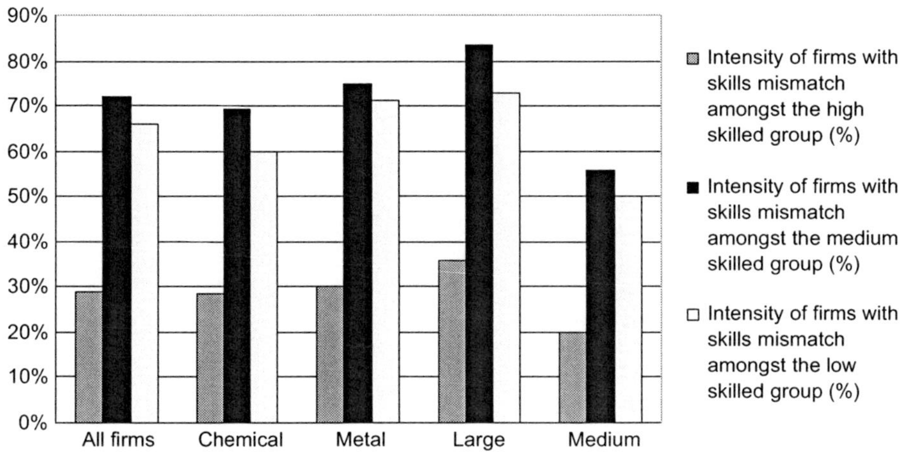

Fig. 6.6 Skills mismatch defined by high medium and low skill levels across firms (%) (2001) (Source: Firm Survey (2002))

educational requirements for medium skills – see Fig. 6.3 above. Moreover, the intensity of mismatch is more prevalent across large size and metal firms compared to medium size and chemical firms. For instance, for metal firms, on average the mismatch intensity for high, medium and low skill groups accounts for 30 %, 75 % and 71 % respectively, while for large size firms the figures are 36 %, 83 % and 73 % respectively. Hence, our results in this section concerning the presence of serious skills mismatch due to the excessive share of unskilled foreign workers at the micro level are consistent with our earlier findings in Chap. 5 above, which indicates the presence of serious skills mismatch at the macro level.

6.3.2.2 Low Skill Levels and Public: Private Duality Within Oil/Chemical Industry

The low skill levels not only lead to skills mismatch across private firms, but probably also have an impact on public-private duality. For instance, when comparing two cases of large public and medium private firms active in the oil/chemical industry, our findings in Table 6.2 illustrate several aspects of the public-private duality at the micro level. The observed duality appears from skill indicators: the share of high skilled workers in total employment; the average years of experience, defined by education and occupation levels; and the distribution of average wages, which are lower in the medium private compared to large public firm. Moreover, the low skill levels in the medium private firm when compared to the large public firm are accompanied by further discrepancies in the trend of labour productivity and sales diversification. Over the period 1999–2001 the labour productivity shows an increasing trend in the large public firm, but an opposite declining trend in the medium private firm. These results are consistent with our earlier findings in

Table 6.2 Public- private duality: differences in skill indicators, diversification and productivity (1999–2001) (% and Dirhams)

Sector	Public large			Private medium		
(a) Skill indicators (2001)	High	Medium	Low	High	Medium	Low
Share of high skilled workers in total employment (education definition) (%)	0.885	0.115	0	0.34	0.25	0.41
Share of high skilled workers in total employment(occupation definition) (%)	0.82	0.155	0.025	0.27	0.10	0.63
Experience (education definition)	18.5	7	n/a	12	11	12
Experience (occupation definition)	10.75	0	5	11.5	7	10
Wages (education definition) (Dirhams)	11850	3662.5	Na.	1280	768	512
(b) Labour productivity (output/labour) and Sales diversification (1999–2001)	1999	2000	2001	1999	2000	2001
Labour productivity (output/labour) (1999–2001)	0.102[a]	0.111[a]	0.113[a]	0.135[b]	0.128[b]	0.110[b]
Sales diversification (2001)			1.5			1

Source: Firm Survey (2002)

Notes: (1) Productivity measured in physical term the unit refers to [a]million barrels per day; [b]metric tonne; (2) Both diversification and productivity are measured for all high, medium and low skilled workers

Chap. 5, which implies a public-private and a macro–micro duality with respect to both upskilling efforts and the transfer of knowledge; our findings are also consistent with the findings in the Gulf literature (cf. Gray, 1999; Khorshid, 2000; Abdelkarim & Haan, 2002). Table 6.1 above shows the limited contribution of the public sector in the chemical industry in our sample; therefore, one can assume that the low skill and respective implications of private firms probably reflect the dominant trend, at least across the respondents and chemical firms in particular.

Furthermore, our results from the firm survey – not reported in Table 6.2 below – indicate that the low skill levels occurred along with low spending on ICT in the medium private firm compared to the large public firm. Our findings indicate a higher technology level (spending on ICT) and upskilling (ICT training) along with higher skill levels in the large public firm compared to the medium private firm. These results are plausible in view of the complementary relationships between skill, technology and upskilling – see our discussion below. One should also note the large swings in computers, telecommunication and training expenses. The substantial decline in total ICT expenses over the period 1999–2001 is probably due to a lack of plans for critical expansion in ICT sector or a general decrease in total spending across all firms. Another interpretation for the big decline in these components in the large public firm is probably related to a change in the strategy of the firm, which may have already established a sound basis for these components and probably needed to shift priority to increase spending on maintenance and other items. The explanation for the substantial decline in total expenses on computers in the private medium firm can be attributed to the big decline in total ICT expenses and probably to the need to shift priority to increase expenses on training.

Table 6.3 The value and trend of labour productivity, output/labour and capital/labour ratios across firms 1999–2001

Variables		Value (1999–2001)			Trend (1999–2001)		
Average ratio of	Group of firms	1999	2000	2001	1999–2000	2000–2001	1999–2001
Capital/labour	Chemical	0.131	0.138	0.132	+	−	+
	Metal	0.0523	0.0574	0.0520	+	−	−
	Large	0.084	0.087	0.077	+	−	−
	Medium	0.090	0.103	0.101	+	−	+
	All firms	0.087	0.095	0.0896	+	−	+
Sales value (output)/labour	Chemical	0.258	0.332	0.321	+	−	+
	Metal	0.146	0.116	0.123	−	+	−
	Large	0.176	0.231	0.229	+	−	+
	Medium	0.2337	0.2272	0.2335	−	+	−
	All firms	0.202	0.229	0.231	+	+	+
Labour productivity (output/labour ratio) for selected firms[a]	Chemical large	0.616	0.622	0.606	+	−	−
		0.102	0.111	0.113	+	+	+
		0.582	0.535	0.409	−	−	−
		0.241	0.289	0.333	+	+	+
	Chemical medium	0.470	0.482	0.410	+	−	−
		0.551	0.520	0.582	−	+	+
		0.117	0.124	0.136	+	+	+
		0.249	0.266	0.226	+	−	−
		0.135	0.128	0.110	−	−	−
	Metal large	0.035	0.032	0.031	−	−	−
		0.052	0.051	0.043	−	−	−
	Metal medium	0.116	0.084	0.106	−	+	−
		0.0325	0.0143	0.0142	−	−	−
		0.229	0.204	0.309	−	+	+

Source: Firm Survey (2002)
[a]Productivity is measured in physical terms (tonne, litre, etc.) for selected firms according to availability of data

6.3.2.3 Low Skill Levels and the Declining Trend of Labour Productivity (Output/Labour and Capital/Labour Ratios)

The low skill levels may contribute to productivity decline across private firms. Table 6.3 below illustrates the value and trend of labour productivity (output/labour ratio) and the average ratios of capital/labour and output (total sales value)/labour across firms. Over the period 1999–2001, the trends of these ratios show considerable variation across firms, and, in particular, the average capital/labour ratio and average labour productivity for numerous firms show a considerable decline.[10]

[10] Due to the small number of observations on the declining trend of labour productivity, our results should be interpreted carefully as probably this may not be the only case; other possible explanations are either the steady or increasing trends amongst the non-respondent firms.

The declining labour productivity across many firms may not be surprising since the majority of employed workers are low skilled/educated foreign workers – see our discussion above– and a low skill level may lead to further decline in productivity. For instance, the bottom half of Table 6.3 above illustrates that, over the period 1999–2000 and 2000–2001, the declining trend of labour productivity is reversed across 3 out of 14 (21.4 %) of the respondent firms and the increasing trend continues across 3 out of 14 (21.4 %) firms; however, the increasing trend turns into a declining one across 3 out of 14 (21.4 %) firms, or the declining trend continues across 5 out of 14 (36 %) of the respondent firms. Therefore, for the majority 8 out of 14 (57 %) of the respondent firms either the increasing trend turns into a declining one or the declining trend continues.[11] These findings on the declining labour productivity at the micro level are consistent with the results regarding the declining value added and productivity at the macro level, as indicated in the Gulf literature (cf. Wadi, 2001; Abdelkarim & Ibrahim, 2001).[12]

Therefore, our findings in this section verify the first hypothesis that high skill requirements and low skill levels – due to high share of unskilled foreign workers – lead to skills mismatch, public private duality and also probably contribute to productivity decline across private firms. In the next sections we examine the second and third hypotheses.

6.4 Relationships Between the Required Education (Occupation), Attained/Actual Education, Experience and Average Wages

Based on the above findings, in this section we examine a part of the second hypothesis that an increase in skill levels and firm size lead to improved relationships between actual and required education, and between actual education, experience and wages across firms.

We begin with the relationship between occupation and education. Using the above definitions of occupation and education/actual and required education respectively, we translate the required qualifications for each of the occupation groups into average years of schooling and use the OLS regression, assuming that the required schooling in each occupation class is dependent on the actual/attained education. Our findings in Table 6.4 and Fig. 6.7 below illustrate that improvement

[11] In Table 6.3 we limit our analysis of the productivity decline to compare only the change in labour productivity over the period 1999–2000 and 2000–2001 across 14 of the respondent firms. Since our data only reflects skill levels for the year 2001, but does not reflect the change in skill levels over the period 1999–2001. That means we cannot compare the change in productivity with the change in skill levels, so as to attribute the declining trend in productivity over the period 1999–2001 to the declining trend in skill levels.

[12] For instance, the results of Wadi (2001), Abdelkarim and Ibrahim (2001) indicate the declining growth rates and declining labour productivity in Kuwait and the UAE respectively.

Table 6.4 Required and actual/attained education and experience across firms (2001)

		Coefficient (t-value)			R^2	N[a]
Independent variable		Actual education	Required education	Constant		
Dependent variable	Group of firms and skill					
Required education	Chemical	0.982*		0.876	0.275	9
		(1.628)		(0.114)		
All groups (high, medium and low)	Large	0.716**		3.763	0.621	6
		(2.559)		(1.028)		
	All firms	0.543		6.573	0.168	14
		(1.557)		(1.480)		
Average years experience	All groups (high, medium and low)	0.108		5.276	0.108	22
		(1.557)		(6.148)		
	(All firms)		0.127*	4.654	0.355	9
			(1.964)	(5.179)		
All firms	High and medium (all firms)	0.309**		−2.142	0.377	23
		(3.567)		(−1.789)		
			0.104	0.451	0.177	11
			(1.390)	(0.424)		
			0.104	0.451	0.177	11
			(1.390)	(0.424)		

Correlation is significant *at the 0.05 level (one-tailed) **at the 0.01 level (one-tailed)

[a]For this regression we use relatively few observations, because some of the respondent firms were particularly reluctant to provide adequate quantitative data on skill indicators. Sometimes we exclude some observations due to inconsistency or unreliability; for instance, one observation is excluded in row 3. As we explained in Chap. 4 above, the main problem is the varying response rate for different questions (e.g. to measure education, occupation and wages) across firms. Moreover, the classification of firms into chemical/metal, medium/large also divided the few observations between them and so allow for only few observations for regression for each group independently

in occupational status (measured by the required education) is positively correlated with education (measured by actual/attained education) across all firms. In addition, Table 6.4 illustrates that an increase in firm size and industry level lead to improved relationships between required and actual education. For instance, the required education appears to be more sensitive to and increasing in actual education within both large and chemical firms, but less sensitive within all firms. This result is plausible since the skill level – share of high skilled measured by educational attainment – is higher within large size and chemical firms compared to metal and medium size firms – see Fig. 6.1 above. This is also probably because large size firms are more prevalent in the chemical industry – see Table 6.1 above – and may have more consistent recruitment strategies. These results confirm our earlier observations that skill levels and requirements (actual and required education) are non-homogenous across firms and are determined by size and industry.

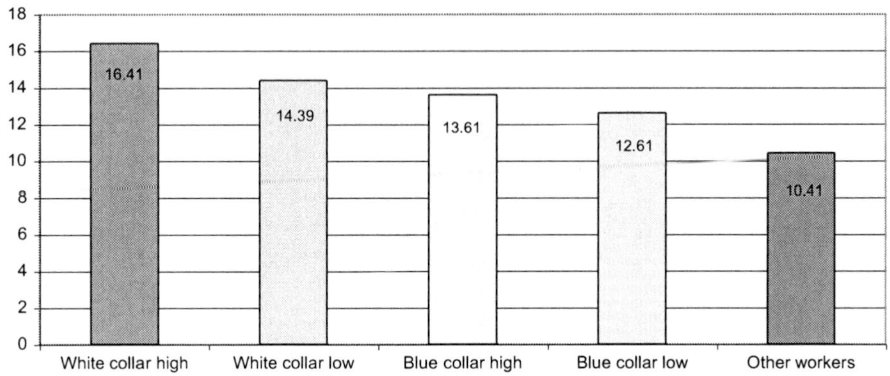

Fig. 6.7 The distribution of occupation classes according to the translated average years of schooling across firms (2001) (Source: Firm Survey (2002))

Concerning the relationship between education, occupation and experience, Table 6.4 above shows that the average years of experience are positively correlated and increasing in education and occupation i.e. attained/actual and required education respectively. In particular, the average years of experience seem more sensitive to high and medium educational attainment and it is also sensitive to high, medium and low educational requirements. This finding is consistent with Fig. 6.5 above, and probably reflects the fact that skill indicators – education and experience – are complementing rather than substituting each other.

Table 6.5 below illustrates a considerable variation in the distribution of average wages amongst high, medium and low skill – educational and occupational – levels across firms. When using the occupational rather than the educational definition, the distribution of wages shows less fluctuation across firms. Therefore, the effect of occupation/required education on the distribution of average wages across firms seems to be less sensitive to differences in firm size and industry. In contrast, when using the educational definition, we observe that the effect of the actual/attained education on the distribution of average wages across firms seems to be more sensitive to differences in firm size and industry.

The above results are consistent with the OLS regression reported in Table 6.6 below, which indicates that the average wages are positively correlated with and more sensitive to attained/actual education. For instance, Table 6.6 below illustrates that the average wages are increasing in actual/attained education and experience (cf. Mincer, 1974) and therefore, is biased against less educated and experienced workers. These findings support our results from the firm survey, which indicate that wages are increasing in education and biased against low educated workers because the ratios of high skilled to low skilled wages, which can be interpreted as

Table 6.5 Differences in the distribution of average wages defined by firm size and industry level (2001)

Skill variables	Education				Occupation			
Characteristics	Size		Industry		Size		Industry	
Wages defined by skill level	Large	Medium	Chemical	Metal	Large	Medium	Chemical	Metal
High educated/white collar high								
10,001–25,000	8.3 %	41.7 %	14.3 %	40 %	11.1 %	15.4 %	15.4 %	11.1 %
5,001–10,000	58.3 %	33.3 %	42.9 %	50 %	88.9 %	61.5 %	69.2 %	77.8 %
2,001–5,000	33.3 %	8.3 %	28.6 %	10 %	0	23.1 %	15.4 %	11.1 %
1,001–2,000	0	16.7 %	14.3 %	0	0	0	0	0
Medium educated/white collar low								
10,001–25,000	0	9,1 %	0	10 %	0		0	0
5,001–10,000	8.3 %	9.1 %	7.7 %	10 %	0	8.3 %	0	11.1 %
2,001–5,000	33.3 %	18.2 %	23.1 %	30 %	55.6 %	50 %	58.3 %	44.4 %
1,001–2,000	58.3 %	18.2 %	46.2 %	30 %	44.4 %	41.7 %	41.7 %	44.4 %
0,500–1,000	0	45.5 %	23.1 %	20 %	0	0	0	0
Low educated/blue collar high								
5,001–10,000	0	10 %	0	12.5 %	0	0		0
2,001–5,000	0	10 %	7.7 %	0	33.3 %	20 %	45.5 %	0
1,001–2,000	45.5 %	20 %	23.1 %	50 %	66.7 %	70 %	45.5 %	100 %
0,500–1,000	54.6 %	60 %	69.2 %	37.5 %	0	10 %	9.1 %	0
Blue collar low								
2,001–5,000					11.1 %	30 %	33.3 %	0
1,001–2,000					66.7 %	50 %	41.7 %	85.7 %
0,500–1,000					22.2 %	20 %	25 %	14.3 %
Others								
1,001–2,000					42.9 %	33.3 %	58.3 %	28.6 %
0,500–1,000					57.1 %	66.7 %	41.7 %	71.4 %

Sources: Firm Survey (2002)

wages/skills premium, exceeds one.[13] These results are consistent with the findings in the new growth literature, particularly skilled biased technical change theorems (cf. Aghion & Howitt, 1992, 1998; Acemoglu, 1998; Autor, Katz, & Krueger, 1998). Our results that required education has no significant impact on wages are somewhat surprising and different from our expectation in view of the results of the overeducation literature (Hartog, 2000; Muysken & ter Weel, 1998; Muysken & Ruholl, 2001; Muysken, Hoppe, & Rieder, 2002; Muysken, Weissbrich, & von Restorff, 2002; Muysken, Kiiver, & Hoppe, 2003). We find that the positive correlations between actual education, experience and wages are particularly significant for large size firms, which may not be surprising since these firms have sufficient scope for a coherent wage policy (Muysken & Nour, 2006). This is also

[13] From the Firm Survey (2002) we find that the proportion of high skilled wages/low skilled wages accounts for 7.5, 6.9, 8.1, 6.3 and 8.4 for all firms, chemical, metal, large and medium size firms respectively.

Table 6.6 Correlation between wages (log) actual and required education and experience (2001)

		Coefficient (t-value)			R^2	N[a]
Independent variable	Group of firms	Actual education	Experience	Required education[b]		
Dependent variable: Average wages (log)						
Average wages (log) high, medium and low skilled	All firms	0.231** (2.259)			0.195	23
	Large	0.284** (4.545)			0.674	12
	All firms			0.159 (1.275)	0.119	14
	All firms	0.170* (1.471)	0.048 (1.107)		0.242	23
	Large	0.193** (2.175)	0.053* (1.374)		0.730	13
	Chemical	0.243** (2.001)	0.05469 (1.102)		0.557	13
	All firms	0.192* (1.199)	0.011 (0.172)	0.063 (0.412)	0.254	14

Correlation is significant *at the 0.05 level (one-tailed) **at the 0.01 level (one-tailed)

[a]For this regression we use relatively few observations, because some of the respondent firms were particularly reluctant to provide adequate quantitative data to measure skill indicators. For instance, there are few observations when combining attained education, experience and required education, particularly so for required education. As we explained in Chap. 4 above, we excluded some observations due to inconsistency or unreliability. One major problem is the varying response rate for different questions (to measure attained and required education, experience and wages) across firms. Moreover, the classification of firms into chemical/metal, medium/large also divided the few observations between them and, therefore, allow for only a few observations for regression for each group independently

[b]The required education is not used as a variable in the upper half of Table 6.6, because, we want to check the relation with respect to actual/attained education and experience independently and then compare the result when the required education is also included in the regression

probably because large size firms may have more consistent recruitment strategies and high skill levels – share of high skilled workers in total employment – see Fig. 6.1 above. These results imply that an increase in skill level/actual education and firm size leads to an improved relationship between actual education, experience and wages.

Therefore, our findings in this section corroborate the first part of the second hypothesis that an increase in skill levels and firm size leads to improved relationship between actual and required education and experience; and between actual education, experience and wages. In the next section we proceed to examine the second part of the second hypothesis that an increase in skill levels and firm size lead to improved relationships between skill, upskilling and technology (ICT). Finally, we test our third hypothesis on the relationship between technology (ICT) and input–output indicators at the micro/firm level.

6.5 Skill, Upskilling (ICT Training) and Technology (ICT) and Input–Output Indicators

Based on the above results, in this section we examine the other part of the second hypothesis that an increase in skill levels and firm size lead to improved relationships between skill, upskilling and technology (ICT) across firms. Before examining this hypothesis, it is useful to briefly show the variations in the use of technology (spending on ICT) and upskilling (spending on ICT training) across firms, because the observed differences in skill and spending on ICT and ICT training can be used to interpret the complementary relationships between skill, technology and upskilling across firms.

6.5.1 Skill and the Share of Spending on Technology (ICT) and Upskilling (ICT Training)

Table 6.7 shows considerable variations in the share and trend of total spending on ICT including computers, telecommunications, training, maintenance and other items defined by firm size and industry. The share of telecommunication exhibits continuous increasing trend for all firms, while that of training shows an opposite declining trend. Table 6.1 above shows that, on average, the share of large size and chemical firms represents about 98 % and 76 % of total spending on ICT respectively and about 98 % and 94 % of total spending on ICT training respectively. However, despite the big share of spending on ICT and ICT training, large size and chemical firms experienced declining trends of ICT and ICT training – cf. Figs. 6.8 and 6.9. The decline in total ICT spending can be interpreted as being due to a lack of plan for critical expansion in ICT sector or probably due to a general cutback in total spending across chemical and large size firms. The declining expenses on both ICT training and computers follow the general decline in total ICT spending, which can also be attributed to a lack of plan for critical expansion a possible change in the strategy of firms that, having already established a sound basis for these components, probably need to shift priority to increase spending on both telecommunications and maintenance.

We now proceed to examine the second part of our second hypothesis that an increase in skill levels and firm size leads to improved complementary relationships between skill, technology (ICT) and upskilling (ICT training)– see Table 6.8 below. For instance, we observe the complementary relationship between the share of high education and the share of expenditure on ICT, which can be seen and understood as complementarity between skill and technology (cf. Goldin & Katz, 1998; Acemoglu, 1998). We find a complementary relationship between the share of high education and the share of expenditure on ICT training, which can be interpreted as complementarity between skill and upskilling. Tables 6.8 and 6.9 show complementary relationships between the share of expenditure on ICT and

Table 6.7 Spending on ICT defined by firm size and industry (1999–2001) (% share in total spending)

ICT	Computers			Telecommunications			Training			Maintenance			Other		
Firms/years	1999	2000	2001	1999	2000	2001	1999	2000	2001	1999	2000	2001	1999	2000	2001
Chemical	17 %	15 %	11 %	11 %	29 %	25 %	59 %	22 %	10 %	11 %	30 %	54 %	2 %	4 %	0.5 %
Metal	19 %	6 %	9 %	21 %	6 %	27 %	7 %	2 %	13 %	53 %	86 %	51 %	0.1 %	0.02 %	0.1 %
Large	17 %	13 %	11 %	11 %	22 %	24 %	57 %	17 %	11 %	13 %	45 %	54 %	2 %	3 %	0.5 %
Medium	20 %	7 %	10 %	27 %	9 %	32 %	6 %	2 %	12 %	47 %	82 %	46 %	0	0	0
All firms	17 %	11 %	11 %	12 %	19 %	25 %	54 %	13 %	11 %	15 %	55 %	53 %	2 %	2 %	0.4 %

Source: Firm Survey (2002)

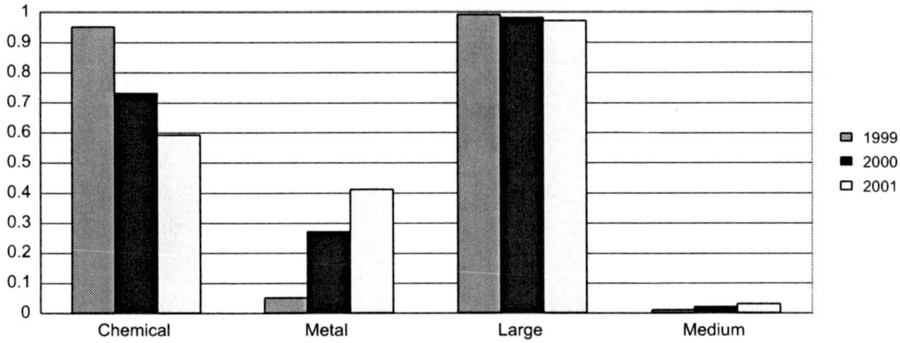

Fig. 6.8 The share and trend of total spending on ICT across firms (1999–2001) (Source: Firm Survey (2002))

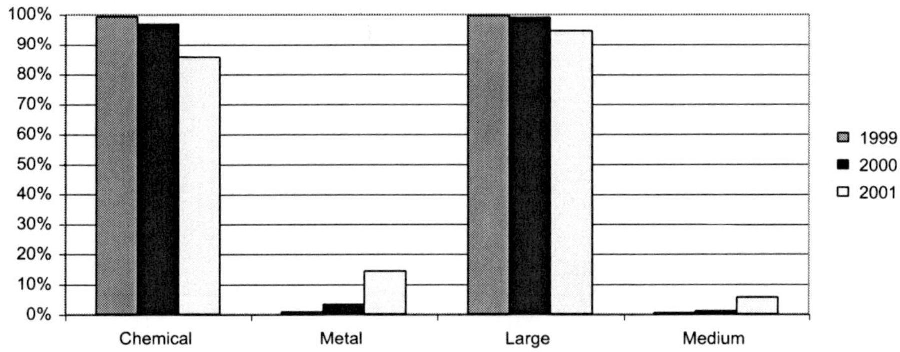

Fig. 6.9 The share and trend of spending on ICT training across firms (1999–2001) (Source: Firm Survey (2002))

ICT training, and between spending on computers, telecommunications and training, which can be read as complementarity between technology and upskilling (cf. Colecchia & Papaconstantinou, 1996; Bresnahan, Brynjolfsson, & Hitt, 1999). Our findings, that these complementarities are particularly significant for large size firms, are plausible since these firms have more spending on ICT and ICT training – see Table 6.1 above – and have high skill levels – share of high skilled workers in total employment – see Fig. 6.1 above. These results are consistent with the second part of our second hypothesis that an increase in skill levels and firm size lead to improved complementary relationships between skill, upskilling and technology (ICT) (cf. Acemoglu, 1998). The results also imply the importance of a good education/high skill level for the enhancement of skill, technology and upskilling complementarity at the micro level. That also seems consistent with the endogenous growth framework and stylized facts concerning the relationships between human capital, technical progress and upskilling – see our theoretical framework in Chap. 3 above.

Table 6.8 The relationship between ICT, skill and upskilling across firms (2001)

		Coefficient (t-value)			R^2	N
Independent variables		ICT expenditures	Training expenditures	Constant		
Dependent variables	Group of firms					
High education	All firms (linear)	0.210** (5.965)		−0.055 (−4.219)	0.703	17
	Chemical (linear)	0.029* (2.612)		0.356 (6.317)	0.363	14
	Large (linear)	0.0316** (2.484)		0.318 (4.632)	0.382	12
	Medium (linear)	0.330 (1.248)		0.265 (4.556)	0.163	10
High education	All firms (linear)		0.03350** (4.089)	0.266 (6.733)	0.563	15
	Chemical (linear)		0.280* (2.040)	0.353 (4.871)	0.294	12
	Large (linear)		0.310* (2.258)	0.304 (4.107)	0.338	12
Training expenditures	All firms (linear)	0.09425** (16.894)		38783.341 (1.615)	0.944	19
	Chemical (log)	0.683** (3.875)		2.365 (1.047)	0.600	12
	Large (log)	0.743** (3.677)		1.472 (0.564)	0.530	14

Correlation is significant *at the 0.05 level (one-tailed) **at the 0.01 level (one-tailed)

6.5.2 The Use of Technology, ICT, Skill and the Demand for Skilled Workers Across Firms

One implication of the above complementary relationship between skill and technology is that the demand for skilled workers has changed in response to the increasing uses of ICT and other technologies. For instance, during the period 1999–2001 the uses of ICT (61 %) increased faster than that of other technologies (56 %); however, the corresponding rise in the demand for skilled workers needed for ICT (57 %) was less than that for other technologies (61 %) across all respondents firms – see Fig. 6.10 below. This trend may reflect the fact that the real demand for skilled workers needed for ICT is less than that of other technologies across firms, which may not be surprising given the recent history of IT diffusion in the Gulf countries. For instance, according to the UNDP-HDR (2004), in 1990 there was a zero/no access/use of Internet (per 1,000 population) amongst the Gulf population, which may imply that the use of Internet started after 1990. Moreover, data from MADAR Research Group (2002) indicates that the introduction of Internet was between 1992 and 1996 and the commercial or public use of Internet was between 1994 and 1999 in the Gulf countries. The introduction

Table 6.9 The relationship between computers, training and telecommunications expenditures across firms (1999–2001)

		Coefficient (t-value)				R^2	N
Independent variables		Computer expenditure	Training expenditure	Telecommunication expenditure	Constant		
Dependent variables (All firms)							
Computer expenditure: All firms	1999		0.620**	0.198	2.484	0.815	10
			(2.489)	(0.626)	(1.097)		
	2000		0.487	0.431	0.633	0.677	12
			(1.325)	(1.007)	(0.220)		
	2001		0.847*	−0.0564	2.178	0.670	14
			(1.627)	(−0.125)	(1.141)		
Training expenditure: All firms	1999	0.820**		0.343	−2.544	0.830	10
		(2.489)		(0.985)	(0.957)		
	2000	0.369		0.639*	−0.936	0.755	12
		(1.325)		(1.972)	(−0.376)		
	2001	0.247*		0.661**	0.546	0.911	14
		(1.627)		(5.219)	(0.504)		
Telecommunication expenditure: all firms	1999	0.309	0.405		3.720	0.675	10
		(0.626)	(0.515)		(1.377)		
	2000	0.261	0.512**		3.601	0.735	12
		(1.007)	(1.972)		(1.934)		
All firms	2001	−0.0276	1.107**		−0.127	0.888	14
		(−0.125)	(5.219)		(−0.090)		

Correlation is significant *at the 0.05 level (one-tailed) **at the 0.01 level (one-tailed)

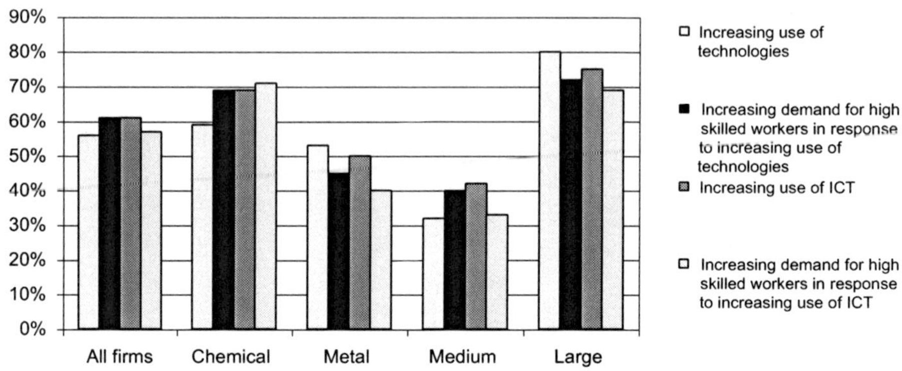

Fig. 6.10 The increasing use of technology, ICT and the demand for high skilled workers across firms, 1999–2001 (Source: Firm Survey (2002))

and commercial use started in 1992 and 1994 respectively in Kuwait, they both started in 1995 in both the UAE and Bahrain, and in 1996 in both Qatar and Oman and finally they started in 1996 and 1999 respectively in Saudi Arabia (cf. MADAR Research Group, p. 4)

According to the respondent firms, the increasing use of new technologies caused an increase in both the demand for more skilled workers and the required skill levels of the respective workers involved with them. Table 6.10 indicates that the increasing use of new technologies has important effects on increasing the general skill levels and the demand for skilled workers amongst 79 % and 62 % of the respondent firms respectively.[14] However, it has only slight effects on increasing skill levels mainly for unskilled workers, and decreasing and substituting the demand for unskilled workers due to reduction and elimination/substitution of some unskilled jobs. This implies change in the structure of employment/demand for workers in response to the increasing uses of new technologies and is also evidence of skilled-biased technical change theorem.[15]

Moreover, from the firm survey we find that the increasing use of new technologies has not only raised the demand for high skilled workers in the past years, but also encouraged firms to predict a future/long run increase in the demand for high skilled workers. For instance, for 61 % of the respondent firms the interpretations of the predicted long run increase in the demand for skilled workers are related to planned/expected expansion of production, product diversification, implementation of new process, output technologies, purchases of new machines

[14] Firms reported the use of different types of new technologies such as mass petrochemicals plants, advanced process controls, gas plants installation, CNC machines, new advanced machines and ICT.

[15] This result is consistent with SBTC theorem and our earlier findings indicating that wages are increasing in education and biased against unskilled workers.

Table 6.10 The effects of new technologies on skill level and the demand for workers in the UAE, 2001

The effects of new technologies in:	All firms	Chemical	Metal	Medium	Large
Increasing the general skill level	79 %	79 %	80 %	63 %	94 %
Increasing skill level mainly for unskilled workers	59 %	63 %	53 %	56 %	61 %
Increasing the demand for skilled workers (more educated, trained and experienced workers)	62 %	58 %	67 %	63 %	61 %
Increasing the demand for more professional workers	62 %	53 %	73 %	50 %	72 %
Decreasing the demand for less skilled workers (less educated, trained and experienced workers)	35 %	32 %	40 %	31 %	39 %
Decreasing the demand for production workers	29 %	16 %	47 %	25 %	33 %
Substituting the demand for less skilled workers	29 %	26 %	33 %	31 %	28 %
Reduction in some unskilled jobs	53 %	53 %	53 %	69 %	39 %
Elimination/substitution of some unskilled jobs	47 %	47 %	47 %	69 %	28 %
Total response	34	19	15	16	18

Source: Own calculation based on the Firm Survey (2002)

and equipment and increasing R&D activities.[16] This result seems consistent with the assumption made by Aghion and Howitt (1992) that an expectation of more research in the next period must correspond to an expectation of higher demand for skilled labour in research in the next period.

6.5.3 *The Share of Spending on ICT and Input–Output Indicators*

Finally, in this section we investigate the third hypothesis on the positive relationships between technology (total expenditures on ICT) and input–output indicators across firms and over time. For instance, when investigating the relationship between ICT and input variables, we find from Tables 6.11 that the total spending on ICT is positively correlated and more sensitive to labour (firm size), and industry level and less sensitive to capital (net worth) throughout the period 1999–2001. The relationship between ICT and labour (firm size) is particularly significant for the large size and chemical firms. The different results across chemical and metal or large and medium size firms is plausible and can be attributed to differences in the skill levels – share of high skilled workers in total employment – see Fig. 6.1 above. This is also because large size firms are more

[16] Moreover, other factors are: the expected increases in market share, turnover, sales, adoption of international standards and enhancement of production, advanced control systems, shortage of manpower, competition, increasing motivation to reduce costs, achieving high standard precision work, improving productivity, quality of work and demand for more specialized skills in IT.

Table 6.11 Total spending on ICT, labour and capital across firms (1999–2001)

		Coefficient (t-value)			R^2	N
Independent variables		Labour	Capital	Constant		
Dependent variable (ICT expenditures)						
ICT expenditures	Large	1.523**		4.008	0.641	14
		(4.625)		(2.138)		
	Medium	9.418**		−29.257	0.610	9
		(3.307)		(−2.454)		
	Chemical	2.065**		1.179	0.485	14
		(3.361)		(0.370)		
	Metal	1.167**		5.655	0.505	9
		(2.674)		(2.537)		
ICT expenditures (All firms) (log)[a]	1999	0.860**	0.241*	3.805	0.630	13
		(2.636)	(1.651)	(1.805)		
	2000	1.068**	0.189	3.763	0.517	13
		(2.461)	(0.978)	(1.290)		
	2001	0.739**	0.175	5.491	0.541	12
		(2.243)	(1.264)	(2.573)		

Correlation is significant *at the 0.05 level (one-tailed) **at the 0.01 level (one-tailed)
[a]Log value for all estimated variables: ICT, labour and capital

prevalent in the chemical industry, they have high share in total ICT spending, employment, capital, output and profit – see Table 6.1 above – and probably have more consistent entrepreneurial/organizational strategies.

We examine the relationship between the total expenditures on ICT, profit and output: Table 6.12 illustrates plausible positive[17] significant correlations between total expenditures on ICT and capital and total output (total sales value) and positive insignificant correlations with profit. These results prove our third hypothesis concerning the positive correlation between ICT and input–output indicators at the micro/firm level. However, our results should be interpreted carefully as they probably have a two-ways causality and may leave open the possibility for reversed causality. Mainly because more profit and output would imply more financial capacity that permits more spending on ICT, on the other hand, more spending on ICT implies higher costs and lower profit.

Our findings concerning the significant positive correlations between ICT and output and the insignificant correlation between ICT and profit imply an inconclusive effect at the micro level. These results agree with our observations at the aggregate level, which imply that the growing expenditures on ICT in the Gulf countries raises the shares of the population using the Internet, enhances e-business, e-education and e-government. However, despite the growing ICT expenditures, their effects are inconclusive at the aggregate level, probably due to low skill levels

[17] Except in 2000, where the correlations between ICT and both output and profit are negative.

Table 6.12 Total spending on ICT, labour capital, output and profit across firms (1999–2001)

		Coefficient (t-value)				R^2	N
Independent variables		Labour	Capital	ICT spending	Constant		
Dependent variables All firms (log)							
Total output (total sales value)	1999	−45897.058	1.207**	53.858**	8423985.9	0.993	12
		(−1.606)	(5.623)	(11.852)	(2.570)		
	2000	−52249.455	2.120**	−1.473	7906055.0	0.978	12
		(−1.477)	(7.150)	(−1.615)	(1.891)		
	2001	−48147.057*	1.808**	13.133*	10655725	0.984	11
		(−1.936)	(8.189)	(1.922)	(3.004)		
Profit	1999	−1527.002	0.140	1.988	129363.28	0.730	11
		(−0.130)	(0.560)	(0.496)	(0.101)		
	2000	−5014.495	0.310*	−0.710	15621.632	0.652	11
		(−0.641)	(1.820)	(−0.921)	(0.012)		
	2001	−11348.674	0.182	1.561	1888472.6	0.515	10
		(−1.236)	(0.608)	(0.240)	(1.657)		

Correlation is significant *at the 0.05 level (one-tailed) **at the 0.01 level (one-tailed)

and inadequate investment in education.[18] The macro observations are consistent with the recent literature indicating the growing but limited effects of ICT diffusion in the developing countries due to a lack of sufficient investment in the complementary infrastructure such as education, skills and technical skills (cf. Pohjola, 2002; Kenny, 2002). Therefore, these results prove the third hypothesis in Chap. 1 above about the inconclusive effect of ICT at the micro level.

6.6 Conclusions

In this chapter we use the data from the Firm Survey (2002) to examine skill indicators, their implications and relationships with average wages, and with upskilling (ICT training) and technology (ICT), ICT and input–output indicators at the micro/firm level.

Our findings in Sect. 6.2 illustrate the low skill levels –due to the excessive share of unskilled foreign workers (Figs. 6.1 and 6.2) – and the implications on skills mismatch (Fig. 6.6), public-private duality and productivity decline across private firms (Tables 6.2 and 6.3). These results are consistent with the micro–macro findings in Chap. 5 above, which indicate the low share of high skilled in total population and employment – measured by both educational and occupational

[18] At the aggregate level, when using the most recent data (2002) on the share of spending on ICT relative to GDP across four Gulf countries: Bahrain, Saudi Arabia, UAE, and Kuwait, we find an inconclusive effect of ICT. Because the share of spending on ICT/GDP shows a significant positive correlation with GDP, but a significant negative correlation with GDP per capita across the four Gulf countries.

levels – and the serious implications on skills mismatch and the macro–micro duality with respect to upskilling efforts. These findings together with those in Chap. 5 above verify hypotheses 3.b and 4.a in Scheme 1.1 Chap. 1 above regarding the implications of the interaction between the deficient educational system and high use of unskilled foreign workers. These findings then confirm our first hypothesis, which we proved in Chap. 2 above, concerning the pressing need for upskilling, particularly within the private sector.

Our results in Sect. 6.3 show positive correlations between actual and required education, experience and average wages (Tables 6.4, 6.5, and 6.6). We verify hypothesis 4.b. in Scheme 1.1. Chap. 1 above that an increase in skill level and firm size lead to improved relationships between actual and required education (Table 6.4), and between actual education, experience and wages (Table 6.6).

In Sect. 6.4 our findings with respect to the positive complementary relationships between skill, technology (ICT) and upskilling (ICT training) and between computers, telecommunications and ICT training (Tables 6.8 and 6.9) are consistent with the findings in the new growth literature. We illustrate and corroborate hypothesis 4.c. in Scheme 1.1. Chap. 1 above that an increase in skill level and firm size lead to an improvement in the complementary relationships between skill, upskilling and technology (ICT).

Taken together, all these results imply the importance of a good education for bridging differences between firms and also for enhancing skill, technology and upskilling complementarity at the micro level. These findings seem consistent with the endogenous growth framework and stylized facts concerning the relationships between human capital, technical progress and upskilling and our theoretical framework in Chap. 3 above.

Finally, our results in Sect. 6.4 indicate positive significant correlations between total spending on ICT and output, but insignificant correlations between total spending on ICT and profit at the micro/firm level (Table 6.12). This result confirms the fifth hypothesis in Scheme 1.1 Chap. 1 above, which implies an inconclusive effect of ICT at the micro level and supports the observations at the macro level in the Gulf countries and the recent literature in the developing countries.

Moreover, our results in Sects. 6.3 and 6.4 show the relationships between actual and required education, experience and wages; and between skill, technology (ICT) and upskilling (ICT training) defined by firm size and industry level. These results are consistent with our findings in Chap. 5 above, which imply that both skill and technology indicators vary across firms and increase with firm size and industry level.

Therefore, our findings in this chapter are consistent with hypotheses 3.b. and 4.a. in Scheme 1.1 Chap. 1 above with respect to the implications of the excessive use of unskilled foreign workers at the micro level. In addition, our results verify hypotheses 4.b. and 4.c. in Scheme 1.1 Chap. 1 above concerning the relationships between actual and required education and experience and between actual education, experience and wages and the relationships between technology (ICT), skill and upskilling (ICT training). Finally, we corroborate the fifth hypothesis in Scheme 1.1 Chap. 1 above regarding the inconclusive effect of ICT at the micro level.

References

Abdelkarim, A. & Haan, H. (2002, January). *Skills and training in the UAE: The need for and the dimensions of institutional intervention* (Policy Research No. 5). Dubai: Centre for Labour Market Research and Information.

Abdelkarim, A. & Ibrahim, S. (2001, December). *Productivity problems in the UAE: The role of productivity organization* (Policy Research Series, No. 4). Dubai: Centre for Labour Market Research and Information.

Acemoglu, D. (1998). Why do new technologies complement skills? Directed technical change and wage inequality. *Quarterly Journal of Economics, 133*(4), 1055–1089.

Aghion, P., & Howitt, P. (1992). A model of growth through creative destruction. *Econometrica, 60*(2), 323–351.

Aghion, P., & Howitt, P. (1998). *Endogenous growth theory*. Cambridge, MA: MIT Press.

Autor, D. H., Katz, L. F., & Krueger, A. B. (1998). Computing inequality: Have computers changed the labour market? *The Quarterly Journal of Economics, 113*(4), 1169–1213.

Braga, H., & Willmore, L. (1991). Technological imports and technological efforts: An analysis of their determinants in Brazilian firms. *The Journal of Industrial Economics, 39*(4), 421–432.

Bresnahan, T. F., Brynjolfsson, E., & Hitt, L. M. (1999). *Information technology, workplace organization, and the demand for skilled labour: Firm- level evidence* (NBER Working Paper Series, No. 7136). Cambridge, MA: National Bureau of Economic Research. http://www.nber.org/papers/w7136.pdf?new_window=1

Colecchia, A. & Papaconstantinou, G. (1996). *The evaluation of skills in OECD countries and the role of technology* (STI Working Paper 1996/6). Paris: OECD, OECD/GD (96) 183.

Firm Survey. (2002, April). *Technological change and skill development: A comparative study of chemical and metal medium and large scale enterprises in the UAE*. UAE: Firm Survey.

Goldin, C., & Katz, L. F. (1998). The origin of technology skill complementarity. *The Quarterly Journal of Economics, 113*(3), 693–732.

Gray, L. (1999, April). *Private sector training and employment: Evaluation and intervention strategies* (Specialist Report No. 4- Dubai). Dubai: The Ministry of Labour and Social Affairs National Strategy for Labour Force Development and Employment Project.

Hartog, J. (2000). On returns to education: Wandering along the hills of Oru land. In H. Heijke & J. Muysken (Eds.), *Education and training in a knowledge based economy*. England: MacMillan.

Kenny, C. (2002, August). *The internet and economic growth in least developed countries* (UNU-WIDER discussion paper series, Vol. DP2002/75). Helsinki, Finland: UNU-WIDER.

Khorshid, M. (2000). *A prototype labour market economic interaction model for a Gulf Cooperation Council Country: Impact of structural imbalances and policy measures on medium term performance*. Paper presented at The Seventh Annual Conference of the Economic Research Forum (ERF) Jordan, Amman, 26–29 Oct 2000.

Kumar, N., & Saqib, M. (1994, January). *Firm size, opportunities for adaptation, and in-house R&D activity in developing countries: The case of Indian manufacturing* (UNU/INTECH working paper, Vol. 13). Maastricht, The Netherlands: UNU-INTECH.

MADAR Research Group. (2002). *E-market trends: Internet coming of age in Arab World with Advent of the Third Wave* (*MADAR Research Journal* Knowledge Economy Research on the Middle East, Vol. 1, Issue Zero Oct 2002, p. 4.

Mincer, J. (1974). *Schooling, experience and earnings*. New York: Columbia University Press.

Muysken, J., Hoppe, M., & Rieder, H. (2002). *The impact of education and mismatch on wages: Germany, 1984–2000* (MERIT research memoranda 2002–031). Maastricht: Maastricht University.

Muysken, J., Kiiver, H., & Hoppe, M. M. (2003). The impact of education and mismatch on wages: Germany, 1984–2000. In F. Büchel, A. de Grip, & A. Mertens (Eds.), *Overeducation in Europe: What do we know?* (pp. 109–132). Cheltenham: Edward Elgar.

Muysken, J., & Nour, S. (2006). Deficiencies in education and poor prospects for economic growth in the Gulf Countries: The case of the UAE. *The Journal of Development Studies, 42*(6), 957–980. Routledge: Taylor and Francis Group Ltd., UK.

Muysken, J., & Ruholl, J. (2001). *The impact of education and mismatch on wages: The Netherlands, 1986–1998* (MERIT research memoranda 2001–030). Maastricht: Maastricht University.

Muysken, J., & ter Weel, B. (1998). *Overeducation and crowding out of low skilled workers* (MERIT Research Memorandum 98–023). Maastricht: Maastricht University.

Muysken, J., Weissbrich, A., & von Restorff, C. H. (2002). *The impact of education and mismatch on wages: the USA, 1986–1996* (MERIT Research Memoranda 2002–015). Maastricht: Maastricht University.

OECD. (1997). *The second European report on science and technology indicators (1997)* (pp. 37, 90–91). Paris: OECD.

Pohjola, M. (2002, July). *New economy in growth and development* (UNU- WIDER Discussion Paper series: DP2002/67). Helsinki.

UNDP-HDR. (2004, July). Human development report (2004): Cultural liberty in today's diverse world. New York/Oxford: Oxford University Press.

Utton, M. A. (1979). *Diversification and competition*. The National Institute of Economic and Social Research 1979 (pp. 15–16, 104–105). Cambridge: Cambridge University Press.

Wadi, M. A. (2001). *Education and labour market: The need for reform: The case of Kuwait* (Arab Planning Institute Working Paper Series, No. 0104). Kuwait: Arab Planning Institute.

Chapter 7
The Importance (Impacts) of Knowledge at the Macro–Micro Levels

7.1 Introduction

Our earlier findings in Chap. 5 indicate that the transfer of knowledge is successful within firms, but is somewhat doubtful between firms and universities and within society at large. Our analysis shows that within society at large, the transfer of knowledge is hindered by low skill levels, deficient educational and training systems, lack of incentives and an imbalanced structure of the population. The transfer of knowledge between universities and firms is hindered by the lack of incentives such as subsidies, and the lack of a networks, information systems, cooperation and interest in conducting joint research between universities and firms and matching the relevance of universities' research to firms needs.

One implication of our earlier analysis is that the Gulf countries need to stimulate the incidence and transfer of knowledge at the aggregate level by providing more incentives, for example through subsidies, to education and training to upgrade skill levels, and also by raising spending on R&D and ICT, organization, coordination and cooperation. Further incentives, such as subsidies, should be provided to stimulate the transfer of knowledge between universities and firms that requires a good knowledge base within firms and further incentives, for example subsidies to education and training to enhance skill levels, and subsidies to R&D, networks organization, information, coordination and cooperation. In this Chapter we extend our earlier analysis and explain the importance (impacts) of knowledge at both micro and macro levels in the Gulf countries in more detail. In addition, we show the factors contributing to improve the tacit knowledge within firms. Due to the lack of relevant data to assess the transfer of knowledge amongst firms and between firms and universities, we focus only on the impacts of knowledge within the firms and at the aggregate/macro level.

The rest of this chapter is organized as follows: Sect. 2 briefly shows the importance and sources of knowledge in the growth literature; Sect. 3 presents hypothesis 7 in Chap. 1 above to test some stylized facts about the importance of

S. Mohamed Nour, *Technological Change and Skill Development in Arab Gulf Countries*, Contributions to Economics, DOI 10.1007/978-3-319-01916-1_7,

knowledge and explains the data used to test them; Sect. 4 discusses the main findings; and Sect. 5 provides the conclusions.

7.2 Definition, Importance, Sources and Measurement of Knowledge in the Growth Literature

Endogenous growth literature recognized the importance of knowledge and its accumulation as a unique source of endogenous technological progress, innovation and economic growth. For instance, in the Lucas (1988) model, knowledge accumulation is vital for the growth process, for knowledge creation, accumulation and acceleration, contribution to scientific and technological progress, innovation, economic growth performance and development.

In defining 'knowledge' the literature makes a distinction between codified and tacit knowledge (Dasgupta and David (1994)). "Codified knowledge implies that knowledge is transformed into information which can either be embodied in new material goods (machines, new consumer goods) or easily transmitted through information infrastructure. While, the tacit knowledge refers to that which cannot easily transferred because it has not been stated or measured in an explicit form, skill is an important kind of tacit knowledge"[1] (cf. Freeman & Soete, 1997, pp. 404–405).

In addition, the definition of codified knowledge in the literature is closely related with investment in public spending on education, training, R&D and ICT. Several studies perceive knowledge as a public good, produced through R&D activities that generate spillover and thereby increasing returns (Romer, 1994; Grossman & Helpman, 1994). Other studies use broader terms to interpret knowledge created and embodied in institutions (cf. Langlois, 2001). For instance, Nelson (1993) and Lundvall (1992) emphasize the importance of institutions for the flows of knowledge and information to innovative capability. According to Smith (2002): "R&D is but one component of knowledge and innovation expenditures, and by no means the largest. Because, R&D data tend to either overemphasize the discovery of new scientific or technical innovations, or to exclude a wide range of activities that involve the creation or use of new knowledge in innovation. Thus, innovation rests not only on discovery and R&D but also on learning, external environment (network) of the firm, non-R&D expenditures such as training, market research, design, trail production and tooling up and IPR costs. In addition to capital expenditure, which is a key mode of 'embodied' knowledge spillover from the capital good sector to using industries"(Smith, pp. 14–18).

Moreover, the evolutionary framework developed by Nelson and Winter (1982) makes the nature of knowledge and firms' investment in it a central factor in

[1] Disembodied flows of knowledge can be transmitted through movement of people, publications, etc.

explaining the size, structure and dynamics of industries. Recent empirical literature (cf. Lööf & Heshmati, 2002) shows that knowledge capital (defined as the ratio of innovation sales to total sales) is found to be a significant factor contributing to performance heterogeneity and a firm's innovative level. Knowledge capital rises with innovation input, the firm's internal knowledge for innovation and cooperation with domestic universities on matters of innovation. Some empirical studies indicate that survival and growth amongst firms is determined by/or at least influenced by differential rates of investment in knowledge (such as R&D) (cf. Klepper & Simons, 1997) or intersectoral differences in the size and R&D intensity of firm (cf. Levin, Cohen, & Mowery, 1985). In addition, Brusoni, Marsili, and Salter (2002) and David and Foray (1995) show that an increasing codification of knowledge stock would increase a firm's innovative performance.

In addition, differential in the productivity and growth of different countries is significantly related to improvement in the quality of human capital, technical progress, factors of production and the capacity to create new knowledge and ideas and incorporate them in equipment and people. "Recent growth literature show increasing evidences of the growing relative importance of intangible capital in total productive wealth and the rising relative share of GDP attributable to intangible capital (Abramovitz & David, 1996, 1998). Intangible capital largely falls into two main categories: on the one hand, investment geared to the production and dissemination of knowledge (i.e. training, education, R&D, information and coordination); on the other hand, investment geared to sustaining the physical state of human capital (health expenditures). In the US, the current value of the stock of intangible capital (devoted to knowledge creation and human capital) began to outweigh that of tangible capital (physical infrastructure and equipment, inventories, natural resources) at the end of the 1960s. Moreover, since 1960s annual investment rates in R&D, public education and software have grown steadily at an annual rate of 3 % in the OECD countries" (David & Foray, 2001, pp. 1–2).

Furthermore, Drucker (1998, p. 15) suggests: "knowledge is now becoming the one factor of production, sidelining both capital and labour". In addition, the OECD (1999, p. 7) has suggested "... the role of knowledge (as compared with natural resources, physical capital and low skill labour) has taken on greater importance".[2] Smith (2002) argues that in recent years, learning and knowledge have attracted increasing attention as a result of the claims that knowledge-intensive industries are now at the core of a growth, knowledge driven economy or even a knowledge society. The role of knowledge as an input to economic processes has fundamentally changed, probably due to rapid technological changes/advances in ICT; ICT is seen as factor increasing knowledge and increasing the common availability of codified knowledge (David & Foray, 1995; Smith, 2002). For instance, van Zon (2001) extends Lucas (1988) model by incorporating the effects of ICT – capital investment and assuming that ICT has positive influence on growth performance,

[2] See Drucker (1998, p. 15) and OECD (1999, p. 7) respectively.

both by improving the intensity of production and total factor productivity and enhancing the efficiency of knowledge accumulation and learning process.

Moreover, the empirical literature shows that knowledge is positively related to human capital (mainly tacit skill or skill level). For instance, Winter (1987) suggests that tacit and codified knowledge need not be substitutes, but can be seen as complements in the learning process. Brusoni et al. (2002) show a strong positive relationship between the codification of the knowledge base of the industry and its investment in skilled people (high levels of investment in tacit skills) and R&D.

In addition, Cowan, Soete, and Tchervonnaya (2001, p. 9) examine knowledge transfer in the services sector as a process by which knowledge travels from a knowledge holder (a person or organization possessing the knowledge)" to a knowledge recipient (a person or organization receiving the knowledge). In their analysis "knowledge holder is important as the "point of departure" of the knowledge being transmitted since they can influence knowledge flows".

Furthermore, the literature indicates a substantial contribution to innovation and therefore to economic growth and public welfare that can be related to an unintended spillover associated with knowledge flows.[3] Distinction has been made between three sources for the flows and transfer of knowledge: for instance, Brusoni et al. (2002) highlight the importance of knowledge sources within the enterprise for innovation among innovative firms in Europe, in particular, the internal divisions (including R&D, design, sales and marketing and senior management). Several other studies have focused on knowledge flows between firms through inter-firm research collaborations (Hagedoorn, Link, & Vonortas, 2001), user-producer networks (Lundvall, 1992), or linkages between competing firms (Von Hippel, 1988). Yet other studies examine knowledge flows between firms and public research organizations such as universities, public research institutes, government laboratories, and publicly-funded technical institutes (cf. Arundel & Geuna, 2001; Mansfield, 1991; Mansfield & Lee, 1996). At the aggregate level, the transfer of knowledge is related to several variables such as the overall quantity of scientific research (publications) and the public research base as measured by the ratio between the total amount of higher education R&D expenditure and the country GDP (cf. Arundel & Geuna, 2001, p. 3, 5).

The notion that knowledge is a public good, produced through education, training and R&D activities that generate spillovers and increasing returns, provides a plausible justification for government intervention to compensate the private sector for the positive externalities they generate and to provide more incentives to support investment and accumulation of knowledge. While Lucas (1988) model emphasizes investment in human capital, it only implicitly allows for a role for public policy through subsidies (Haslinger & Ziesemer, 1996, p. 230). Subsequent studies attempted to fill this gap in Lucas (1988) model and explicitly indicate a potential role for government intervention and public policies to support

[3] Verspagen and Schoenmakers (2000) use patent citations to measure knowledge spillover.

the creation and accumulation of knowledge. The main channels are through taxation or subsidisation to the provision of R&D (cf. Romer, 1990; Barro & Sala-i- Martin, 1992, 1995), public knowledge: basic education and basic scientific research (cf. Ziesemer 1990, 1995) and subsidising training (cf. Chatterji, 1995) – see our discussion in Chap. 3 above.

7.3 The Hypothesis, Stylized Facts and Data

Based on the above background, this Section presents hypothesis 7 in Chap. 1 above to test some stylized facts about the importance of knowledge in the Gulf countries and explains the data used to test them.

7.3.1 The Importance (Impacts) of Knowledge at the Micro–Macro Levels in the Gulf Countries

In recent times, few studies discuss the status of knowledge in the Arab countries. The UNDP- AHDR (2003) examines the weak status of demand, production and dissemination of knowledge in the Arab states. Aubert and Reiffers (2003) assess the challenges and underline a strategy for the development of knowledge-based economies in the Middle East and North Africa countries (MENA). Both reports provide significant contribution, but a somewhat general analysis at the aggregate/ macro level that refers to all Arab and MENA countries respectively. Since the Gulf countries show considerable disparity from the other Arab and MENA countries, at least in respect of some indicators such as structure and size of the economy, level of income and structure of labour market, it might be useful to look at them separately. Thus, one obvious advantage of our analysis is that we provide a more specific analysis that focuses only on the Gulf countries. Moreover, different from earlier studies, we provide a new empirical investigation of both the importance (impacts) of tacit knowledge at the micro level – see our discussion below – as well as the discrepancy in the transfer of knowledge/external schooling effects at the macro–micro levels – see our discussion in Chap. 5 above.

In this chapter we use the literature presented above to examine hypothesis 7 in Scheme 1.1 in Chap. 1 above concerning the importance (impacts) of tacit and codified knowledge at the macro (within society)–micro (inside the firms) levels. In particular, our aim is to test the following stylized facts:

1. At the macro level codified knowledge is positively correlated with economic growth (GDP), and tacit knowledge is positively correlated with schooling.
2. At the macro level codified knowledge and Full Time Equivalent Researchers (FTER) are positively correlated with each other and also with technology (patents), publications and cooperation.

3. At the micro (firm) level tacit knowledge is positively correlated with technology (ICT), upskilling (training), profit, productivity, output and output diversification.
4. At the micro (firm) level tacit knowledge is positively correlated with market size (firm size; capital; and investment) and firm age.

7.3.2 Definition of Data and Variables

We use the broad definition of knowledge found in the new growth literature that highlights both the tacit and codified components of knowledge. In particular, we define tacit knowledge by the percentage share of high skilled workers in total employment at the micro level[4] and the share of enrolment in tertiary education at the macro level. In addition, we use the number of full time equivalent researchers (FTER[5]) as another indicator of tacit knowledge at the macro level.[6] We define codified knowledge by the embodied knowledge distributed in many indicators, including the share of spending on R&D, education and ICT as percentage of GDP at the macro level.[7] In addition, we use several variables related to knowledge such as patents, publications, cooperation – measured by joint publications, and schooling years – defined by school life expectancy – across the Gulf countries. Table 7.1 below presents the data and variables, which we use in our analysis of the importance (impacts) of knowledge at the macro/aggregate level in the Gulf countries.

As in Chap. 6 above, we obtain our micro/firm data from the Firm Survey (2002) and use three sets of indicators, including tacit knowledge (technical and non technical skills), technology and input–output variables. We define tacit knowledge by the share of high skilled/educated workers in total employment, and technology by expenditures on ICT; inputs indicators are labour (employment size) and capital (net worth), output (total sales value), output diversification (sales diversification), productivity and profit.[8]

[4] As in Chap. 6 above, our definition of high skilled workers refer to workers with post secondary educational attainment: university degree and above (16 years of schooling).

[5] The concept of full–time equivalent researcher is adopted by UNESCO statistics on R&D personnel.

[6] The main limitations of our data at the macro/aggregate level are the definition of tacit knowledge by the share/ ratios of enrolment in tertiary education (despite their drawback), the adjustment of the variables for different years and the use of unified ratio of ICT spending, due to scarcity of data.

[7] At the micro level, the definition of codified knowledge by the relative term or the share of these indicators to total output or sales value does not provide relevant results.

[8] As in Chap. 6 above, we use the same definitions of educational qualifications, ICT, diversification, output, capital, labour (firm's size) and firm's age (total years in operation) – see our definitions in Chapter 6 above. In addition, we obtained information on investment variables from GOIC databases.

Table 7.1 The determinants of knowledge in the Gulf societies (1990–2001)

Variable/country	UAE	Kuwait	Bahrain	Oman	Qatar	Saudi Arabia
GDP(US$ billion)(2001)[a] (1)	69.23	32.0	7.9	19.8	16.5	186.5
Schooling years (2000)[b] (2)	10.7	8.7	13	8.7	13.1	9.5
High skilled (share of enrolment in tertiary education) (%) (1998)[b] (3)	12	21	25	8	28	21
FTER (1996)[c]	107	440	86	82	34	846
Publications (1990–1995)[d]	579	1936	453	466	377	8306
Cooperation (1995)[d]	55	117	29	37	36	294
Share of public spending on R&D as % of GDP (1996)[e]	0.02	0.22	0.06	0.07	0.06	0.14
Share of public spending on education as % of GDP (1995–1997)[f]	1.7	5.0	4.4	4.5	3.4	7.5
Spending on ICT/GDP(2001)[g]	3.6	3.6	3.6	3.6	3.6	3.6
Codified knowledge	5.32	8.82	8.06	8.17	7.06	11.24
Patents (1991–1999)[h]	15	27	2	3	0	103

Notes: (1) data for the UAE obtained from The UAE Ministry of Planning (2002) (2) data for Saudi Arabia refers to 1997 from ERF (2002) (3) data for Oman refers to 2000–2001
[a]UNDP (2003) "UNDP Human Development Report", [b]UNESCO-UIS (2003): www.unesco.org, [c]ESCWA-UNESCO (1998), [d]Zahlan (1999a, b), [e]Qasem (1998a, b) and GOIC (2000), [f]UNDP (2002) "UNDP Human Development Report", [g]WITSA (2002), [h]US Patent and Trademark Office web site: www.uspto.gov

7.4 The Empirical Results

We use the data presented above and the linear and log linear OLS regression techniques to test and compare the importance (impacts) of tacit and codified knowledge at the micro and macro levels respectively and compare the relevance of our findings to those in the knowledge literature. Based on Table 7.1 above, Tables 7.2 and 7.3 below present a panel data analysis reflecting the average across the Gulf countries over the period 1990–2001. Based on data from the Firm Survey (2002), Tables 7.4, 7.5 and 7.6 reflect the results across firms.

Tables 7.2, 7.3, 7.4, and 7.5 present our results, which indicate the importance (impacts) of tacit and codified sources of knowledge at the macro (aggregate) and micro (firm) levels respectively. Some of these results are consistent with the findings in the literature (cf. Abramovitz & David, 1996, 1998; David & Foray, 2001; Lööf & Heshmati, 2002). Our results in Tables 7.2 and 7.3 illustrate the importance of knowledge at the aggregate/macro level. Table 7.2 shows that tacit knowledge – defined by the number of FTER – and codified knowledge show significant positive correlations with publications, cooperation and technology (patents). The correlations between tacit knowledge -defined by the number of FTER- and these variables appear more significant than those with codified knowledge. When defining the number of FTER as one form of tacit knowledge, we find a

Table 7.2 The impacts of FTER and codified knowledge on publications, cooperation and patent across the Gulf countries (1990–2001)

	Coef (t-value)			R^2
	Constant	Tacit knowledge (2) (Number of FTER)	Codified knowledge (share of education, R&D and ICT in GDP)	
Number of FTER	−843.173 (−2.272)		136.717** (3.060)	0.701
Codified knowledge	6.749 (10.202)	0.005** (3.060)		0.701
Number of publications	−477.469 (6.729)	9.393** (6.729)		0.919
	−8692.351 (−2.314)		1320.549** (2.921)	0.681
Cooperation	10.640 (0.928)	0.316** (10.884)		0.967
	−248.444 (−1.924)		42.298** (2.722)	0.649
Technology (patents)	−6.755 (−1.074)	0.119** (7.502)		0.934
	−101.592 (−1.909)		15.606** (2.436)	0.597

Correlation is significant **at the 0.01 level (one-tailed)
Notes: N = 6

Table 7.3 The impacts of tacit and codified knowledge on schooling and GDP across the Gulf countries (1990–2001)

	Coefficient (t-value)			R^2
	Constant	Tacit knowledge (1) (tertiary school enrolment ratios)	Codified knowledge (share of education, R&D and ICT in GDP)	
Schooling	7.296 (3.605)	17.326* (1.747)		0.433
Growth of GDP	−112 (−0.976)		20.7[a] (1.493)	0.358

Correlation is significant * at the 0.05 level (one-tailed)
[a]When excluding the observations for the UAE, the coefficient in the regression equation turns significant. This result is plausible since the UAE has a low share of public spending on education and R&D relative to GDP, when compared to other Gulf countries. This result can then be used to argue that an increase in public spending on these components would imply an increase in GDP

significant positive correlation between the number of FTER and codified knowledge, which can be interpreted as complementary relationship between tacit and codified knowledge (cf. Winter, 1987; Brusoni et al., 2002). Moreover, Table 7.3 indicates a positive significant correlation between tacit knowledge – defined by tertiary school enrolment ratios – and schooling years, while codified knowledge

Table 7.4 The significance of tacit knowledge across firms, 2001

	Coefficient (t-value)		R^2	N
	Constant	Tacit knowledge (share of high skilled in total employment)		
ICT expenditures	−0.055 (−4.219)	0.210** (5.965)	0.703	17
Training expenditures	−0.036 (−2.276)	0.168** (4.089)	0.563	15
Total profit	−0.041 (−2.590)	0.278** (5.858)	0.710	16
Total output (total sales value)	0.071 (0.371)	0.141** (2.038)	0206	18
Productivity (total sales value per workers)	0.0529 (0.768)	0.637** (2.985)	0.358	18
Output diversification (sales diversification)	1.178 (8.029)	0.634* (1.901)	0.194	17

Correlation is significant * at the 0.05 level (one-tailed) ** at the 0.01 level (one-tailed)

Table 7.5 The increased use and effect of skilled workers, scientists and engineers across firms in the UAE, 2002 (measured in % as indicated by respondents)

The increased use of skilled workers and their effects	All firms	Chemical	Metal	Medium	Large
(a) Increased use of skilled workers (1999–2001)	44 %	33 %	60 %	29 %	58 %
(b) The effects of increased use of skilled workers					
Increase in firm production	90 %	78 %	100 %	75 %	100 %
Effective utilization of technologies	75 %	89 %	64 %	75 %	75 %
Improve product quality	60 %	67 %	55 %	63 %	58 %
Improve the level of competitiveness in the local market	90 %	78 %	100 %	88 %	92 %
Faster adaptation of technologies	80 %	78 %	82 %	88 %	75 %
Improve the level of competitiveness in the international market	50 %	78 %	27 %	50 %	50 %
Total response	20	9	11	8	12
(c) The effects of scientists and engineers on firm production and acquisition of knowledge					
The effects of scientist and engineers	All firms	Chemical	Metal	Medium	Large
Add technical, scientific or marketing knowledge to areas where firms already had expertise	80 %	90 %	67 %	76 %	83 %
Shorten development time	57 %	60 %	53 %	53 %	61 %
Add new technical, scientific or marketing knowledge to areas where firms lacked expertise	51 %	60 %	40 %	41 %	61 %
Total response	35	20	15	17	18

Source: Own calculation based on the % as indicated by respondent firms to Firm Survey (2002)

Table 7.6 The determinants/factors enhancing tacit knowledge across firms, 2001

	Coefficient (t-value)		R^2	N
	Constant	Tacit knowledge (share of high skilled in total employment)		
Firm size	−2.887 (−3.804)	0.273* (1.832)[a]	0.150	21
Capital	0.195 (6.689)	0.0016** (2.353)	0.257	18
Investment	−4.520 (−3.167)	0.195** (2.139)[a]	0.260	15
Firm age	0.262 (2.693)	0.004 (0.670)	0.018	26

Correlation is significant * at the 0.05 level (one-tailed) ** at the 0.01 level (one-tailed)
[a]The logarithm of the variable is taken

shows a positive correlation with GDP.[9] In addition, we observe from Table 7.1 above that the share of public spending on R&D is associated with an increase in the number of FTER, publications, cooperation and technology (patents), while cooperation is associated with an increase in both publications and technology (patents). Therefore, these results verify the first and second stylized facts that at the macro/aggregate level knowledge is positively correlated with GDP (economic growth), schooling years and technology (patents) across the Gulf countries.

Table 7.4 verifies the third stylized fact that at the micro/firms level tacit knowledge shows positive significant correlations with technology (total expenditures on ICT) and skill upgrading (total expenditures on training), total output (defined by total sales value), output diversification (defined by sales diversification), productivity and profit.[10] From the perspective of the new growth literature, the positive correlation between tacit knowledge and output is important to prevent the diminishing returns to scale and to ensure the increasing returns and dynamic growth in the production function. This would imply that with the assumption of a potential role for public policies, the government could prevent the diminishing returns to scale and ensure increasing returns to scale, mainly through improving tacit knowledge by stimulating investment in education (basic, secondary and tertiary).

Our results from the Firm Survey (2002) in Table 7.5 bear out the assumption that the increased use of tacit knowledge – defined by skilled workers, scientists and engineers – shows significant effects across firms. In particular, this contributes towards the improvement in firm production, the level of competitiveness in the local market, faster adaptation of foreign technology, utilization of technology and

[9] In contrast to our expectations, the findings at the macro level indicate insignificant correlations between codified knowledge and schooling, and between tacit knowledge – defined by tertiary enrolment ratios – and both GDP and codified knowledge.

[10] There are also positive correlations between tacit knowledge and output, output diversification, productivity and profit that exceed the combined correlations of traditional inputs such as labour and capital not reported in Table 7.4; these results are consistent with the findings in the literature (cf. Drucker, 1998; OECD, 1999).

product quality. Moreover, Table 7.5 indicates that the increased use of scientists and engineers would imply additions to acquisition of existing knowledge within the firm, as well as the shortening of development time and acquisition of new knowledge, the latter regarded as of somewhat less importance.[11]

Our findings in Table 7.6 prove the fourth stylized fact that at the micro/firm level tacit knowledge is significantly and positively correlated with market size: total investment, capital and firm size. Therefore at the micro/firm level an increase in total investment, capital and firm size would coincide with more tacit knowledge.

7.5 Conclusions

In this chapter we use the Firm Survey (2002) data at the micro level and secondary data at the macro level to examine hypothesis 7 in Scheme 1.1 in Chap. 1 above concerning the importance/impacts of tacit and codified sources of knowledge at the micro and macro levels respectively in the Gulf countries. Our results prove this hypothesis and show that at the macro level tacit knowledge is positively correlated with schooling years, while codified knowledge is positively correlated with GDP (economic growth). Moreover, we find that at the macro level codified knowledge and the number of FTER show positive correlations with the number of publications, cooperation and technology (patents). Furthermore, at the aggregate level, our results imply a significant positive complementary relationship between the number of FTER and codified knowledge, which we interpret as a complementary relationship between tacit knowledge and codified knowledge. At the micro (firm) level, we illustrate the importance of tacit knowledge, which shows positive significant correlations with technology (expenditures on ICT) and upskilling (expenditures on training), output, output diversification, productivity and profit. Finally, we find that at the micro (firm) level, tacit knowledge shows positive significant correlations with total investment, capital, and firm size. This can be interpreted that higher levels of total investment, capital and firm size would correspond to more tacit knowledge across firms. Our results at the micro and macro levels verify the four stylized facts presented in the introduction, which are consistent with the general findings in the knowledge literature. The major implication of our findings is that knowledge shows positive significant correlations with many variables at both the micro and macro levels. Therefore, this would imply that public policy should provide further incentives to improve tacit and codified sources of knowledge at both the macro and micro levels. Another implication is that the positive impact of tacit knowledge also underlines the importance of good education, since tacit knowledge is often embodied in educated people and thus human capital. Moreover, from the perspective of the new growth literature, the positive correlation between tacit knowledge and output is important to prevent the

[11] Knowledge includes technical, scientific or marketing knowledge.

diminishing returns to scale and to ensure the increasing returns and dynamic growth in the production function. This would imply that, with the assumption of a potential role for public policies, governments could prevent the diminishing returns to scale and ensure increasing returns to scale, mainly through improving tacit knowledge by stimulating investment in education (basic, secondary and tertiary). In addition, at the aggregate/macro level, the positive correlation between GDP and codified knowledge –the share of public spending on education, R&D and ICT relative to GDP – would imply a positive role for public policy to support codified knowledge by increasing spending on education, R&D and ICT. These results are consistent with the literature that substantiate the role of public policies to support the creation and accumulation of knowledge, as we explained in Sect. 2 of this chapter and Sect. 5 in Chap. 3 above.

References

Abramovitz, M., & David, P. A. (1996). Technological change and the rise of intangible investments: The US economy's growth –path in the twentieth century. In D. Foray & B.-A. Lundvall (Eds.), *Employment and growth in the knowledge based economy (OECD documents)*. Paris: OECD.

Abramovitz, M., & David, P. A. (1998). American macro economic growth in the era of knowledge based progress: The long –run perspective. In S. L. Engerman & R. E. Gallman (Eds.), *An economic history of the United States: The twentieth century* (Vol. 3, pp. 1–92). New York: Cambridge University Press.

Arundel, A., & Geuna, A. (2001). *Does proximity matter for knowledge transfer from public institute and Universities to firms?* ((SPRU electronic working paper series No. 73, pp. 3, 5)). Brington: SPRU, University of Sussex.

Aubert, J-E. & Reiffers, J-L. (Eds.). (2003). Knowledge economies in the Middle East and North Africa: Toward new development strategies, Vol. 1. In *World Bank Institute learning resources series*. The World Bank (2003) Report No. 28038.

Barro, R. J., & Sala-i-Martin, X. (1995). *Economic growth*. New York: McGraw Hill.

Barro, R. J., & Sala-i-Martin, X. (1992). Public finance in models of economic growth. *The Review of Economic Studies, 59*(4), 645–661.

Brusoni, S., Marsili, O., & Salter, A. (2002). The role of codified sources of knowledge in innovation: Empirical evidence from Dutch manufacturing. *SPRU electronic working paper series*, No. 80, University of Sussex.

Chatterji, M. (1995, September). *Training subsidies, technical progress and economic growth* (pp. 274–282). Manchester: The Manchester School, LXIII(3). Blackwell Publishers Ltd. The Victoria University of Manchester.

Cowan, R., Soete, L., & Tchervonnaya, O. (2001). *Knowledge transfer and the services sector in the context of the new economy* (MERIT-INFONOMIC Research Memorandum 2001–021, p. 9). Maastricht: Maastricht University.

Dasgupta, P., & David, P. (1994). Toward a new economics of science. *Research Policy, 23*(5), 487–521.

David, P. A., & Foray, D. (1995). Accessing and expanding the science and technology knowledge base. *STI Review, 16*, 13–68. OECD, Paris.

David, P. A., & Foray, D. (2001). *An introduction to the economy of the knowledge society* (MERIT –INFONOMIC Research Memorandum series No. 2001–041). Maastricht: Maastricht University.

Drucker, P. (1998). From capitalism to knowledge society. In D. Neef (Ed.), *The knowledge economy* (p. 15). Woburn: Butterworth.

Economic Research Forum for the Arab Countries, Iran and Turkey (ERF). (2002). *Economic trends in MENA region 2002*. Chapter Five: Labor market and Human Resource Development: The GCC Labor Market: Private vs Public. The ERF and the American University in Cairo.

ESCWA- UNESCO. (1998). Research and development system in the Arab States: Development of science and technology indicators. 1998 *(E/ESCWA/TECH/1998/3)*. In ESCWA (1999) *Review of science and technology in ESCWA member countries*. Issue No. 1. 1999 *(E/ESCWA/TECH/1999/Rev. 1)*. Jan 1999: pp. 3–4.

Firm Survey. (2002). Technological change and skill development: A comparative study of chemical and metal medium and large scale enterprises in the UAE. UAE, April, 2002.

Freeman, C. & Soete, L. (1997). *The economic of industrial innovation*, (3rd ed., pp. 2–24, 404–405). London: Cassell.

Grossman, G. M., & Helpman, E. (1994). Endogenous innovation in the theory of the growth. *Journal of Economic Perspectives, 8*(1), 23–44.

Gulf Organization for Industrial Consulting GOIC. (2000). *Gulf statistical profile 2000: Industrial Data Bank*. Doha: GOIC.

Hagedoorn, J., Link, A. N., & Vonortas, N. (2001). Research partnership. *Research Policy, 29*, 567–86.

Haslinger, F., & Ziesemer, T. (1996). Endogenous growth and distributional conflict. In C. Gore, G. Köhler, U. Peter Reich, & T. Ziesemer (Eds.), *Questioning development* (pp. 223–40). Marburg: Metroplis Verlag.

Klepper, S., & Simons, K. (1997). Technological extinctions of industrial firms: An enquiry into their nature and causes. *Industrial Corporate Change, 6*, 379–460.

Langlois, R. N. (2001). Knowledge, consumption, and endogenous growth. *Journal of Evolutionary Economics, 11*, 77–93.

Levin, R., Cohen, W. M., & Mowery, D. C. (1985). R&D appropriability, opportunity and market structure: New evidence on some Schumpeterian hypotheses. *American Economic Review, 75*, 20–24.

Lööf, H., & Heshmati, A. (2002). Knowledge capital and performance heterogeneity: A firm-Level innovation study. *International Journal of Production Economics, 76*(2002), 61–85.

Lucas, R. E. (1988). On the mechanics of economic development. *Journal of Monetary Economics, 22*, 3–42. North Holland.

Lundvall, B.-Å. (Ed.). (1992). *National systems of innovation: Towards a theory of innovation and interacting learning*. London: Printer Publishers.

Mansfield, E. (1991). Academic research and industrial innovation: An update of empirical findings. *Research Policy, 26*, 773–76.

Mansfield, E., & Lee, J.-Y. (1996). The Modern University: Contributor to industrial innovation and recipient of industrial R&D support. *Research Policy, 25*, 1047–58.

Nelson, R. (Ed.). (1993). *National innovation systems: A comparative study*. New York: Oxford University Press.

Nelson, R. R., & Winter, S. G. (1982). *An evolutionary theory of economic change*. Cambridge, MA: Harvard University Press.

OECD. (1999). The knowledge based economy: A set of figures and facts. Paris: OECD. OECD. (1999). L'économie fondée sur le savoir: des faits et des chiffres. Paris: OECD.

Qasem, S. (1998a). Research and development in the Arab states: Development of science and technology indicators. In *Review of science and technology in ESCWA member countries, ESCWA* (1999), Issue No. 1. New York, NY: United Nations.

Qasem, S. (1998b). Research and development systems in the Arab states: Development of science and technology indicators, Chapter 4. In *Economic Trend in MENA Region 2002*. Cairo: Economic Research Forum and the American University in Cairo.

Romer, P. M. (1990). Endogenous technological change. *Journal of Political Economy, 98*(5), Part 2, 71–102.

Romer, P. M. (1994). The origin of endogenous growth. *Journal of Economic Perspectives, 8*, 3–22.

Smith, K. (2002, June). What is knowledge economy'? Knowledge intensity and distributed knowledge bases. *UNU-INTECH Discussion Paper Series* No. 2002–6.

The UAE Ministry of Planning. (2002). Statistical data for the years (2002). Abu Dhabi, UAE.

The U.S. Patent and Trademark Office (USPTO). (2005). Annual reports – Various issues 1991–1999. U.S.: US Patent and Trade mark office: http://www.uspto.gov. Accessed April 10, 2005.

UNDP. (2002). Human development report (2002): Deepening democracy in a fragmental world. New York/Oxford: UNDP/Oxford University Press.

UNDP. (2003). Human development report (2003): Millennium development goals: A compact among nations to end human poverty. New York/Oxford: UNDP/Oxford University Press.

UNDP- AHDR. (2003). Arab Human Development Report (2003): Building a knowledge society. New York/Amman: UNDP – RBAS/National Press.

UNESCO-UIS. (2003). The UNESCO education data and statistics indicators 1998–2001. www.unesco.org

van Zon, A. (2001). *ICT- investment, knowledge accumulation and endogenous growth* (MERIT – INFONOMIC research memorandum series, No. 2001–038). Maastricht: Maastricht University.

Verspagen, B. & Schoenmakers, W. (2000). *The spatial dimension of knowledge spillovers in Europe: Evidence from firm patenting data.* Paper prepared for AEA conference on intellectual property econometrics, Alicante, 19–20 April 2000.

Von Hippel, E. (1988). *The sources of innovation.* New York: Oxford University Press.

Winter, S. G. (1987). Knowledge and competence as strategic assets. In D. J. Teece (Ed.), *The competitive challenge: Strategies for industrial innovation and renewal* (pp. 159–184). Cambridge, MA: Ballinger Publishing Company.

WITSA. (2002, February). Digital planet 2002: The global information economy. In *The world information technology and services alliance.* Arlington.

Zahlan, A. B. (1999a). *The Arabs and the challenges of science and technology: Progress without change.* Beirut: The Centre for the Study of Arab Unity.

Zahlan, A. B. (1999b). Science policy for the twenty-first century: Mobilization and development. In *ESCWA proceedings of the expert group meeting on science and technology policies and strategies for the twenty- first century,* 10–12, 14–16. Beirut: ESCWA, March 1999.

Ziesemer, T. (1990, January). Public factors and democracy in poverty analysis. *Oxford Economic Papers*, 1990, Special Issue on Public Economics, Vol. 42, pp. 268–280. Reprinted in: P.J.N. Sinclair & M.D.E. Slater (Eds.). (1991). *Taxation, private information and capital.* Oxford: Clarendon Press.

Ziesemer, T. (1995). Endogenous growth with public factors and heterogeneous human capital producers. *Finanzarchiv, 52*(1), 1–20. Neue Folge.

Part IV
Policy Recommendations, Summary and Conclusions

Chapter 8
Education, Training and Skill Development Policies in the Gulf Countries: Macro–Micro Overview

8.1 Introduction

Chapter 5 investigates the causes and consequences of deficient educational and training systems, the lack of knowledge transfer and upskilling. The results that are set out in Chaps. 6 and 7 imply the importance of a good education. From that perspective, therefore, it is convenient to conclude our study by discussing the educational policies in the Gulf countries, and the training and skill upgrading plans, mechanisms and policies implemented to improve them. In particular, this chapter examines hypothesis 8 in Scheme 1.1 in Chap. 1 above concerning the need for skill and technological upgrading through relevant policies for skills development: enhancing the educational system, and provision of training and transfer of knowledge/external schooling effects at the macro–micro levels in the UAE.

The rest of this chapter is organized as follows: Sect. 8.1 discusses the supply–demand sides: major characteristics and implications of educational policies in the Gulf countries based on data and information obtained from the UNESCO, UNDP and other relevant sources. Section 8.2 examines the training and skill upgrading policies implemented by the large public firms in the UAE based on data and information obtained from these firms. Section 8.3 uses the results of the macro and firm surveys (2002) and the follow-up interviews to present the macro–micro views and suggestions for relevant mechanisms and policies for skill development: enhancing the educational system, provision of training and transfer of knowledge/external schooling effect. Section 8.4 provides the conclusions.

S. Mohamed Nour, *Technological Change and Skill Development in Arab Gulf Countries*, Contributions to Economics, DOI 10.1007/978-3-319-01916-1_8,

8.2 Characteristics of Educational Policies in the Gulf Countries: Supply, Demand, Quality and Impacts

Before proceeding to discuss upskilling policies, it may be useful to begin with a brief explanation of the major characteristics of educational policies in the Gulf countries, in particular the structure and pattern of educational policies, the supply side as measured by resources or priority of financial and human investment in education. In addition, we examine the demand for education as indicated by enrolment ratios and access to schooling and the impacts on literacy, school life expectancy, training and quality of education.

The UNESCO-UIS (2004a) information on the structure/nature of educational system implies an insufficient duration of compulsory education in most of the Gulf countries.[1] For instance, the duration of compulsory education in the UAE, Saudi Arabia and Kuwait lasts for 6–8 years and falls behind the international standard of 12–13 years of compulsory education attendance in the advanced countries such as the USA, UK and Germany, and 9–11 years in Korea and Singapore respectively.[2]

"Moreover, the educational policies in the Gulf countries are characterizing by central administration pattern, which implies a high degree of centralization and intervention from the governments/ ministries of education to control all the educational institutions" (cf. Al-Sulayti, 2002, pp. 29–30). "The ministries of education administer around 95 % of educational affairs, consequently the educational institutions are lacking independence, moreover, the educational institutions are characterizing by bureaucracy, routine, institutional rigidity and lacking perfect understanding of educational policies, dynamism, flexibility, planning, organizational development, monitoring, assessment, cooperation and problems solving ability. (cf. Fahmey and Mahmoed, 1993)" (cf. Al-Sulayti, 2002, p. 30).

8.2.1 The Supply Side of Educational Policies: Financial and Human Resources

We use the UNESCO definition to show the supply side/priority of educational investment as measured by financial resources (public and private educational investment, the percentage share of public spending on education in GDP and total government spending) and human resources (teaching staff). Next, we show the demand for education (enrolment ratios) and the impacts in the Gulf countries.

Priority of public investment in education is measured by financial resources devoted to education, which is indicated by the share of public spending on

[1] Al-Sulayti (2002, p. 15) indicates the insufficient laws/regulations regarding compulsory education attendance.

[2] See the UNESCO Education Statistics: UNESCO- UIS (2004a) UIS web site global statistics on education: www.unesco.org.

education as a percentage of GDP and total government expenditures. For instance, Table 8.1 illustrates that the priority of public spending on education, as measured by public spending on education as a percentage of total government spending, in some of the Gulf countries are close to the levels in the developed countries. However, only in Saudi Arabia and Kuwait is this spending as a percentage of GDP close to the levels prevalent in the developed countries, while the rest of the Gulf countries lag behind in this respect. Public spending on education as a percentage of GDP shows considerable disparity and fluctuation across the Gulf countries. For instance, in the period 1998–2002, the highest public spending on education as percentage of GDP in Saudi Arabia was close to five and three times those of the UAE and Bahrain respectively. Moreover, the wide variations also hold for public spending on education as a percentage of total government expenditure, particularly evident between Saudi Arabia (22.8 %) and Bahrain (12 %). In addition, the trends of public spending on education as a percentage of total government expenditures vary across most of the Gulf countries, with large increase in Kuwait, Saudi Arabia and the UAE but a decline in Bahrain.

Moreover, the priority and trend of distributing the public spending varies over time between the Gulf countries. Table 8.2 shows that one common characteristic of educational policies in the Gulf countries is that the distribution/allocation of public spending on various educational levels tend to prioritize either primary or secondary education and seriously neglect tertiary education. Despite the recent gradual change in the distribution of public funding on education to increase spending on secondary education, in general the share of spending on tertiary education remains marginal and insufficient and even shows a declining trend in Saudi Arabia and Oman. Generally, there is a wide gap between Saudi Arabia, Kuwait and other Gulf countries, namely Oman and the UAE. Table 8.2 shows that the distribution of public spending by educational levels may be related to the costs of various educational levels measured by spending per pupils, thus the low spending in tertiary education is probably related to high costs of spending on tertiary compared to secondary and primary pupils.

One common characteristic of educational policies in the Gulf countries is the lack of incentives or marginal contribution of the private sector on educational investment. Table 8.3 shows that the educational investment is almost entirely dependant on the public sector, with a very minimal contribution from private sector. More recently though, following the declining trends of public spending, private spending on education shows an opposite increasing trend to fill the gap in most of the Gulf countries. The extent of privatization shows an increasing trend in the UAE, Qatar and Oman but a declining trend in Bahrain.

The adequacy of human resources in education or teaching staff can be defined by pupil-teacher ratios; Table 8.4 shows that the adequacy of teaching staff varies across the Gulf countries and is generally better for secondary education when compared to primary education and, in most cases, to tertiary education. One serious common problem with respect to human resources in education is the low quality of teaching staff as reported in the Gulf literature. "The educational system in the Gulf countries suffers from serious weak performance/low quality of teachers

Table 8.1 Public expenditures on education in the Gulf countries compared to world countries (1990–2001/2002)

	Public expenditure on education as percentage of					
	GDP[a, b, c]			Total government expenditures[a, b]		
Country	1990[a]	1998/1999[b]	1999–2001[a]	1990[a]	1995/1997[d]	2000/2001[b]
Bahrain	4.2	3.67	3.00	14.6	12	11.41
Kuwait	4.8	n/a	n/a	3.4	14	n/a
Oman	3.1	3.87	4.2	n/a	16.4	n/a
Qatar	3.5	3.58	3.6[c]	11.1	n/a	n/a
Saudi Arabia	6.5	9.47	8.3[c]	17.8	22.8	n/a
United Arab Emirates	1.9	1.95	1.9[c]	14.6	20.3	n/a
United States	5.2	5.01	5.6	12.3	14.4	n/a
Sweden	7.4	7.98	7.6	13.8	12.2	13.40
Norway	7.1	7.68	6.8	14.6	16.8	16.18
Republic of Korea	3.5	4.07	3.6	22.4	17.5	17.38
United Kingdom	4.9	4.71	4.6	n/a	11.6	n/a

[a]UNDP Human Development Report (2004)
[b]UNESCO–UIS (2003)
[c]UNESCO–UIS (2004b) country profile: data refers to the most recent years between 1998–2002
[d]UNDP Human Development Report (2002)

Table 8.2 Percentages distribution of current expenditure and current expenditure per pupil as a percentage of GNP per capita by educational level and in the Gulf countries (1990–2001)

	Distribution of current expenditure by level (%)[a, b, c]						Expenditure per pupil as % of GNP per capita[b]					
	Pre primary and primary		Secondary		Tertiary		Pre primary and primary		Secondary		Tertiary	
Country	1990	1999/ 2001	1990	1999/ 2001	1990[b]	1999/ 2001[c]	1990	1996	1990	1996	1990	1996
Bahrain	n/a	68.8[d]	45.8	n/a	n/a	n/a	9	8	23	19	n/a	n/a
Kuwait	53.4	68.5[d]	13.6	n/a	16.0	30.2[f]	16	14	n/a	n/a	n/a	87
Oman	54.1	36.4	37.0	51.4	7.8	1.8	12	n/a	21	n/a	68	n/a
KSA	78.8	82.2[d]	n/a	84.4[e]	21.2	15.6[f]	25	19	n/a	n/a	126	58
UAE	53.8[e]	51.9	46.2[e]	46.4	n/a	n/a	n/a	n/a	n/a	n/a	n/a	n/a

[a]UNDP Human Development Report (2004)
[b]UNESCO–UIS (2000) World Education Report (2000)
[c]UNESCO–UIS (2003)
[d]Data refers to 1996
[e]Data refers to 1995–1997
[f]Data refers to 1998

due to a lack of teaching skills and knowledge of recent teaching and learning techniques. For instance, a study investigates the teaching skills amongst university graduates who applied for Arabic, English and Mathematics teaching jobs in the

Table 8.3 The Distribution of public and private expenditures on education and percentage ratio of private enrolment ratio in the Gulf countries (1990–2000)

	Public and private spending on education (%)[a]				Private enrolment at secondary and primary levels (%)[b]			
	Public		Private		Secondary level		Primary level	
Country	1990	1996	1990	1996	1990/1991	1999/2000	1990/1991	1999/2000
Bahrain	94.3	94.8	5.7	5.2	8.8	15.8	13.2	19.1
Kuwait	n/a	n/a	n/a	n/a	n/a	27.9	25.0	31.1
Oman	92.0	89.7	8	10.3	0.7	n/a	1.7	4.5
Qatar	97.3	91.8	2.7	8.2	12.3	n/a	23.4	n/a
KSA	94.4	93.4	5.6	6.6	2.8	n/a	4.1	6.4
UAE	95.4	92.3	4.6	7.7	20.6	32.0	32.2	45.0

[a]UNESCO–UIS (2000) World Education Report (2000): UNESCO's World Education Indicators
[b]UNESCO- UIS (2003)

public schools in Bahrain (1995/1996) shows that applicants success[3] in engineering studies, science, social science, commercial science and English are respectively 10 %, 43 %, 49 %, 39 % and 59 %".[4]

8.2.2 *The Demand Side of Educational Policies: The Demand for and Enrolment in Education*

Apart from the supply side, it is also important to examine the demand for education as measured by enrolment ratios. Table 8.5 illustrates that enrolment ratios vary across the Gulf countries, decline with the increase of educational level and, on average, lag far behind the levels in the developed countries. In particular, average enrolment ratios in tertiary education in all Gulf countries (21.35–18.52 %) remain very low and lag far behind the levels of the developed countries (58.39–85 %). That also holds for net enrolment ratios in primary and secondary education in the Gulf, except Bahrain and Qatar, which have enrolment ratios approaching those of the developed countries and are higher than in other Gulf countries.[5]

One major problem of educational system in the Gulf countries is the recent stagnation in enrolment in tertiary education, for instance, after considerable improvement in enrolment in tertiary education in the UAE until around 1994, the enrolment figures have stagnated in recent years – see Fig. 8.1 below. Therefore, this implies an ample role for policy making to improve enrolment in tertiary education. In addition,

[3] The applicants who passed the exams.

[4] See the Ministry of Education in Bahrain State (1995–1996) Unpublished Report in Al-Sulayti. (2002, p. 28).

[5] "Probably, the low enrolment at secondary level is attributed to high drop out in transition from primary to secondary schooling and lack of effective actions in educational policy to legitimize the compulsory education" (Al-Sulayti, 2002, p. 15).

Table 8.4 Pupil-teacher ratio by level of education in the Gulf countries (1990–2001/2002)

	Primary			Secondary			Tertiary	
Country	1990[a]	1998/2002[b]	2001/2002[c]	1990[a]	1996[a]	2001/2002[c]	1998/1999[c]	2001/2002[c]
Bahrain	19	16	16	16	15	12	n/a	n/a
Kuwait	18	14	14	10	11	10	15	n/a
Oman	28	23	23	16	18	18	n/a	31
Qatar	11	12	12	9	10	10	14	13
KSA	16	12	12	13	13	13	18	20
UAE	18	15	16	n/a	13	13	13	n/a

[a]UNESCO– UIS (2000), World Education Report (2000): www.unesco.org
[b]UNESCO– UIS (2004b) country profile: Data refers to most recent years between 1998–2002
[c]UNESCO– UIS (2004c) Educational statistics (1998–2002)

as in most other developing countries, one serious problematic feature concerning the tertiary education in the Gulf is that enrolment and graduation ratios in tertiary education are biased against scientific, technical, engineering, agriculture, medical and natural sciences and focused on art, humanities, law and social sciences. For instance, in the period 1990–1996, enrolment and graduation ratios in medical sciences, natural sciences, engineering and agriculture accounted for only 28 % as compared to 72 % for art, humanities, law and social sciences; these biases are particularly serious in Saudi Arabia, Qatar, Oman and the UAE – see Table 8.5 above.[6] The share of tertiary students enrolled in sciences, math and engineering in the Gulf is low compared to Korea (34 %), Algeria (50 %) and China (53 %) – cf. Fig. 8.2 below. A further problematic feature of higher education in the Gulf appears from the relative distribution of tertiary education students by attainment levels. Figure 8.3 below shows that for the majority (96 %) of tertiary students the attainment was less than a university degree, while only a few (4 %) obtained the first university degree or higher, falling far behind China (48 %) and Korea (41 %).

Further serious problems include the negligence of vocational education across the Gulf countries (except Bahrain) and the problem of the declining trend in the enrolment ratios in vocational education in the Gulf countries (except the UAE and Kuwait), see Table 8.5 above.

Moreover, another problematic feature is the lack of incentives/minimal enrolment in private schooling compared to intensive enrolment in public schooling, which may be related to the high cost of private schooling and the minimal contribution of the private sector spending in total spending on education compared to the public sector. Similar to public enrolment, private enrolment ratios decline with the increase of educational level, i.e. are higher at primary level and lower at

[6] "The irrelevant wrong policy for admission in higher education leads to focus on humanities and social science and biases against science, technology and engineering studies leads to mismatch, unemployment, shortage of technical skills that leads to dependence on foreign technical skills" (Al-Sulayti, 2002, pp. 16–18). "The low share of enrolment in technical education relative to total enrolment in tertiary education, is probably attributed to both social/cultural aspect in the society that discourage the involvement in technical work and the weak relationship between educational policies and development planning" (Alfakhery, 1999, p. 82).

Table 8.5 Enrolment ratios by educational level in the Gulf compared to world countries (1990–2001/2002) (%)

Educational level	Primary level[a]		Secondary level[a]		Tertiary level[a, b]		Tertiary students in Science, Math and Engineering[a, b]			Vocational education (1990–1995)[d]	
Year/ Country	1990/1991	2001/2002	1990/1991	2001/2002	1998/1999[b]	2000/2001	1994/1997	1996[c, h]	1996[c, i]	1990/1991	1994/1995
Bahrain	99	91	85	81	25.20	n/a	n/a	n/a	42	13.25	12.69
Kuwait	49	85	n/a	77	21.08	n/a	23	27	n/a	0.62[f]	0.69
Oman	69	75	n/a	68	n/a	8.49	30	36	32	2.79	1.41[j]
Qatar	89	94	70	78	27.66	24.62	n/a	n/a	19	2.92	1.78
KSA	59	59	31	53	20.71	22.4[g]	18	21	24	2.78	2.34[j)]
UAE	100	81	58	72	12.10	n/ a	27	29	25	0.71	1.41
Average Gulf	77.5	80.83	61	71.5	21.35	18.52	24.5	28.3	28.4	3.85	3.39
US	97	93	85	85	75.66	72.62	n/a	n/a	n/a	n/a	n/a
Sweden	100	102	85	99	62.30	70.04	31	n/a	n/a	n/a	n/a
Korea	104	101	86	89	65 [e]	77.62	34	n/a	n/a	18.04	18.64
UK	100	101	81	95	58.39	59.53	29	n/a	n/a	n/a	n/a
Finland	98	100	93	95	83 [e]	85 [e]	37	n/a	n/a	n/a	n/a

[a]UNDP Human Development Report (2004)
[b]UNDP Human Development Report (2002),
[c]UNESCO– UIS (2000) UNESCO's: World Education Report (2000),
[d]UNESCO (1996) Statistical Yearbook and UNESCO Statistics: www.unesco.org
[e]UNESCO- UIS (2004a) UIS web site global statistics on education: www.unesco.org
[f]Data refers to 1992/1993
[g]Data refers to 1999/2000
[h]Data refers to (%) of tertiary students in natural science, engineering, agriculture and medical sciences 1996
[i]Data refers to (%) of tertiary graduates in natural science, engineering, agriculture and medical sciences 1996
[j]Data refers to 1993/1994

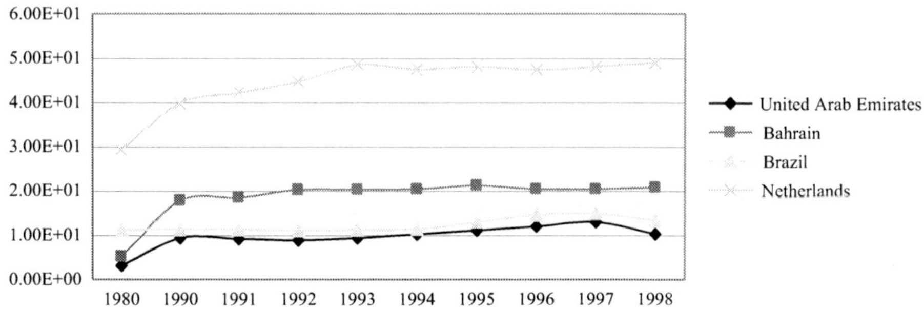

Fig. 8.1 Gross enrolment in tertiary education in the UAE, Bahrain, Brazil and the Netherlands (1980–1998) (%) (Source: The World Bank, World Development Indicators Database (WDI) (2004))

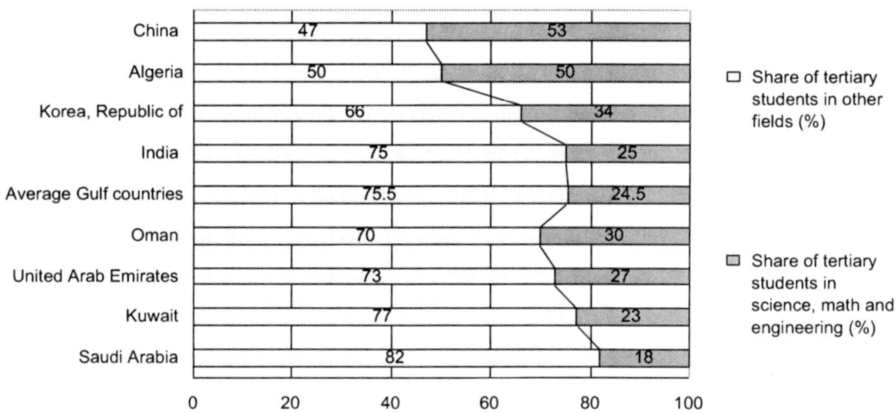

Fig. 8.2 Relative distribution of tertiary education students (%) by fields in the Gulf countries compared to Algeria, India, China and Korea (1994/1997 - 1999/2000) (Source: UNDP (2004))

secondary level. Private primary and secondary enrolment ratios show an increasing trend over time with considerable variation across the Gulf countries, namely between the UAE and Saudi Arabia and Oman, see Table 8.3 above.[7]

[7] The scarcity of reliable information limited our analysis from discussing two interesting issues related to educational policies: the contribution of private sector in both spending and enrolment in tertiary education; and the enrolment of the citizens from the Gulf countries in overseas educational institutions. The high GDP per capital has encouraged a considerable number of the citizens from the Gulf countries to seek higher education abroad. The only available information indicates that during the period 1999–2002/2003 the number of students from Saudi Arabia, Qatar and Oman who study in the United States declined by 31 %, 26 % and 25 % respectively – see the UNDP – AHDR (2003, Table 1, p. 23). This may substantiate the need for improving domestic higher educational institutions to fill the gap and absorb the students who have returned.

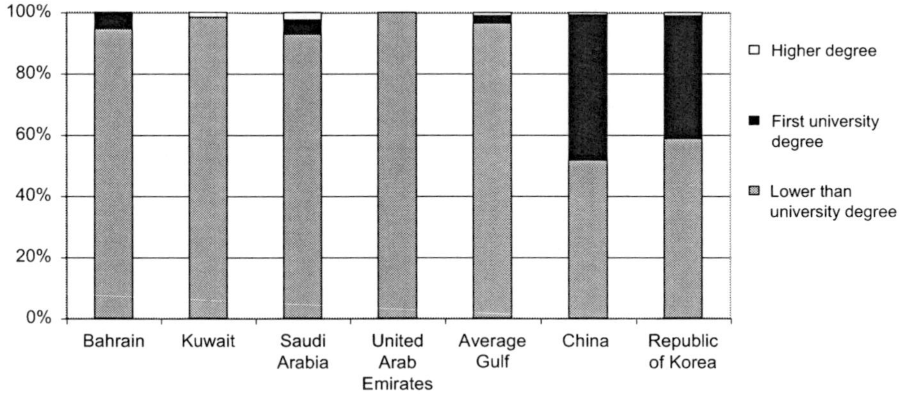

Fig. 8.3 Relative distribution of tertiary education students (%) by attainment levels of higher education in the Gulf countries compared to China and Korea (1999/2000) (Sources: UNDP – AHDR (2003) and UNESCO-UIS (2003): UNESCO web site (www.unesco.org))

8.2.3 Return and Quality of Educational Policies

Another common characteristic of the educational system in the Gulf countries is the weak internal efficiency/quality of both primary and secondary education; the severity of the problem varies across the Gulf countries.[8] For instance, Table 8.6 illustrates that in the period 1990–2002, the percentage of repeaters in primary schooling is higher in both Saudi Arabia and Oman, while the percentages of transition to secondary and tertiary education are low in both Saudi Arabia and UAE.[9]

The average for all Gulf countries in terms of quality of education has improved over time, as is apparent from the considerable decline in the percentage of repeaters in primary schooling and increase in the percentages of transition from primary to secondary education, however, across individual Gulf countries poor quality is still obvious. For instance, Table 8.6 indicates that throughout the period 1990–2002, the percentages of repeaters in primary schooling remained the same in Kuwait. In half of the Gulf countries – namely, Bahrain, Oman and Qatar- the percentages of transition from primary to secondary education has declined.

[8] No relevant data and information are available to allow an assessment of the quality of tertiary education.

[9] "The poor quality is attributed to: (a) High repetition rates, for instance, repetition rate at primary level for female in Saudi Arabia is around 14 %, at some secondary level in Kuwait increased to 31 % and at industrial education level in Bahrain increased to 38 %. (b) Weak absorptive capacity and performance level of students at all levels. (c) Failure of educational strategy to motivate innovative skills and problem solving ability/skills. (e) Weak monitoring and examination systems due to traditional, inefficient and subjective assessment methods and lack of international recognition/ bases. (f) Lack of monitoring systems/ institutions to measure and assess the performance of educational and training institutions" (Al-Sulayti, 2002, pp. 21–24).

Table 8.6 Quality of Education in the Gulf countries: percentage of repetition and transition (1990–2002)

Indicator	Percentage of repeters: primary education (%)		Percentage of reaching secondary and tertiary education (%)		Primary to secondary transition rates (%)
Country/year	1990[a]	1998–2002[b]	(Secondary) 1995[a]	(Tertiary) 1995[a]	1998–2002[b]
Bahrain	5	4	99	95	98
Kuwait	3	3	97	96	98
Oman	9	4	99	96	98
Qatar	7	3	100	98	96
Saudi Arabia	9	5	96	89	97
UAE	4	3	93	83	98
Average Gulf	6.17	3.67	97.33	92.83	97.5

[a]UNESCO–UIS (2000) UNESCO's World Education Report (2000)
[b]Calculated from UNESCO –UIS (2004b) country profile: statistics refer to the most recent year between 1998 and 2002

Therefore, further efforts are needed to enhance the quality of education at all levels, in order to avoid the exacerbation of the problems that will result in the event of a failure to implement some effective polices to improve the quality of education.

In addition, the poor quality of education can be observed from the results of the Third International Mathematics and Science Study Score for students during 1994–1995, where the poor performance of Kuwait [taken to represent the Gulf countries] in terms of mathematics and science school training fell far behind Singapore, USA, Japan and Europe. For instance, of the 41 countries in which half a million 13 years old were tested, Kuwait with Colombia and South Africa took the last three places in both subjects, while Singapore reached first place in both subjects ahead of the USA, Europe and Japan, which scored third place in both subjects. These figures indicate that there are indeed large quality differences in two subjects of critical importance to technological and skill development (cf. Lall, 1999, pp. 22–23).

8.2.4 The Impacts of Educational Policies on Literacy and Access to Schooling (School Life Expectancy)

Educational policies in all the Gulf countries lead to only slight improvements in school life expectancy in the UAE, Kuwait and Qatar and enrolment in all educational levels in Bahrain and Qatar. However, the educational policies have insufficient effects on improving school life expectancy, which remains low and lags behind when compared to the international standard. One important positive implication of educational policies is the increase in literacy rates; however, the

Table 8.7 Educational outcomes: Youth illiteracy rate and school life expectancy in the Gulf countries (1990–2002)

	Youth illiteracy rate (% ages 15–24)[a]		Youth literacy rate (% ages 15–24)[a]		School life expectancy[b, c]	
Country	1990	2002	1990	2002	1992[b]	1998[c]
Bahrain	4.4	1.4	95.6	98.6	13.5	13.0
Kuwait	12.5	6.9	87.5	93.1	7.0[d]	8.7
Oman	14.4	1.5	85.6	98.5	n/a	8.76–9.0[e]
Qatar	9.7	5.2	90.3	94.8	11.8	13.1
Saudi Arabia	14.6	6.5	85.4	93.5	8.5	n/a
UAE	15.3	8.6	84.7	91.4	10.6	10.7

[a]Calculated from UNDP Human Development Report (2004)
[b]UNESCO–UIS Statistical Yearbook (1999): www.unesco.org
[c]UIS–UNESCO (2003): www.unesco.org
[d]Data refers to 1991
[e]Data refers to 2000/2001

educational policies have so far only managed to alleviate rather than fully eliminate the youth illiteracy problem in the Gulf countries. For instance, Table 8.7 illustrates that in the year 2002, the illiteracy rates amongst the youth population are in excess of 5 % in Qatar (5.2 %), Saudi Arabia (6.5 %), Kuwait (6.9 %) and the UAE (8.6 %), and are lower than 2 % only in Oman (1.5 %) and Bahrain (1.4 %). This implies that there is an ample room for policy to increase the literacy rate among the young population.

Furthermore, when comparing the supply and demand sides, we observe that the supply side or public spending seems to be only one component in the educational policies, because higher public spending per se does not imply a higher demand, participation and enrolment ratios, access to schooling/school life expectancy and higher literacy rate. For instance, despite higher spending on all these counts, Saudi Arabia falls behind Bahrain, which reports moderate spending but better demand/enrolment ratios at all educational level, access to schooling/school life expectancy and literacy rates.

8.3 The Impact of Educational Policies on Training Policies: Large Public Firms and Public Policies of Training and Skills Upgrading

Educational policies in the Gulf countries have insufficient effect on training provision and failed to integrate sufficiently with training policies. "The relationship between the educational and training policies vary across the Gulf countries, as technical education and training are either integrated with or separated from educational institutions.[10] Despite these differences, however, in both cases the educational policies in the Gulf countries are still in need to enhance the fruitful cooperation, co-ordination and integration with training policies" (Al-Sulayti, 2002, pp. 20–21).

Earlier findings in Chap. 5 show that the lack of interaction between educational and training systems hinders the provision of training and upskilling plans within private firms, and also leads to duality/discrepancy between macro–micro views with respect to implementation of upskilling plans. We will illustrate below that the interaction between educational and training policies appears to be effective only within large public firms that adopt training policies consistent/in line with public policies.

Table 8.8 illustrates that the three largest public enterprises in the UAE, namely, the Gulf Pharmaceutical Industries (JULPHAR), Abu Dhabi National Oil Company (ADNOC) and Dubai Aluminium Company (DUBAL), all seem committed to implement diversified training and skill upgrading policies that are quite consistent with the line taken by public policies. In particular, they adopt similar strategies that highlight training and upskilling of workers, linkages with universities to absorb national graduates, active human resources development units and recruitment policies to set up and implement regular internal and external training plans and wide use of ICT to upskilling workers especially national workers. Therefore, in contrast to the private firms, the large public firms (JULPHAR, ADNOC and DUBAL) have successfully contributed to serve the public policies for enhancing training and skill upgrading, especially amongst the national workers – cf. Table 8.8 below. However, it is less clear whether the large public firms induce positive effects on upskilling workers in private firms. In our view, the interpretation of the serious public-private discrepancy can be attributed to presence of high resources, support and incentives within public firms, which are probably lacking within private firms.[11, 12]

The major policy implication from these findings is that the improvement of the educational systems in the Gulf countries is essential and requires improvement of

[10] In most of the Gulf countries – Bahrain, Qatar, Oman and the UAE – both the educational and training institutions are integrated within one entity administered by the ministries of education, whereas in both Saudi Arabia and Kuwait the technical education and training are administered by independent institutions headed by the minister of labour and social affairs and the minister of education respectively (Al-Sulayti, 2002, p. 20).

[11] For instance, the selected three largest public firms have several common characteristics such as large market size, namely size of employment, capital (local capital), market, products, sales, sales revenues; investment in ICT, use of advanced technologies and active R&D/technology development unit.

[12] From the results of the firm survey (2002) and the selected three cases of large public firms studied in this chapter, it may be true that public firms are systematically larger than private firms. It is therefore plausible to expect that the large public firms to have higher financial capacity to support training and skill upgrading than private firms. However, it is less clear and hard to make generalization to conclude whether this applies to all other public firms as well, because the available information for the UAE indicate the classification of firms according to size, activities and ownership (nationality of main owner(s)) rather than public- private sectors.

Table 8.8 Human resources development and training policies in the large public firms in the UAE

Firms	Human resources development strategies and training policies in JULPHAR, DUBAL, and ADNOC
1. JULPHAR	JULPHAR's human resources development unit aims to upgrade skill levels via the following: 1. Offering high school training programmes for the high secondary school students 2. Offering educational grants to different educational institutions and individuals to encourage competition and positive impact in society 3. Attracting university trainees and experts in the field of science and pharmacy from the emirates and from abroad 4. Offering short and medium on the job induction training programmes based on training needs 5. Offering staff ongoing internal and external ICT training/ upgrading opportunities 6. Providing specialized long term training programmes 7. Employing graduate UAE nationals to acquire knowledge and experience under the supervision and training of professional and skilled experts 8. Facilitating, transferring and sharing of knowledge in the medical/ pharmaceutical fields, via: a. Arranging scientific seminars and educational programmes for various pharmacists and doctors in different specialities b. Participating in both local and international medical conferences c. Participating in continuous education through a network of *scientific offices* in the UAE, Middle East, Europe and USA d. Providing grants to research organizations and universities of international repute that are actively involved in the development and discovery in the field of pharmaceutical technology e. Encouraging an active R&D unit to be continuously involved in the development of ways and means to explore new application of generic dosage forms f. Employing over 20 scientists, including Ministry of Health approved pharmacists to be involved in the development of new products, which have resulted in the registration of more than 600 dosage forms worldwide
2. DUBAL	DUBAL's human resources development unit aimed at upskilling workers through the following: 1. Offering various training programmes, such as on the job training within the plant itself. For instance, about 95 % of the workforce has participated in some form of training 2. Offering the employees training opportunities through on going project work, as well as visits to other leading producers around the world 3. Emphasis on continuing to employ UAE nationals; contributing to the development of the national workforce by hiring, training and further developing young nationals 4. Collaborating with colleges and universities in the UAE and abroad to recruit national graduates 5. Providing pre-employment courses and graduates and management development programmes, in addition to special training programmes (in-house and abroad) for UAE nationals supported by a dedicated team of trainees and professional experts

(continued)

Table 8.8 (continued)

Firms	Human resources development strategies and training policies in JULPHAR, DUBAL, and ADNOC
	6. Providing external accreditation training courses and learning units for special learning courses
	7. Offering teamwork operation, such as the suggestion scheme (SS), Performance, Enhancement Programme (PEP), Continuous Improvement Team (CIT) and Total Quality Management (TQM) programmes designed to involve all workers in the ongoing process of continuous improvement
3. ADNOC	ADNOC's human resources and development implementation policy is based on the following:
	1. Promoting an active human resources development unit, establishing competency based career development programmes and the national recruitment committee to attract and encourage the recruitment and development of national workers in the oil and gas industries
	2. Emphasis on continuing to employ UAE nationals; the firm survey (2002) indicates that the current share of national workers is 37 % and is expected to increase to 50 %, 60 % and 75 % in the short, medium and long terms respectively
	3. Offering various internal and external training opportunities to create and maintain a learning environment within the organization. Offering special training programmes to UAE national employees in order to meet the targets of public policy to upgrade national workers. ADNOC supports its training institute (ADNOC Training Institute (A.T.I.)), which established in 1979 to contribute to meeting the needs of ADNOC group of companies for skilled national manpower. For instance, the number of graduates from ATI increased continuously from 386 in 1994 to 1150 in 2000
	4. Providing career development programmes to promote work performance
	5. Offering an annual scholarship program, which started in 1974, with the aim of motivating interested and excellent UAE secondary school students to study abroad in the fields related to oil and gas industries. The number of scholarships increased rapidly from 100 in 1994 to 527 in 2000; most of these are offered for studying abroad in the USA (84 %), UK (8 %) and Australia (2.9 %). In addition, local scholarships are offered in collaboration with the local universities, such as the UAE University (4.7 %) and Higher Colleges of Technology (0.4 %)
	6. Linking education and industry via establishing the Petroleum Institute in Abu Dhabi (2001) to offer undergraduate and postgraduate programmes in the fields of engineering, applied science and research, particularly related to the petroleum industry. The Petroleum Institute is established in collaboration with international industry partners including BP, JODCO, Shell, Total and Colorado School of Mines (CSM) in the U.S.

[a]Gulf Pharmaceutical Industries (JULPHAR). (2000). JULPHAR achievement report. Unpublished report, http://www.julphar.net, Ras Al Khaimah, UAE. Accessed April 20, 2002.
[b]Dubai Aluminium Company (DUABL). (2000). DUBAL achievement report. Unpublished report, http://www.dubal.ae, Dubai, UAE. Accessed April 20, 2002.
[c]ADNOC Achievement Report (1995–1999), ADNOC Human Resources Development book, publications and web sites

the quality/internal efficiency, supply (investment) and demand (enrolment) sides, particularly with respect to tertiary and technical education. From that perspective, we explain below the views of the policy makers and experts regarding the relevant plans and policies to reform the educational system, which is essential for skill development. After that, we show that policy makers, experts and firms all view the improvement of education as important for enhancing the provision of training and knowledge transfer/external schooling effects.

8.4 Plans, Policies and Mechanisms for Skill Development: The Macro- Micro Views

It is useful in this section to discuss and compare first the relevant plans and then policies and mechanisms for skill development from both macro and micro perspectives/views.

8.4.1 Plans for Skill Development: The Macro- Micro Views

In light of the above findings, we now use the results of the macro and firm surveys (2002) to provide insights to help generate policies to enhance skill levels by implementation of short and long terms plans at the macro–micro levels. We then compare and integrate the macro (official: policy makers and experts) and micro (firms) views concerning the important tools and plans for skills development in the current, short run and long run.

The policy makers and experts suggest several important instruments for skills development, some of which have already been implemented and others being implemented now or in the near future. For instance, Table 8.9 shows that the policy makers and experts highlight investment in vocational training and formal education, improving the quality of teachers, trainers and mentors, and investment in training of existing employees. This is to be coupled with learning on the job, sending teachers and mentors abroad to acquire knowledge and skills, using ICT to upgrade skill levels, enhancing the system of accreditation and licensing and enhancing the system or programme of apprenticeship. Measures such as sending students abroad to acquire knowledge and skills, supporting long distance learning, sending workers abroad to acquire skills and bringing/attracting new foreign skills, scientists and engineers from abroad are viewed as somewhat less important factors. Plans currently implemented include investment in education, investment in training of existing employees, using ICT to upgrade skill levels, encouraging learning on the job, investment in vocational training, bringing/attracting new foreign skills, scientists and engineers from abroad and sending students abroad to acquire knowledge and skills. However, our earlier discussion in this chapter and in Chap. 5 above, illustrates the serious shortcomings of some of these components, particularly with respect to investment in education, training and vocational education. Hence, the officials' view suggests further efforts in the short run to motivate investment in education, investment in training of existing employees, investment in vocational training, sending workers abroad to acquire skills and improving the quality of teachers, trainers and mentors. Further efforts considered important in the long run to enhance the system or programme of apprenticeship, support long distance learning, encourage the system of accreditation and licensing, send teachers/instructors and trainers abroad to acquire knowledge and skills and to improve the quality of teachers, trainers and mentors.

On the other side, at the micro level/across firms, the results of the firm survey suggest differing points of view with different priorities that highlight learning on the job as main priority,[13] especially in the short run.[14] Where as, investment in training of existing employees, using ICT to upgrade skill levels, bringing/attracting new foreign skills, scientists and engineers, supporting long distance learning, sending trainers, mentors and workers abroad to acquire skills and knowledge are receiving less attention, particularly in the short run. Firms highlight these components and learning on the job in the long run – see Table 8.10 below.

From Tables 8.9 to 8.10 we observe the discrepancy in the macro–micro views/perspectives concerning the selection of both tools and plans for skill development. For instance, the macro/policy makers and experts' view tends to highlight investment in vocational training and formal education, improving the quality of trainers and mentors and investment in training of existing employees as top priorities. Their next priorities are: encouraging learning on the job, sending trainers and mentors abroad to acquire skills, using ICT to upgrade skill levels. Supporting long distance learning, sending workers abroad to acquire skills and bringing/attracting new foreign skills, scientists and engineers from abroad are viewed as somewhat less important tools. On the other side, the micro (firm) view highlights learning on the job as main priority. The rank of the firms' other priorities are: investment in training of existing employees, using ICT to upgrade skill levels, bringing/attracting new foreign skills, scientists and engineers, supporting long distance learning, and sending trainers, mentors and workers abroad to acquire skills and knowledge.

From the policy makers, experts and firms' perspectives the top priorities in the short run are investment in education, training (including vocational training), sending workers abroad to acquire skills, improving the quality of teachers, trainers and mentors, learning on the job, using ICT to upgrade skill levels and bringing new foreign skills, scientists and engineers. From the policy makers, experts and firms' perspectives the top priorities in the long run highlight enhancing the system or programme of apprenticeship, supporting long distance learning, encouraging the system of accreditation and licensing, sending teachers, mentors, workers and students abroad to acquire knowledge and skills.

[13] As reported by 86 % of the respondents firms.

[14] As indicated by 61 % of the respondents firms.

Table 8.9 Plans and tools for skill development: macro-policy makers and experts view

Tools for skill development (%)	Importance	Has been already implemented	Short run/current plan	Long run/future plan
Investment in formal education	96 %	61 %	29 %	11 %
Investment in vocational training	100 %	46 %	29 %	14 %
Investment in training of existing employees	93 %	57 %	29 %	7 %
Improving the quality of teachers, trainers and mentors	96 %	36 %	25 %	25 %
Sending teachers/instructors/trainers abroad to acquire knowledge and skills	79 %	25 %	21 %	32 %
Sending students abroad to acquire knowledge and skills	68 %	43 %	14 %	21 %
Sending worker abroad to acquire skills	61 %	36 %	29 %	18 %
Bringing/attracting new foreign skills, scientist and engineers	57 %	46 %	21 %	11 %
Using ICT to upgrade skill levels	75 %	54 %	11 %	14 %
Encouraging Learning on the job	86 %	50 %	21 %	18 %
Supporting long distance learning	64 %	25 %	7 %	39 %
Enhancing the system of accreditation and Licensing	75 %	25 %	11 %	36 %
Enhancing the system or programme of apprenticeship	75 %	21 %	–	43 %
Total response	28	28	28	28

Source: Own calculation based on the macro survey (2002)

From the macro/policy makers and experts' perspective, the top priorities in the short run are investment in education, training (including vocational training) of existing employees, sending workers abroad to acquire skills and improving the quality of teachers, trainers and mentors. Less emphasis would be placed on learning on the job, bringing new foreign skills, scientists and engineers, sending trainers and mentors abroad to acquire skill, using ICT to upgrade skill levels, supporting long distance learning and sending trainers, mentors and workers abroad to acquire skills. On the other side, firms highlight encouraging learning on the job as top short run priority, followed by investment in training of existing employees, using ICT to upgrade skill levels and bringing new foreign skills, scientists and engineers. Less emphasis would be placed on supporting long distance learning and sending trainers, mentors and workers abroad to acquire skills.

Furthermore, from the macro/policy makers and experts perspective, the top priorities in the long run would be on enhancing the system or programme of apprenticeship, supporting long distance learning, encouraging the system of accreditation and licensing. This followed by sending teachers/instructors and trainers abroad to acquire knowledge and skills and improving the quality of teachers, trainers and mentors. Less emphasis would be on sending students and workers abroad to acquire skills, supporting learning on the job, using ICT to

Table 8.10 Plans and tools for skill development: micro-firm view

Tools for skill development	Of special Importance (%)					To be pursued now/in the short run (%)					To be pursued in the near future/ long run (%)				
	All Firms	Chemical	Metal	Large	Medium	All Firms	Chemical	Metal	Large	Medium	All Firms	Chemical	Metal	Large	Medium
Response Rate:															
Investment in training of existing employees	53	50	57	56	50	39	40	36	50	27	55	60	45	44	67
Sending trainers and mentors abroad to acquire skills	22	14	36	17	28	6	10	0	6	7	71	60	91	75	67
Sending workers abroad to acquire skills	11	5	21	11	11	3	5	0	6	0	61	50	82	63	60
Bringing/attracting new foreign skills, scientists and engineers	42	32	57	39	44	29	15	55	19	40	55	65	36	56	53
Using ICT to upgrade skill levels	47	55	36	61	33	35	45	18	50	20	39	35	45	25	53
Encouraging learning on the job	86	82	93	94	78	61	60	64	56	67	32	35	27	31	33
Supporting long distance learning	33	18	57	28	39	19	20	18	13	27	58	60	55	63	53
Total response	36	22	14	18	18	31	20	11	16	15	31	20	11	16	15

Source: Own calculation based on the firm survey (2002)

upgrade skill levels, bringing new foreign skills, scientists and engineers and investment in training of existing employees. On the other hand, firms tend to highlight sending trainers, mentors and workers abroad to acquire skills as main long run priority, followed by supporting long distance learning, investment in training of existing employees and bringing new foreign skills, scientists and engineers. Less emphasis would be placed by firms on using ICT to upgrade skill levels and encouraging learning on the job.

In addition to the above observed discrepancies between macro–micro views concerning the selection of plans and tools and arrangement of priorities and policies for enhancing skill, we explain below the visible differences in the macro–micro perspectives in suggesting policies for improving the provision of training and transfer of knowledge. Therefore, this implies that further efforts are needed to enhance the consistency between the macro–micro views and public-private sectors, particularly with respect to the arrangement of priorities and plans to ensure more successful and consistent implementation of policies for skills development and encouraging private sector participation in education and training.

8.4.2 Policies and Mechanisms for Skill Development: The Macro- Micro Views

The implementation of the above plans for skills development requires an integration of the macro–micro policies; the results of the macro and firm surveys (2002) are useful for discussing and integrating these policy perspectives. From the macro survey we find that the policy makers and experts' view concerning skill development policies highlights the mechanisms/policies for enhancing the efficiency of educational system, enhancing the provision of training, planning skill needs and enhancing the external schooling effects/transfer of knowledge. Additional mechanisms/policies identified include monitoring skill needs on a regular basis, enhancing social partnership and collaboration between educational and training institutions, employers, workers and the state to determine skill needs and the most effective ways of meeting and financing them, promoting of resources allocation and importing skills from abroad.[15]

Our analysis below discusses the mechanisms for enhancing the educational system, transfer of knowledge/external schooling effects and provision of training. Other components include: planning skill needs, monitoring skill needs on a regular basis, enhancing social partnership in skill development, promoting of resources allocation and importing skill from abroad are somewhat integrated in the above components. We begin with the reform of educational system because we want to

[15] As reported by 97 %, 93 %, 93 %, 83 %, 79 %, 79 %, 76 % and 72 % of the respondent policy makers and experts respectively.

argue that both training provision and transfer of knowledge can be enhanced by an efficient educational system.

8.4.2.1 Reform of Educational System

Beginning with the reform of the educational system, Table 8.11 summarizes the official view concerning the reform of the educational system, which highlights improvement of the quality of teachers and mentors, improvement of infrastructure, encouragement of modernization and dynamism in the educational system and enhancing planning for educational need. In addition, they prioritize the improvement of internal efficiency/quality of basic, secondary and tertiary education; enhancing the linkages (network) between universities, colleges, technical and training institutes; monitoring educational needs on a regular basis; and encouraging the system of flexibility of educational institutions. Further reform measures include increasing the harmony/consistency between educational output and market needs by focusing on particular future skill needs, increasing public spending on education, increasing motivation and incentives to change student attitudes, increasing spending and incentives to encourage enrolment in technical education and increasing private sector involvement on education. Finally, we suggest an improvement of duration of compulsory education and autonomy of educational institutions.

In recent years, there have been several recent initiatives in the Gulf countries aimed at long term solutions to develop human resources, reform educational and training programmes and the labour market. For instance, the UAE has established the National Human Resources Development and Employment Authority (TANMIA)– affiliated to the UAE Ministry of Labour and Social Affairs to help improve the skills of the UAE nationals looking for jobs. In our view, these recent initiatives would be more effective if the governments in the Gulf collaborate with the private sector to work actively to influence both the supply and demand sides by implementing more effective policies to increase incentives, for example through subsidies to improve both education and training. For instance, public policies can influence the demand side for education and change the low enrolment ratios at the tertiary level, especially technical education, by providing more fellowships, scholarships and prizes for engineering and science students, and increasing incentives for students to increase attraction for enrolment into science and engineering at secondary schools levels. The governments should continue to upgrade schooling and increase enrolment at all levels, especially in higher education.

In our view the Gulf countries can benefit from the experiences of other advanced countries to improve the coordination and planning to avoid the mismatch between supply and demand and to meet critical skills needs. For instance, the Gulf countries can benefit from the experiences of the European countries, where the government limits itself to pay teachers' salaries and leaves the coordination problem to employers' federations. The Gulf countries should continue to upgrade schooling and increase enrolment in all levels especially in higher education and

Table 8.11 Policies and mechanisms for skill development: (a) macro/official view: Reform of educational system

Macro policies and mechanisms for enhancing the efficiency of education system:	%
Improve the quality of teachers or mentors	97 %
Encourage the system of modernization and dynamism	97 %
Improve the infrastructures	97 %
Better planning for educational needs	93 %
Improve the internal efficiency/quality of basic education	93 %
Improve the internal efficiency/quality of tertiary education	90 %
Enhance the linkages [networks] between universities, colleges, technical and training institutes	90 %
Monitoring educational needs on a regular basis	90 %
Encourage the system of flexibility of educational institutions	86 %
Increase the harmony/consistency between educational output and market needs by focusing on particular future skill needs	86 %
Increase public spending on education	86 %
Increasing the motivation and incentives to change the attitudes of educated economically active population	83 %
Increase spending and incentives to encourage enrolment in technical education	79 %
Increase private sector spending and involvement on education	72 %
Total response	29

Source: Own calculation based on the macro survey (2002)

should also induce firms to organize in a federation, which has the task to organize branch specific education, by using taxes as a stick and the payment of teachers' salaries as a carrot.

8.4.2.2 Enhancing the Transfer of Knowledge/External Schooling Effect

The reform of the educational system is expected to have a direct positive effect on motivating/enhancing the transfer of knowledge/external schooling effects. For instance, Table 8.12 shows that the macro–micro views highlight the potential positive implications of improving the qualifications of skilled and unskilled workers, the quality of education and training in enhancing the transfer of knowledge/external schooling effects. The macro–micro views differ with respect to the potential effect of improving firm conditions to encourage external effects and sponsoring educational scholarship. Moreover, the macro survey shows that the policy makers and experts' view indicates that the transfer of knowledge/external schooling effect can be motivated via increasing the information about future educational, training and skill needs in the productive sectors. There is also a need to increase awareness about the future value of investments in education and training to minimize the risk aversion: preference of more certain short term returns to available jobs than long term skill investments; in addition to increasing the interaction to market needs and enhancing a system of certification of skills

Table 8.12 Policies and mechanisms for skill development: (b) macro–micro views: factors enhancing the transfer of knowledge/ external schooling effect

Factors enhance external schooling effect/ knowledge transfer	All firms	Chemical	Metal	Large	Medium	Official
Improves the qualifications and ability of unskilled workers to learn from skilled workers	87 %	82 %	94 %	90 %	84 %	100 %
Improves the qualifications of skilled workers to permit the positive effects on unskilled workers	82 %	73 %	94 %	80 %	84 %	95 %
Improves the quality of training to coincide with international standard	62 %	55 %	71 %	65 %	58 %	100 %
Improves the quality of education	56 %	50 %	65 %	55 %	58 %	100 %
Improves firm conditions to encourage the external effects	41 %	36 %	47 %	35 %	47 %	100 %
Sponsors educational scholarship	26 %	27 %	24 %	35 %	16 %	90 %
Total response	39	22	17	20	19	20

Sources: Own calculation based on the macro survey (2002) and firm survey (2002)

acquired. Both the provision of adequate incentives for trainers and minimization of education, learning and training costs are expected to have somewhat less important potential effects in the transfer of knowledge/external schooling effect.[16]

8.4.2.3 Enhancing Training Provision

From the macro-firm surveys it appears that views of the policy makers and experts and those of the firms are consistent in highlighting the reform of educational system as an important mechanism to improve the provision of training, and the reform of educational and training systems for the enhancement of knowledge transfer/external schooling effects. However, on the other hand, there appears to be clear discrepancies between the macro–micro views (and also across firms) concerning the arrangement of priorities of other mechanisms for improving the provision of training. For instance, Table 8.13 presents the policy makers and experts' view to improve the provision of training that highlights enhancing training programmes to fit both the changing skill needs and changing technical needs, and enhancing planning for training needs and availability of trainers and mentors. Other measures towards enhancing the educational qualifications of workers, increasing the availability of training materials and equipment, regular/ adequate assessment and monitoring of training needs, increasing the appreciation of/information on the benefits of training, enhancing the availability of finance to cover training costs and enhancing the specialized training institutions are also highlighted. Further, measures aimed at improving the quality of trainers and

[16] As indicated by 86 %, 83 %, 83 %, 83 %, 69 % and 55 % of the respondent policy makers and experts respectively.

Table 8.13 Policies and mechanisms for skill development: (c) macro- micro views: promotion of training

Policies intervention for enhancing training provision	Official	All firms	Chemical	Metal	Large	Medium
Enhancing the educational qualifications of workers	93 %	56 %	44 %	71 %	40 %	64 %
Enhancing the availability of training materials and equipment	93 %	63 %	67 %	57 %	60 %	64 %
Enhancing training programmes to fit the changing technical needs	97 %	63 %	67 %	57 %	60 %	64 %
Increasing the appreciation of or information on the benefits of training	90 %	63 %	67 %	57 %	60 %	64 %
Regular/adequate assessment and monitoring of training needs	93 %	56 %	67 %	43 %	60 %	55 %
Improving the quality of trainers and mentors	83 %	50 %	56 %	43 %	60 %	45 %
Enhancing training programmes to fit the changing skill needs	100 %	50 %	56 %	43 %	60 %	45 %
Increasing availability of trainers and mentors	97 %	50 %	56 %	43 %	60 %	45 %
Enhancing adequate planning for training programme/needs	97 %	50 %	56 %	43 %	40 %	55 %
Enhancing the availability of finance to cover training costs	90 %	56 %	56 %	57 %	60 %	55 %
Enhancing/encouraging the specialized training institutions	86 %					
Enhancing the interactions between training institutions and firm.	76 %	31 %	22 %	43 %	20 %	36 %
Enhancing the full appropriability of the return from investment in training	76 %	44 %	44 %	43 %	40 %	45 %
Enhancing the system of training certification of skills acquired	76 %	38 %	22 %	57 %	40 %	36 %
Increasing the participation of private training institutions	76 %					
Decentralization of decision-making	72 %					
Restriction the mobility of trainees		38 %	33 %	43 %	40 %	36 %
Total response	29	16	9	7	5	11

Sources: Own calculation based on the macro survey (2002) and firm survey (2002)

mentors, enhancing the interactions between training institutions and firms, enhancing the appropriability of the return from investment in training, enhancing the system of training certification, increasing the participation of private training institutions and decentralization of decision-making are also mentioned.

The firms' view indicates that the provision of training could be improved by enhancing training programmes to fit the changing technical needs, increasing the appreciation of/information on the benefits of training, enhancing the availability of training materials and equipment and enhancing educational qualifications of workers. Mechanisms such as enhancing the availability of finance to cover training costs, regular/adequate assessment and monitoring of training needs, increasing availability and improving the quality of trainers and mentors, enhancing training programmes to fit the changing skill needs and enhancing planning for training needs are viewed by the firms as being of somewhat less importance. That also holds for enhancing the appropriability of the return from investment in training, enhancing the system of training certification, restricting the mobility of trainers and enhancing the interaction between training institutions and firms. Since training is costly, firms prefer policy interventions to finance training; however, it is less clear to what extent firms have a sound policy to contribute to training costs, as only 55 % of all respondent firms have upskilling plan – cf. Table 5.9 in Chap. 5 above.

Finally, in view of the complementary relationship between skill, skill upgrading and technological progress – see our discussion in Chaps. 3 and 6 above – the development of education, training, transfer of knowledge and skill levels may have further positive implications on the development of local technologies. Accordingly, the promotion of local technologies depends on skill upgrading, the promotion of R&D activities and enhancement of networks systems, collaboration between universities, firms, public and private sectors and the implementation of an explicit technology policy.

8.5 Conclusions

In this chapter we use some secondary data and information and the macro and firm surveys (2002) to analyse the educational, training and skill development policies in the Gulf countries. We prove hypothesis 8 in Scheme 1.1 in Chap. 1 above concerning the need for skill and technological upgrading through the reform of the educational and training systems/policies and the transfer of knowledge. In particular, we show that skill development depends on: (a) reforming the educational system; (b) enhancing the provision of training; (c) planning skill needs and matching educational output with market needs; (e) enhancing the transfer of knowledge/schooling effect; and (d) incentives and collaboration between public and private institutions. We explain that the promotion of local technologies and adoption of appropriate foreign technologies and the interaction between both these to foster economic growth in the Gulf countries depends on skill development. Particularly, on an enhancement of: (a) skill upgrading: educational and training systems; (b) R&D activities; (c) the transfer of knowledge/schooling effect; (d) networks system; and (e) incentives to motivate collaboration between universities and firms and between public and private institutions.

Our findings in Sect. 8.1 show that the educational policies in the Gulf countries share several problematic features such as an insufficient duration of compulsory education, the dominance of public sector and the lack of incentives/marginal contribution of the private sector on educational investment. Additional problems include poor quality, insufficient demand (enrolment ratios), an insufficient supply (spending) and the biased structure of tertiary education. However, despite these similarities, we also observe enormous variations, particularly with respect to the supply and demand sides of educational policies. Differences in the supply side include financial resources or priority of public expenditures on education relative to GDP and total government expenditures, allocation/distribution of public spending and spending per pupils at various educational levels, human resources or availability of teaching staff and the extent of privatization. Differences regarding the demand side include enrolment ratios and outcomes or implications on literacy rates, access to schooling/school life expectancy and interaction with training.

We find that the priority of investment in education, as measured by public expenditures on education as a percentage of total government expenditures, is approaching the level prevalent in developed countries; however, the priority of investment as a percentage of GDP in most of the Gulf countries lags far behind the level of the developed countries. When comparing supply–demand sides, it turns out that the supply side or public spending seems to be only one component in educational policies, because higher public spending per se does not lead to higher demand, participation and enrolment ratios, access to schooling/ school life expectancy and higher literacy rates. For instance, despite higher spending in Saudi Arabia, the demand/ enrolment ratios, access to schooling/school life expectancy and literacy rates are all falling behind those in Bahrain, which shows moderate spending, but better demand/enrolment ratios at all educational levels, better access to schooling/school life expectancy and literacy rates.

We observe that while the educational policies in the Gulf countries have raised enrolment ratios and literacy rates, they have failed to show satisfactory outcomes with respect to access to schooling/school life expectancy and training. This is due to serious deficiencies concerning the quality of education, coupled with the serious problems of biased structure and inadequate spending and enrolment in tertiary education in these countries. Hence, the major policy implication from our findings is that the improvement of the educational policies in the Gulf countries is vital and requires an improvement in the quality/internal efficiency, in the supply (investment) and demand (enrolment) sides, particularly in tertiary and technical education, and encouraging private sector investment in education.

Our results in Sect. 8.2 show that the implication and interaction between educational and training policies seem to be effective only within the largest public firms, which appear more committed to implement skill upgrading policies that are consistent with the line of public policies. The large public firms successfully contribute to serve public policies of training and skill upgrading via establishing active human resources development units, recruitment policies and specialized training centres to implement various regular and special internal and external training programmes, especially for national workers. In addition they encourage the use of ICT to upgrade skill levels, offer scholarships and collaborate with universities to absorb young national graduates. These results oppose our earlier findings in Chap. 5, which indicate a lack of effective interaction between educational and training policies and a lack of incentives for provision of training within private firms. Hence, these findings imply a further duality/discrepancy at the micro level/across public-private firms.

In Sect. 8.3 we use the results of the macro and firm surveys (2002) to integrate the divergent macro–micro views concerning plans and mechanisms for skill development in the short and long run and propose some policies and recommendations. The short run plans include investment in education and training of existing employees, the use of ICT to upgrade skill levels, and tools to encourage learning on the job and investment in vocational training. The long run plan highlights sending trainers, mentors and workers abroad to acquire skills, supporting long distance learning, beside continued investment in the above tools to ensure implementation of the short run plan. We show that the macro–micro views and policies for skill development highlight planning and monitoring skills needs on a regular basis, promoting resources allocation, reforming the educational system as an important mechanism for enhancing the provision of training and transfer of knowledge/external schooling effects.

The policy makers and experts' view concerning the reform of the educational system highlights improving the quality of teachers and mentors, improvement of infrastructure, encouragement of modernization and dynamism in the educational system and enhancing planning for educational needs. They also prioritize the improvement of internal efficiency/quality of basic, secondary and tertiary education; enhancement of the linkages (networks) between universities, colleges, technical and training institutes; monitoring of educational needs on a regular basis; and encouraging the system of flexibility in educational institutions.

In recent years, there have been several initiatives in the Gulf countries aimed at long term solutions to develop human resources, reform educational and training programmes and the labour market. In our view, these recent initiatives would be more effective if the governments in the Gulf collaborated with the private sector to work actively to influence both the supply and demand sides by implementing more effective policies to increase incentives, for example subsidies, to improve both education and training. For instance, public policies can influence the demand side for education and change the low enrolment at the tertiary level, especially technical education, by providing more fellowships, scholarships and prizes for engineering and science students, and increasing incentives for students to increase attraction for enrolment into science and engineering at secondary schools levels.

In our view the Gulf countries can benefit from the experiences of other advanced countries to improve the coordination and planning, to avoid the mismatch between supply and demand and to meet critical skills needs. For instance, the Gulf countries can benefit from the experiences of the European countries, where the government limits itself to paying teachers' salaries and leaves the coordination problem to the employer's federation. The Gulf countries should continue to upgrade schooling and increase enrolment in all levels especially in higher education and should also induce firms to organize in a federation, which has the task to organize branch specific education, by using taxes as a stick and payment of teachers' salaries as a carrot.

Moreover, the macro–micro suggestions with respect to knowledge transfer/ external schooling effects stress the improvement of quality of educational and training systems, qualifications of skilled and unskilled workers. In addition, recommendations include increasing information about future skill needs and the value of investments in education and training, interaction/consistency to market needs and a certification system.

Furthermore, the macro–micro views regarding improvement of the provision of training vary in arranging priorities, but generally emphasize the enhancement of training programmes to fit both the changing skill and technical needs, enhancing planning for training needs and quality and availability of trainers and mentors. Other measures include the enhancing of training materials and equipment, and the educational qualifications of workers, assessing and monitoring of training needs regularly/adequately, increasing the appreciation of/ information on the benefits of training, enhancing the availability of finance to cover training costs and enhancing specialized training institutions.

In addition, in view of the complementary relationship between skills, skill upgrading and technological progress – see earlier discussion in Chaps. 3 and 6 – the development of education, training, transfer of knowledge and skill levels may have further positive implications on the development of local technologies. Accordingly, the promotion of local technologies depends on skill upgrading, promotion of R&D activities and enhancement of networks system, collaborations between universities, firms, public and private sectors and the implementation of an explicit technology policy

Finally, our results show a serious discrepancy between private and large public firms regarding the implementation of public policies of training and skill upgrading and also divergent macro–micro views concerning the arrangement of priorities to implement plans, mechanisms and policies for enhancing skill, provision of training and transfer of knowledge. Therefore, we recommend further efforts to be made to enhance the consistency between the macro–micro views and public-private sectors, particularly with respect to arrangement of priorities, plans and mechanisms to ensure more consistent, effective and successful policies for skill development and encouraging private sector participation in education and training.

References

ADNOC Achievement Report. (1995–1999). *ADNOC Human Resources Development book, publications and web sites*. AbuDhabi, UAE: ADNOC.

Alfakhery, J. J. (1999). *Human development indicators in the UAE: A comparative study of UNDP Human Development Reports 1994–1998* (Labour and social research and studies series Vol. 1, pp. 81–82). Dubai, UAE: The UAE Ministry of Labour and Social Affairs – Department of studies, research and statistics. (in Arabic).

Al-Sulayti, H. A. (2002). *Education and human development in the GCC countries: An analytical study* (ECSSR strategic studies, Vol. 71). Abu Dhabi, UAE: ECSSR. (in Arabic).

Dubai Aluminium Company (DUABL). (2000). DUBAL achievement report. Unpublished report, http://www.dubal.ae, Dubai, UAE. Accessed April 20, 2002.

Fahmey, M. S., & Mahmoud, H. A. (1993). Problems of educational administration in the Gulf cooperation council countries. *The Arab Education office for the Gulf countries* – Riyadh

(1993) in Al-Sulayti, H. A. (2002). *Education and human development in the GCC countries: An analytical study* (ECSSR strategic studies, Vol. 71, pp. 29–30). Abu Dhabi: ECSSR. (in Arabic).

Firm Survey. (2002, April). *Technological change and skill development: A comparative study of chemical and metal medium and large scale enterprises in the UAE*. UAE: Firm Survey.

Gulf Pharmaceutical Industries (JULPHAR). (2000). JULPHAR achievement report. Unpublished report, http://www.julphar.net, Ras Al Khaimah, UAE. Accessed April 20, 2002.

Lall, S. (1999). *Competing with labour: Skills and competitiveness in developing countries* (Issues in development discussion paper no. 31, p. 17). Geneva: Development Policies Department, ILO.

Macro Survey. (2002, April). *Skill creation, human resources development and policy intervention: Interviews with policy makers and experts in the UAE*. UAE: Macro Survey.

The Ministry of Education in Bahrain State (1995–1996) Unpublished Report in Al-Sulayti (2002): p. 28.

The World Bank, World Development Indicators Database (WDI). (2004). http://data.worldbank.org/data-catalog/world-development-indicators. Accessed on December 25, 2004.

UNDP. (2002, July). *Human Development Report (2002): Deepening democracy in a fragmental world*. Oxford: Oxford University Press.

UNDP. (2004). *Human Development Report (2004): Cultural liberty in today's diverse world*. New York/Oxford: UNDP/Oxford University Press.

Undp- AHDR. (2003, July). *Arab Human Development Report (2003): Building a knowledge society*. New York/Amman, Jordan: UNDP – RBAS/National Press.

UNESCO- UIS. (2000). World Education Report (2000): UNESCO's World Education Indicators: http://www.unesco.org/education/information/wer/htmlENG/tablesmenu.htm.

UNESCO- UIS. (2004a). UIS web site global statistics on education: www.unesco.org.

UNESCO– UIS. (2004c). Educational statistics (1998–2002).

UNESCO Data and Statistics. (1999). UIS–UNESCO Statistical Yearbook (1999): www.unesco.org

UNESCO Institute of Statistics Data and Statistics. (1996). UNESCO statistical yearbook: "The World Education Indicators on school life expectancy 1992": www.unesco.org

UNESCO -UIS Data and Statistics. (2004b). Country Profile: www.uis.unesco.org.

UNESCO-UIS. (2003). The UNESCO education data and statistics indicators 1998–2001 www.unesco.org.

Chapter 9
Summary and Conclusions

This concluding chapter summarizes the major findings and contributions of the research. Section 9.1 briefly identifies the research problem and the major findings of the research; in Sect. 9.2 we show the relevance of the research findings to the general literature and contribution to the Gulf literature; and, finally, Sect. 9.3 presents short outlines on policy recommendations.

9.1 Research Problem, Methodology and Major Findings

This thesis is composed of four parts and nine chapters: Part I includes both Chaps. 1 and 2 and presents the introduction and motivation of the research; Part II contains Chap. 3, which presents the conceptual and theoretical frameworks; Part III comprises Chaps. 4, 5, 6 and 7 and presents the empirical application; and, finally, Part IV encompasses Chaps. 8 and 9 on policies, recommendations and conclusions. We explain below the main findings of each chapter.

Chapter 1 presents a brief introduction that gives a general overview of the research problem, its importance, relevance, objectives, questions, hypotheses and the structure of the research. We explain that the central themes of discussion in this research are the required skills formation and upskilling of the workers, together with their interaction with technological change in the Gulf countries. In particular, we intend to provide an empirical investigation of the causes and consequences of deficient educational systems, their interaction with the excessive share of low educated foreign workers and their implications on skill levels, skills mismatch, transfer of knowledge, provision of training, level of local technologies and dependence on foreign technologies. In addition, we aim to present an in-depth macro–micro analysis to assess technology and skill levels using a more comprehensive set of indicators.

Following the identification of the research problem in Chap. 1, we then present the background that motivated the research in Chap. 2. In particular, we show some stylized facts about the Gulf countries, to examine the research problem more

S. Mohamed Nour, *Technological Change and Skill Development in Arab Gulf Countries*, Contributions to Economics, DOI 10.1007/978-3-319-01916-1_9,

extensively, along with other strategic problems confronting economic development in these countries. We explain that oil greatly contributed to economic development in the Gulf countries; however, the heavy dependence on oil poses serious challenges since oil is an exhaustible resource and, because of the instability of oil prices, the revenue from oil is uncertain and volatile. Hence, economic growth and sustainable development strategy in the Gulf depends on economic diversification, which in turn is contingent upon the availability of adequate and appropriate skills and technologies. We also illustrate the other serious structural problems in the Gulf countries that relate to the Dutch disease, structural imbalances in the labour market, duality between the public and private sectors, growing unemployment, slowdown in economic growth and declining labour productivity. We illustrate the low skill and technology indicators and the substantial gap prevalent in the Gulf countries when compared to the world's rapidly advanced countries. In our view, the Gulf countries need to upgrade skill levels and encourage the development of local technologies to narrow the technological gap and achieve economic development in the region. In particular, skill upgrading is imperative to facilitating economic diversification, restructuring the labour market, enhancing productivity of labour, lessening dependence on foreign workers and, consequently, duality and unemployment in the labour market. Skill upgrading through enhancing educational and training systems is essential to facilitate the adoption of appropriate foreign technologies in the short run, and to encourage the development of local technologies through encrouging R&D activities to reduce the technological gap and dependence on foreign technologies in the long run. Therefore, our findings in Chap. 2 confirm our first hypothesis in Scheme 1.1 Chap. 1 above: that the Gulf countries need to promote the local skill and local technologies to face the challenges created by the depletion of oil resources. They need to implement the three strategies of diversification, building local technological capacity and restructuring the labour market. Our results confirm part of the second hypothesis in Scheme 1.1 Chap. 1 above: that in the short and medium term, the Gulf countries are unable to rely on local skills and local technologies and remain heavily dependent on both foreign skills and foreign technologies at the macro level.

In light of the findings in Chap. 2, it becomes more plausible to highlight the need for improvement of education or skill upgrading and the development of local technologies or technological progress to facilitate economic diversification and ensure long run economic growth and sustainable development in the Gulf countries. Before commencing with the empirical analysis, Chap. 3 briefly explains the concepts, measures and theoretical and empirical literature in relation to human capital (education), technological change and economic growth. We provide a background for the empirical analysis in the subsequent chapters by surveying the theoretical and empirical literature that emphasize the positive endogenous growth effects of technical change and human capital in increasing and sustaining economic growth. We explain that economic growth theories recognized and provided different perceptions and analytical frameworks for modelling the various effects of technical change, innovation and human capital on economic growth. The major differences arise because exogenous growth theories perceive and model technical progress and human capital as exogenous variables in growth accounting model, while, in contrast, the endogenous growth theory envisages and models technical progress and human capital as endogenous variables determining the rates and differences of economic growth across countries. The endogenous growth theory contributes towards improving the understanding of the interaction between technological change, human capital and economic growth and fills the gap in earlier growth theories by considering the important endogenous effects of human capital, technological progress and innovation. It also predicts that in the long run economic growth at the aggregate level is determined by endogenous sources of technological change: human capital, learning by doing, spillovers of knowledge and external effect of human capital. The presence of increasing returns to scale and externalities prevent diminishing returns to the accumulation of capital and thereby ensure the steady state of growth in the long run. While the feature of spillovers of knowledge supports endogenous growth, it also creates a form of externality and implies that private investments generate a positive external effect and the private returns from investment tend to be lower than the social returns. The outcomes tend not to be Pareto optimal but sub optimal and they require government intervention to correct the distortion using various instruments, such as providing subsidies (which can be financed by taxation) to improve the accumulation of technology and human capital, the incentives and returns from investment for private investors. We illustrate that the inclusion of human capital and technological change in growth accounting models motivate the endogenous growth literature to provide several interesting explanations of the relationship between human capital and technical progress. In particular, it stimulates considerable debate about the complementary relationship between human capital and technical progress, skilled biased technical change, the role of technical progress in skill upgrading and the role of skills and improvement in the accumulation of human capital in skill upgrading. These explanations imply that next to the important endogenous effects of technical progress and human capital in economic growth, the complementary relationships amongst these and between them and skill upgrading are also important for enhancing economic growth. Finally, we show the advantages and limitations of various measures of technological change and human capital that have been used in the theoretical and empirical literature, and we then select the most relevant measures for our empirical analysis in the subsequent Chapters according to the availability of data.

We consider the endogenous growth framework as a useful background for the empirical investigation in the following chapters. Before we go into the empirical analysis, we define the methods of data collection including both surveys and interviews in Chap. 4. We utilize the surveys data in our analysis and use the descriptive, comparative and statistical (OLS regression) methods of analysis. We explain that the basic objective of performing the macro and firm surveys is to obtain specific information to provide insights into the factors influencing or the causes and consequences of low skill and technology and to help to generate policies to improve skill and technology at the macro–micro levels. The macro survey examines the causes and consequences of the deficiency of the educational system and the firm survey discusses the implications of the excessive use of unskilled foreign workers. The field research to collect our primary data was held in the period from February to April 2002 in the UAE as a case study of the Gulf countries. The selection and focus of our analysis on the UAE was attributed to the easy accessibility to data and information, the availability of facilities for the fulfilment of the fieldwork/surveys, because the UAE ranks first in terms of ICT diffusion and has the highest per capita manufacturing product in the Gulf region.

In Chap. 4 we explain the selection of the sample, its composition, operation, coverage, advantages and limitations of the surveys data, and show the structure and design of the questionnaire. The firm survey (2002) on "Technological change and skill development" covers 106 of the medium and large size firms working in two industries in the manufacturing sector: the chemical and metal industries. The selection of both industries was based on many reasons, the most important of which is that the argument for both upskilling and technological upgrading is promising in both sectors and can be used to reduce the dependence on foreign workers. The sample in the firm survey was drawn from the medium and large size firms active in the chemical and metal industries, which are located in three emirates of Abu Dhabi, Dubai and Sharjah. The selection of these emirates was based on their significant average share in total employment, capital investment and total number of factories engaged in the chemical and fabricated metal industries. The macro survey (2002) on "Skill creation, human resources development and policy intervention" was sent to 40 of policy makers and experts in 14 public and university institutions in the UAE. The number of responding firms and policy makers are 44 and 30 respectively.

The data from the firm and macro surveys provide us with the required information, which is particularly useful for presenting a macro–micro comparative analysis to identify the causes and consequences of the skills problem and the policies for skill development from a macro–micro perspective. The results of the macro survey seem quite representative, since the selection covers governments, universities, and educational and training institutions. One advantage of the macro survey is that it examines the problem after integrating the two different perspectives of policy makers and experts. The results of the firm survey are also quite representative, since the selection and coverage of firms in the survey includes a broad range of firms working in the chemical and metal industries, which provides us with relevant data and information that is of considerable use in our analysis. Such coverage also has the advantage of enabling us to compare between firms according to two criteria: the size of employment and the industrial activity. One major limitation with respect to the firm survey is the low response rate for some questions, especially when the answers or data required quantitative measurement. Such problems arise because some of the respondents firms were unwilling to provide complete and reliable quantitative data, while others offered somewhat selective answers.

Apart from this limitation, the data from the firm and macro surveys remains useful, not only for the empirical investigation in Chaps. 5, 6 and 7, but also for the policy analysis and suggestions in Chap. 8. We begin our analysis in Chap. 5, by using the results from the macro and firm surveys to verify our third hypothesis in Scheme 1.1 in Chap. 1 above, about the serious implications of the interaction between the deficient educational system and the high incidence of unskilled foreign workers. In particular, the results from the macro survey show that the deficient educational system is attributed to many causes such as the poor quality of education that leads to many serious consequences including low skill levels, poor provision of training, skills mismatch and low transfer of knowledge at the macro level. In addition, the results from the firm survey illustrate that the excessive use of low educated foreign workers leads to several serious implications such as low skill levels, poor provision of training, skills mismatch, poor technology indicators, weak adaptation of imported technologies and a heavy dependence on foreign technologies. Our findings from the surveys and follow-up interviews indicate that the poor technology indicators/indigenous capability to build the local technology and heavy dependence on foreign technology can be attributed to low skill levels, lack of R&D activities, weak linkages, lack of networks systems, and low transfer of knowledge. These findings at the micro level seem consistent with those at the macro level.

When distinguishing between firms according to firm size and industry level, we find that skill and technology indicators show considerable variation across firms. Our findings show two surprising contradicting macro–micro views. The first contradicting optimistic-pessimistic micro and macro view regarding the incidence and success of knowledge transfer/external schooling effect implies that the transfer of knowledge/the external effects of schooling is probably successful within firms, but is unsuccessful within society at large. This is probably because the transfer of knowledge is hindered by: the low quality of education; the weak linkages and a lack of networks between universities, colleges, technical and training institutes and the productive sectors; and the imbalanced structure of the population and labour market. Our observation of the second contradicting optimistic-pessimistic macro and micro view, concerning the self-reliance on local skill and the role of both technological upgrading and upskilling in reinforcing it, implies that the self-reliance strategy is probably a preferred government strategy but not necessarily favoured by private firms. This is probably because profit maximizing private firms are motivated to continue in hiring cheap readymade skilled foreign workers rather than hiring, training and upskilling expensive national workers. These results corroborate a part of the sixth hypothesis in Scheme 1.1 in Chap. 1 above with respect to the failure and the factors hindering the transfer of knowledge/external schooling effects at the macro level. But, on the other hand, our findings surprisingly reject a part of the sixth hypothesis concerning the failure of the transfer of knowledge/external schooling effect at the micro level, and also reject hypothesis 8. c. in Scheme 1.1 in Chap. 1 above about the consistency of upskilling and transfer of knowledge at the macro–micro levels.

The surprising results from Chap. 5 motivate our research to attempt a more comprehensive analysis of skills problem and the implications of unskilled foreign workers at the micro level/across private firms. Therefore, in Chap. 6, we then use the data from the firm survey (2002) to broaden our earlier analysis in Chap. 5 by providing an in-depth analysis of skill indicators, their implications and relationships with wages, upskilling (ICT training) and technology (ICT) indicators at the micro/firm level. Our findings illustrate the low skill levels – due to the excessive share of unskilled foreign workers – and the implications on skills mismatch, public-private duality and productivity decline across private firms. These results are consistent with the micro–macro findings in Chap. 5, which indicate the low share of high skilled workers in total population and employment – measured by both educational and occupational levels –and the serious implications on skills mismatch and the macro–micro duality with respect to upskilling efforts. Furthermore, we show that difference between required and actual education indicates severe skills mismatch across all firms and all skill levels, especially, across medium and low skilled workers. These findings, together with those in Chap. 5, verify hypotheses 3 and 4.a in Scheme 1.1 in Chap. 1 above regarding the implications of low skill levels and the argument, earlier in Chap. 2, about the pressing need for upskilling, mainly in the private sector.

Our results show positive correlations between skill (actual and required education and experience) and average wages. We show that differences in skill levels/ stock of human capital (share of high skilled in total employment) across firms are related to market size (share in total employment, capital, output/sales and profit). We also find that an increase in skill level –share of high skilled in total employment – and firm size lead to improved relationships between actual and required education and experience and wages. Next, our results show positive complementary relationships between technology (ICT), skill and upskilling (ICT training). We illustrate that an increase in skill level – share of high skilled in total employment –and firm size lead to improved in the complementary relationships between skill, upskilling and technology (ICT). The relationships between skill indicators and wages, and between skill, technology (ICT) and upskilling (ICT training) substantiate our fourth hypothesis (4.b–4.c) in Scheme 1.1 in Chap. 1, and agree with the findings in Chap. 5 concerning the differences in skill and technology indicators across firms according to firm size and industry. These results imply the importance of good education/skill levels for bridging differences between firms and also for improving skills, technology and upskilling complementarity at the micro level.

These results guide us in Chap. 7 to use the firm survey (2002) data at the micro level and secondary data at the macro level to examine and verify hypothesis 7 in Scheme 1.1 in Chap. 1 above concerning the importance/impacts of tacit and codified knowledge at the micro–macro levels respectively. We find that at the macro level tacit knowledge is positively correlated with schooling years, while codified knowledge is positively correlated with GDP (economic growth). Moreover, our results at the macro level show significant positive complementary relationships between codified knowledge and the number of FTER and between these and the number of publications, cooperation and technology (patents). Furthermore, at the micro (firm) level, we illustrate that tacit knowledge is positively correlated with technology (expenditures on ICT), upskilling (expenditures on ICT training), output, output diversification, productivity and profit. In addition, we find that at the micro (firm) level tacit knowledge is positively correlated with market size: total investment, capital and firm size. The major implication of our findings is the positive correlation between knowledge and various variables at both the micro and macro levels. Therefore, further incentives should be provided to improve tacit and codified sources of knowledge at the macro and micro levels. Another implication is that the positive impact of tacit knowledge also implies the importance of a good education since tacit knowledge is often embodied in educated people and so in human capital.

In view of the findings in Chaps. 2–3, and Chaps. 5, 6 and 7, which indicate the importance of a good education, in Chap. 8 we use the data from the firm and macro surveys to conclude our study with policy analysis. We corroborate hypothesis 8 (8. a–8.b) in Scheme 1.1 in Chap. 1 above concerning the need for skill and technological upgrading through the reform of the educational and training systems and the transfer of knowledge. Moreover, we use secondary data and information and the macro and firm surveys (2002) to present a policy analysis of the educational (supply–demand sides) and training systems in the Gulf countries. We show that the educational policies in the Gulf countries shared several problematic features such as the dominance of public sector, the lack of incentives/marginal contribution of the private sector in educational investment, poor quality, insufficient supply (spending) and demand (enrolment) and the biased structure of tertiary education. On the other hand, our results show an enormous variation in the supply–demand sides of educational policies across the Gulf countries. When comparing supply–demand sides, it turns out that the supply side or public spending seems to be only one component in the educational policies, because higher public spending per se does not imply a higher demand for enrolment of children in education. That also does not imply higher participation and enrolment ratios, access to schooling/school life expectancy and higher literacy rates. Moreover, we find that although the priority of spending on education – measured by the share of public spending on education as percentage of total government spending – in some of the Gulf countries is close to the levels in developed countries, the quality of education is low in all Gulf countries. The major policy implication from these findings is that the improvement of the educational systems in the Gulf countries is vital and requires improvement of the quality/internal efficiency, supply (investment) and demand (enrolment) sides, particularly by increasing incentives at tertiary and technical education. We next discuss the macro–micro views concerning plans, mechanisms and policies for skill development through enhancing the educational system, provision of training, transfer of knowledge/external schooling effects, effective collaboration between public and private institutions and increasing incentives for private sector investment in education and training in the UAE. Our results show a serious discrepancy with respect to the implementation of public policies of training and skill upgrading between private and large public firms and divergence in arranging priorities to implement plans, mechanisms and policies for enhancing skill levels, provision of training and transfer of knowledge at the macro–micro levels. These results are consistent with earlier observations in

Chap. 5 concerning the contradicting optimistic-pessimistic macro and micro views with respect to upskilling efforts and/or the self-reliance on local skill and the role of both technological upgrading and upskilling in reinforcing it. Therefore, we recommend further efforts be made to enhance the consistency between the macro–micro views and the public-private sectors, particularly in the arrangement of priorities, plans and mechanisms to ensure more consistent, effective and successful policies for skills development.

9.2 Relevance and Contribution of the Research

Most of our findings in this research are consistent with both the new growth literature and the Gulf literature. Compared to the endogenous growth framework, we provide further evidence in support of the endogenous and new growth literature, in particular with respect to the positive correlation between actual education, experience and wages. Our results in Chap. 6 show positive complementary relationships between technology (ICT), skill and upskilling (ICT training), these findings seem consistent with the theoretical framework in Chap. 3, endogenous growth framework and the stylized facts in the new growth literature concerning the relationships between human capital, technical progress and upskilling. Our findings are broadly consistent with and provide further evidence in support of the findings in the new growth literature concerning the skilled biased technical change theorem. In addition, our results concur both with the general literature that defines both skill and technology in relation to firm characteristics (size and industry), and also the recent literature highlighting the growing effects of new technologies, especially ICT diffusion. Our results in Chap. 7 verify four stylized facts about the importance/impacts of knowledge at the micro and macro levels, and are in line with the recent general findings in the knowledge literature. In particular, the complementary relationship between tacit knowledge and codified sources of knowledge at the macro level and the significant correlations between both tacit knowledge and codified sources of knowledge and output and growth at the micro and macro levels respectively. Tacit knowledge is important not only through its direct effects, but also through its further effects on upskilling and the use of technology (ICT). Our findings are consistent with the recent results in the knowledge literature, which indicate that knowledge components have more significant impacts on output (total sales value) that exceed the effects of traditional variables (i.e. labour and capital).

On the other hand, we find a positive significant correlation between the use of/total spending on ICT and total output, but an insignificant correlation between the use of/total spending on ICT and profit at the micro/firm level. This result proves our fifth hypothesis in Scheme 1.1 in Chap. 1 above and the observations about the insignificant/inconclusive effect of ICT at the macro level in the Gulf countries and the recent literature in the developing countries. However, our results with respect to ICT should be interpreted more carefully as they probably have two-ways causality and may imply a possibility for reversed causality. Mainly because more profit and output would imply more financial capacity that permits more spending on ICT, on the other hand, more spending on ICT implies higher costs and lower profit.

Our findings about the insignificant correlation between the required education and wages are in contrast to the findings in the new growth literature on the importance of job characteristics (skills required) in wages determination.

Compared to the Gulf literature, we provide new evidence and add to the few recent studies in the Gulf that highlight the need for upskilling, the low skill, low technological level and dependency on foreign technologies, and the duality between public and private sectors. Compared to the Gulf literature, our research is important for elaborating and providing a more in-depth analysis, not only for assessing the Gulf technology-skill indicators using a more comprehensive set of indicators than often used in the new growth literature, but also for analysing the causes and consequences of low skills and technology, the relation between them at both the macro and micro levels, and for addressing policy aspects aiming to enhance them. Basically, we identify upskilling as an essential element for the fulfilment of three current strategies in the Gulf: diversification, technological development and restructuring/reducing the imbalances in the labour market. We show that the low skill level is basically attributed to the deficient educational system – due to low quality of education – and high incidence of unskilled foreign workers at the macro and the micro levels respectively. The importance of our analysis is the identification of the numerous implications of the interaction between a poor educational system and an excessive share of low educated foreign workers that leads to low skill levels, poor provision of training, skills mismatch, low transfer of knowledge, poor technology indicators and high dependence on foreign technologies. We add to the findings of Haan (1999) regarding the lack of technology policy, technical skills, R&D, technology culture in the Gulf society and the mismatch in the labour market due to deficient educational system and cultural reasons. One important result from our analysis is that we illustrate that the lack of local efforts for technology development is basically related to low R&D efforts that are attributed to low skill level, lack of networks systems, fruitful cooperation between universities and firms, lack of resources, social awareness and concern. We provide basic and new contributions and fill the gap in the Gulf literature by investigating the significance of the incidence and transfer of knowledge/external schooling effects, the factors hindering and those contributing towards enhancing them at the macro and micro levels in the Gulf. We show the significance of tacit and codified sources of knowledge at the micro–macro levels. Unlike the few recent studies of knowledge in the Arab countries, one advantage of our analysis is that we provide a more specific analysis that focuses only on the Gulf countries. Different from earlier studies, we provide new empirical investigation of both the importance (impacts) of tacit knowledge at the micro level – see our discussion in Chap. 7 – and the discrepancy in the transfer of knowledge/external schooling effects at the macro–micro levels – see our discussion in Chap. 5.

We show the positive correlation between skill indicators (actual and required education and experience) and between these indicators and wages; the distribution of average wages is significantly correlated with the actual education and experience, but is less sensitive to the required education. We add to the literature in indicating the implications of the poor educational system and the high incidence of unskilled foreign workers in the labour market, particularly the skills mismatch problem at the macro level. A novel element of our research, distinguishing it from the few earlier studies, is that we manage to measure the skills mismatch at the micro level/across firms. Our new findings show that at the micro level although occupations are improving with education, schooling requirements are seldom significantly match with the actual/attained schooling, especially within both the medium and low skilled worker groups. The gap that appears between the required and actual/attained schooling indicates a mismatch at the micro level, which is notably higher within both medium and low skilled workers.

Our findings concerning the channels of technology transfer and the wide variation between the level of technology transfer in the different industrial scales and activities/sectors go beyond the findings in the Gulf literature (e.g. Elsabaa, 1997). This is because we identify wide variations in the preferred channels of technology transfer that include not only joint ventures and foreign industrial projects, but also strategic alliances, hiring foreign skill/technologically advanced workers and consultants, technology licensing and FDI. We show that across firms not only the level of technology use and channels of transfer are determined by firm size and industry, but also skill and technology indicators (the use of ICT, R&D, patent, product and process innovations) are significantly defined by firm's characteristics i.e. size and industry. These results are consistent with the general literature, which illustrates that both large size firms and high intensive/active industry (e.g. chemical) are more intensive in terms of the use of technology and skills. However, one should also expect that these results might imply a possibility for reversed causality, mainly because R&D is a fixed cost that requires high financial capacity, which is most likely to be stronger amongst large size firms.

We add to the very few literature in the Gulf concerning the positive impacts the technology transfer brings to output/production (Elsabaa, 1997) and the negative impact the use of technology induces in the demand for unskilled workers/labour saving effect (Haan, 1999). We provide a more elaborate analysis, relying not only on the qualitative effects of the use of technologies, particularly ICT diffusion on the demand for labour and the effects of increasing use of technologies on product and process innovations, but also on the quantitative effects of ICT on output and profit.

Our results provide further evidence that is consistent with the Gulf literature on the duality between the public and private sectors. We show new aspects not only with regard to the public-private duality in skill and technology levels, the use of ICT and upskilling, but also in relation to the macro–micro duality and the surprising contradicting views concerning the transfer of knowledge, upskilling and the impact of ICT.

Our new results from Chap. 8 show that the implication and interaction between educational and training policies seem to be effective only within the largest public firms, which appear more committed to implement skill upgrading policies that are consistent with the line taken by public policies. The large public firms successfully contribute to serve public policies of training and skill upgrading via establishing active human resources development units, recruitment policies and specialized training centres to implement various regular and special internal and external training programmes, especially for national workers. In addition, these firms encourage the use of ICT to upgrade skill levels, offer scholarships and collaborate with universities to absorb young national graduates. These results oppose our earlier findings in Chap. 5, which indicate a lack of effective interaction between educational and training policies and a lack of incentives for provision of training within private firms. Hence, these findings imply a further duality/discrepancy at the micro level/across public-private firms. That also leads to duality/discrepancy between macro–micro views with respect to implementation of upskilling plans. Therefore, we observe that, in contrast to the private firms, the large public firms (JULPHAR, ADNOC and DUBAL) in the UAE have successfully contributed to serve the public policies for enhancing training and skill upgrading, especially among the national workers. However, it is less clear whether the large public firms induce positive effect to upskill workers in private firms. In our view the interpretation of the serious public-private discrepancy can be attributed to the presence of high resources, support and incentives within large public firms, which are probably lacking within private firms.

9.3 Policy Recommendations

The major policy recommendation from this research is that skill development policies can be enhanced by making improvements to the educational and training systems and enhancing the transfer of knowledge/external schooling effects. As for improving of education, the major policy recommendations include the improvement in the quality of teachers or mentors, infrastructure, planning for educational needs, the internal efficiency/quality of basic, secondary and tertiary education, encouraging the system of modernization and dynamism. In addition, measures should be undertaken to enhance the linkages (networks) between universities, colleges, technical and training institutes, monitor educational needs on a regular basis, encourage the system of flexibility of educational institutions, and increase the harmony/consistency between educational output and market needs. In addition, further measures include: increasing incentives for enrolment and spending on education by both public and private sectors, particularly in tertiary and technical education, changing the attitudes of educated economically active population, improvement of regulations/laws to legitimize sufficient duration of compulsory education and decentralization of decision-making.

Concerning the improvement of training, the major policy recommendations include enhancing the educational qualifications of workers, availability of training materials and equipment, planning and regular/adequate assessment and monitoring of training programmes to fit the changing technical and skill needs. Further recommendations include increasing the appreciation of or information on the benefits of training, improving the quality and availability of trainers and mentors, enhancing availability of finance to cover training costs. In addition, there should be measures aimed at encouraging specialized training institutions, the interactions between training institutions and firms, enhancing the full appropriability of the return from investment in training, enhancing the system of training certification of skill acquired, increasing the participation of private training institutions and decentralization of training provision.

With respect to improvement of the transfer of knowledge, the major policy recommendations include an improvement of the quality of education and training and the qualifications of both skilled and unskilled workers to permit the positive effects of skilled workers on unskilled workers. In addition, there are recommendations that aim at the improvement of firms conditions to encourage the external effects, sponsoring educational scholarships, increasing the interaction to market needs through increasing the information about future educational, training and skill needs, especially in the productive sectors and their demand for graduate students. The policy recommendations also aim at increasing awareness about future value of investments in education and training, enhancing a system of certification of skill acquired, providing adequate incentives for trainers and minimization of education, learning and training costs.

Since the skills problem is partially attributed to the high presence of unskilled foreign workers, skill upgrading requires both a reduction in numbers and an upgrading of unskilled foreign workers. There is much to be learned from the successful stories in the rapidly advanced countries, in particular, the experiences of skill upgrading in Singapore and Korea – cf. our discussion in Chap. 3.

Finally, in view of the complementary relationship between skills, skill upgrading and technological progress – see our discussion in Chaps. 3 and 6– the development of education, training, transfer of knowledge and skill levels may have further positive implications on the development of local technologies. Accordingly, the promotion of local technologies depends on skill upgrading, promotion of R&D activities and the enhancement of networks systems, collaboration between universities, firms, public and private sectors and implementation of an explicit technology policy.

9.4 Direction for Future Research

We plan to utilize and extend the major findings of this study for future empirical research to improve understanding of the causes and consequences of low skill and technological level in other developing countries with similar circumstances. It is hoped that our future research makes reference/would be relevant to more than one country and the results could be generalized and extended to be of value/use and benefit to other developing countries. It is also hoped that the results would generate some useful insights for international comparisons across developing countries and contribute to enhancing the accumulation of human capital, external schooling effects/transfer of knowledge, uskilling, technological capacity, social welfare and economic development in the developing countries.

References

El Sabaa, S. (1997, November). Linking technology to industrial development in the United Arab Emirates. *Trade and Industry Magazine, 22*(263), 16–29. Dubai, UAE.

Firm Survey. (2002, April). *Technological change and skill development: A comparative study of chemical and metal medium and large scale enterprises in the UAE*. UAE: Firm Survey.

Haan, H. (1999, January/March). *The UAE: Assessment of technology use in some selected sectors- Towards introduction and explaining capital and skill intensive technologies* (Specialist Rep. No. 6). Dubai/Amsterdam: National Human Resources Development and Employment Strategy Project.

Macro Survey. (2002, April). *Skill creation, human resources development and policy intervention: Interviews with policy makers and experts in the UAE*. UAE: Macro Survey.

Appendices

S. Mohamed Nour, *Technological Change and Skill Development in Arab Gulf Countries*, Contributions to Economics, DOI 10.1007/978-3-319-01916-1,

Appendix 1: Questionnaire of the Firm Survey (2002)

"Technological Change and Skill Development: A Comparative Study of Chemical and Metal Medium and Large Scale Enterprises in the United Arab Emirates"

1. General Background Information

1. Code (File No.): ……………. ………. (For Coding Only: Please do not write in this item)

2. Name of firm: ………….

3. Years in operation (since the establishment): ……………….

4. If your firm has started in the UAE but has changed names, changed management, changed ownership, merged with other firms, or experienced any other changes, or if it is started in another country and then moved to the UAE, please specify the years in operation?……………………….

5. Location: Name of Emirate where the firm is located (please tick one box)

Abu Dhabi.	Dubai	Sharjah.
1	2	3

6. If your firm has branches in many parts of the country, please name the location?…………………………
Sector (please tick one box)

Public.	Private.	Mixed
1	2	3

7. Main Product(s): (please tick up to four boxes)

Chemical	Petroleum	Petrochemical	Plastic	Rubber	Metal / Iron – Steel	Metal/ Aluminium	Others [please specify below]
1	2	3	4	5	6	7	8

8. Name up to four main products and the approximate proportion that each contributes to your total sales and total employment?

Product Name				
% Of total sales				
% Of employment				

9. Is your firm a subsidiary or an affiliate of a multinational enterprise? (Please tick one box)

Yes	No
1	2

10. If your firm is an affiliate of a multinational enterprise, please give the origin of your parent company? (Please tick one box)

Arab	Non–Arab Asian	European	North American	Australian or New Zealand	Others [please specify below]
1	2	3	4	5	6

11. Ownership of the firm. (Please give the percentage)

Local	Foreign	Total
…… %.	… %.	100%

12. Nationality of the main owner(s). (Please tick the relevant box / boxes)

Local	Arab	Non – Arab Asian	European	North American	Australian or New Zealand	Others [please specify below]
1	2	3	4	5	6	7

Firm size [Employment size]. (Please tick one box)

50 – 99	100 –499	500 +
1	2	3

15. Firm Production and Firm Performance: (please give an approximate estimate of the following items)

	1999	2000	2001 (approximately)
Total employment[1]			
Net Worth[2]			
Total Profit [approximately]			
Total Sale [approximately]			
Total Output [approximately]			

2. The use of Technology[3] and Firm Product

2.1 General information: the use of technology, spending on ICT, dependence on foreign technology

16. Firm's own appreciation of its level of technology: (Please tick one box)

Very advanced production technology.	1
Advanced production technology.	2
Basic/ simple production technology.	3
Mixed: simple and advanced production technology.	4

17. Compared to the international standard of technology used in the activity in which you operate, how do you rate the level of technology used in firm production in the last three years? (Please tick one box)

Higher than the International Standard.	1
Similar to the International Standard.	2
Lower than the International Standard.	3

18. In the last three years, approximately how much did your firm spend on ICT: Computer and Telecommunication hardware and software technologies and other ICT related Services?

Expenditure on:	1999	2000	2001 (approximately)
Computer.			
Telecommunication			
Training and Software Development			
Maintenance services			
Hosting and other relevant ICT services			

19. Does your firm have an adequate capacity / ability to produce and develop local technologies[4] at this moment? (Please tick one box)

Yes	No
1	2

20. Does your firm purchase equipment, machines and techniques from abroad? (Please tick one box)

Yes	No
1	2 → skip to question [22]

21. If any, what are the main reason (s) of purchasing from abroad? (Multiple Answers Possible [MAP])

Not available from local supplier.	1
Better quality.	2
Better price.	3
Others.....[please specify below].	4

....

22. What was the percentage value of imported capital equipment to total capital equipment in the year 2001?

---

[1] This term includes total number of workers including subcontractors, support services and other workers employed by the firm.

[2] Net worth equals total assets minus total liabilities, this item refers to Capital which reflects the current market value of Fixed Assets, paid up capital in operation and investment / inflow.

[3] Technology is more than just machinery and equipment. One can distinguish the following elements which in one form or combination constitutes a technology:

Hard ware refers to materials, production tools and end-product.

Soft ware concerns the documented – processes, techniques, methods, blue prints, etc.

Human ware is the know- how [i.e. knowledge, skills and experiences] held by group of people.

Institution ware includes institutions and wider networks/ systems of management structures, business services [e.g. consulting and design firms], research and development [e.g. laboratories], policies and regulations [i.e. the political and legal framework], etc., that activate the interaction of the production system with the physical and social environment.

[4] Local technology refers to ability / capability to build, develop, master, enhance and utilize the production and promotion of technology locally / for local purposes.

23. What was the percentage value of capital equipment to total capital equipment that has been built by foreign companies?
24. What kind(s) of technology transfer[5] did your firm use over the last three years? (Multiple Answers Possible [MAP])

Transfer that based on direct investment made by foreign firm(s) to facilitate the inflow of technologies.	1
Transfer that based on an earlier contractual agreement to jointly share the losses [risks/ dangers] and profits.	2
Transfer that required an issuance of a formal licensing.	3
Transfer that based on an allied between foreign firm and local firm to transfer strategic technologies to local firm	4
Transfer that made by hiring foreign skills/ technologically advanced workers/ consultants to build the local technology.	5
Others…..[please specify below].	6

……………………………………………………………………………………………………

25. How important is/ are the effect(s) of technology transferred in enhancing firm production and enhancing the capacity to develop the local technologies in your firm over the last three years? (Please tick one box for each statement)

	Very important	Important	Important only in restricted filed	Unimportant
1. Enhancing firm production	1	2	3	4
2. Enhancing the capacity to develop the local technologies	1	2	3	4

26. Did your firm hire technologically advanced workers/ consultants over the last three years? (Please tick one box)

Yes	No
1	2 → skip to question [28]

27. If any, how important is / are the effect(s) of technologically advanced workers/ consultants in enhancing firm production and enhancing the capacity to develop the local technologies in your firm over the last three years? (Please tick one box for each statement)

	Very important	Important	Important only in restricted filed	Unimportant
1. Enhancing firm production	1	2	3	4
2. Enhancing the capacity to develop the local technologies	1	2	3	4

28. Does your firm have a plan to introduce, develop or improve the local technologies benefiting from the imported technologies[6]? (There are three statements below, Please respond to each one by ticking yes or no box corresponding to each one).

	Yes	No
In the short run your firm needs to depend on imported technology.		
In the medium term the use of imported technologies and accumulation of knowledge and learning will allow your firm to begin produce its own technology or to use other sources of local technologies.		
In the very long run to some extent your firm will manage to partially develop its own technologies or to use other sources of local technologies.		

[5] The transfer of technology from the developed countries to the developing countries takes different forms, such as:

Foreign Direct Investment [FDI]: refers to a direct investment made by foreign firm to facilitate the inflow / transfer of technology to the hosting / local firm.

Joint ventures is a contractual agreement to facilitate the transfer / inflow of technology to local firm based on an earlier agreement to share the [risk/ danger] losses and profits between local firm and foreign firm.

Technology Licensing is a form of technology transfer that required a permission or consent to permit or authorize the transfer of technology by issuance of a formal license.

Strategic Alliances is a state or condition under which the local firm and the foreign firm formed an allied to transfer strategic technologies to the hosting / local firm.

Import and hire foreign skills and foreign technologically advanced workers/consultants to build the local technology.

[6] Short run refers to next three years, medium term refers to the next three to five years and long run refers to the next ten years.

29. Does your firm have a plan to pursue the following strategies to accelerate the development/ promotion of local technologies? (There are three statements below, Please respond to each one by ticking yes or no box corresponding to each one).

	Yes	No
Autonomous strategies [national – led strategy] to guide learning in domestic firms.		
Foreign Direct Investment- dependent strategies that rely on foreign companies to guide learning/promotion of local technologies subject to government policies / regulations.		
Foreign Direct Investment- dependent strategies that rely on foreign companies to guide learning / promotion of local technologies subject to market conditions.		

30. How important are the effects of technology upgrading in fulfilling the following long run strategies? Please, tick the relevant answer(s) in the respective columns (Multiple Answers Possible [MAP])

	Importance Extremely 3	Moderately 2	Slightly 1	**Not Relevant 0**
Enhancing firm production.				
Raising skill level.				
Reinforcing firm ability to promote its own technologies.				
Upskilling national workers in the firm.				
Hiring more skilled national workers.				
Others [please specify below].				

……

2.2 *Technology Indicators*

31. How many patents[7] did your firm apply for in the last three years? (Please tick one box)

Zero.	1	2	3	4 to 10	11 and above
1	2	3	4	5	6

32. Does your firm perform research [including outsourcing research activities] for the purpose of development of production, development and adaptation of technology [R & D[8]]? (Please tick one box)

Yes, Continuously	Yes, Occasionally as needed	Not at all.
1	2	3 → skip to section (c), question [40]

If the answer is [1] or [2] for question [32] continues in answering questions [33] – [39].

33. If any, approximately how much did your firm spend on these research activities [including outsourcing research activities] during the year 2001?

………………………………………………………………………………………………

34. Approximately what was the percentage of research expenditure [including outsourcing research activities] to total output expenditure in the year 2001?

………………………………………………………………………………………………

35. In the year 2001 approximately what percentage of your research efforts and percentage of research expenditures [including outsourcing research activities] is devoted to the following activities? Please approximate the percentage.

	New product	Improved product	New process	Improved process	Total
1. % Of Research Efforts	………%	………%	………%	………%	100%
2. % Of Research Expenditures	………%	………%	………%	………%	100%

36. How many employees are engaged in research [including outsourcing research activities] in your firm? (Please tick one box)

Full – Time				Part –Time			
Zero	1-5	6-10	11+	Zero	1-5	6-10	11+
1	2	3	4	1	2	3	4

37. Does the performance of the research unit [including outsourcing research activities] in your firm contribute to adaptation of imported technologies to fit the industrial need in your firm? (Please tick one box)

Yes, to large degree	Yes, to acceptable degree	Yes, to minimum degree	Not at all
1	2	3	4

[7] Patent is a protection of property rights especially for inventions.

[8] R & D is a combination of activities / efforts or practical researches carried out with the aim to [1] develop and enhance the productive capacity; [2] introduce new technologies, or improve the old technologies and [3] allow optimal adaptations of imported technologies to industrial / local needs. This item includes the outsourcing research activities.

38. If the research unit in your firm did not contribute to adaptation of imported technologies, how important is the shortage of skilled & qualified workers in the performance of the research activities in your firm? (Please tick one box)

Very important	Important	Unimportant
1	2	3

39. How important is the effect of research output in your firm in affecting research output in other firms working in your sector? (Please tick one box)

Very important	Important	Important only in restricted filed(s)	Unimportant.
1	2	3	4

2.3 Technology and Firm Product / Process Innovation[9]

40. In the last three years has the use of both technology and the ICT in firm production … (please tick one box)

(a) The use of technology			(b) The use of ICT technology		
Increased	Decreased	Remained stable	Increased	Decreased	Remained stable
1	2	3	1	2	3

If the answer is [1] for question [40] continue answering questions [41]-[43], if not proceed to section 3.a, question [44]

41. If the use of both technology and the ICT increased, did they require more workers with higher skills? (Please tick one box for each)

(a) The use of technology required more workers with higher skills		(b) The use of ICT required more workers with higher skills	
Yes	No	Yes	No

42. In the last three years did the increasing use of technology enable your firm to introduce any new product / process[10] or any product / process changes? If any, what were they? Please tick the relevant answer(s) in the respective columns (Multiple Answers Possible [MAP])

	Yes	No
To produce a new product.		
To produce a new process.		
To produce a new combination of old output.		
To produce a new service.		
To produce a new method of production.		
To produce a new organizational method.		
To produce more output with low cost.		
To produce the same output with low cost.		
To open a new market.		
To improve the quality of firm product.		
To improve the process of personal selection.		
To improve training within the firm.		
To improve communication within the firm.		

43. If any, approximately, how much did these products / processes decrease / increase firm's costs, sales and profits? Please tick the relevant answer in the respective columns.

	Decrease by			Increase by			No change
	1%- 10%	11%– 25%	Over 25%	1%- 10%	11% - 25%	Over 25%	No change
Per unit energy costs							
Per unit material costs							
Total costs							
Total sales							
Total profits.							

[9] Innovation is defined as firm ability to involve in one or all of the following activities: introduction / production of a new product / process, a new combination of old output, a new method of production, a new organizational method, a significant improvement in the quality of old product/ process, ability to produce at low costs and to open a new market.

[10] New product/ process even just for your firm or for local market and not necessarily new for the international market.

3. Human Capital (Skill) and Firm Production[11]

3.1 Human Capital [Skill] Indicators

44. Please give the approximate percentage of workers according to educational level in your firm in the year 2001?

Level of Education	National	Foreign
With Post Secondary education		
With Secondary education		
With Less than Secondary education		
Total Percentage	100%	100%

45. Please give the approximate percentage of workers according to occupation classification in your firm in the year 2001?

Group of Occupation	National	Foreign
Managers		
Professional / Management Executive/ Scientific / Technical and Engineers		
Clerical/ administrative		
Skilled craftsmen		
Plant machinery operators, assemblers and elementary occupation		
Other workers		
Total Percentage	100%	100%

46. Please approximate the average years of experience and average wages according to educational level in your firm in the year 2001?

Level of Education	Average years of experiences		Average wages	
	National	Foreign	National	Foreign
With Post Secondary education				
With Secondary education				
With Less than Secondary education				

47. Please approximate the qualifications [level of education], average years of experience and average wages according to occupation classification in your firm in the year 2001?

Group of Occupation	Qualifications (Level of Education)	Average years of experience	Average Wages
Managers			
Professional / Management Executive/ Scientific / Technical and Engineers			
Clerical/ administrative			
Skilled craftsmen			
Plant machinery operators, assemblers and elementary occupation			
Other workers			

3.2 Skilled Workers and Firm Product

48. Did scientists & engineers hired by your firm contribute to firm activities in any of the following ways?

	Yes	No	Partially
Shorten the development time.			
Add technical, scientific or marketing knowledge to areas where your firm already had expertise			
Add new technical, scientific or marketing knowledge in area where your firm lacked expertise			
Other types of knowledge [please specify below].			

....

49. Over the last three years has your firm experienced any shortage of skilled workers? (Please tick one box)

Yes	No
1	2 ⟶ skip to question [51]

---

[11] Skilled workers are educated workers with college/ university degree [i.e. sixteen or more years of schooling]

50. If any, over the last three years has at least one project been seriously affected by the shortage of skilled workers, qualified personnel and expertise? (Please tick one box) (Multiple Answers Possible [MAP]).

	Yes	No
Seriously delayed		
Abolished		
Not even started		

51. In the last three years has the proportion of skilled workers in your firm ....(Please tick one box)

Increased	Decreased	Remained Stable
1	2 ⟶ skip to question [55]	3 ⟶ skip to question [55]

If the answer is [1] for question [51], continue answering questions [52], [53] and [54].

52. If the use of skilled workers in your firm has increased, in the last three years, has this increase lead to any of the following effects? Please tick the relevant answer(s) in the respective columns. (Multiple Answers Possible [MAP])

	Yes	No
Increase firm production.		
Effective utilization of technologies.		
Easier and faster adaptation of technologies.		
Improve product quality.		
Improve the level of competitiveness in the local market.		
Improve the level of competitiveness in the international market.		
Others [please specify below].		

....

53. Does the increasing use of skilled workers induce any negative effect(s) in your firm? (Please tick one box)

Yes	No
1	2 ⟶ skip to question [55]

54. If any, please specify the effect(s)?

....

3.3 The incidence of external effect of schooling/ transfer of knowledge the hindering and other promoting factors

55. In your opinion, does the use of skilled workers induce a significant positive effect[12] on unskilled workers in your firm? (Please tick one box).

Yes	No
1 ⟶ skip to question [57]	2

56. If no, in your opinion, how important are the following factors in reducing the effect in your firm? Please tick the relevant factors in the respective columns. (Multiple Answers Possible [MAP])

	Importance Extremely **3**	Moderately **2**	Slightly **1**	**Not Relevant 0**
Skilled workers failed to deliver their knowledge and experiences to benefit unskilled workers.				
Unskilled workers were unable to acquire the knowledge and experiences from skilled workers.				
Low return from / quality of education.				
Low return from/ quality of training compared to international standard.				
Firm conditions do not encourage the external effects.				
Others [please specify below].				

....

[12] This is a non-intentional external effect made by skilled worker and lead to an enhancement of the productivity of unskilled worker.

57. In your opinion, how important are the following policies / solutions in inducing the effect in your firm? Please tick the relevant answer(s) in the respective columns. (Multiple Answers Possible [MAP])

	Importance: Extremely 3	Moderately 2	Slightly 1	Not Relevant 0
Improves the qualifications of skilled workers to permit the positive effects on unskilled workers.				
Improves the qualifications and ability of unskilled workers to learn from skilled workers.				
Improves the quality of education.				
Improves the quality of training to coincide with international standard.				
Improves firm conditions to encourage the external effects.				
Improves firm selection in both recruitment and termination.				
Sponsors education scholarship.				
Others [please specify below].				

....

3.4 Plan and strategy for skill upgrading and potential effects

58. Does your firm have a plan for the next three years to raise the general level of skill? (Please tick one box).

Yes	No
1	2 → skip to chapter [4] question [61]

59. If any, how important is the effect of upskilling [raising skill level] in fulfilling the following strategies in your firm? Please tick the relevant answer in the respective columns.

	Importance: Extremely 3	Moderately 2	Slightly 1	Not Relevant 0
Enhance / Increase firm production.				
Upskilling national workers in the firm.				
Hiring more skilled national workers.				
Reduce future demand for foreign skilled workers.				
Others [please specify below].				

....

60. If the strategies [2] and [3] in question [59] are important, how important are their effects in fulfilling the following strategies in your firm? Please tick the relevant answer in the respective columns.

	Importance: Extremely 3	Moderately 2	Slightly 1	Not Relevant 0
a. Upskilling national workers in the firm:				
Increase the employment of national workers.				
Reduce future demand for foreign skilled workers.				
b. Hiring more skilled national workers:				
Increase the employment of national workers.				
Reduce future demand for foreign skilled workers				
Others [please specify below].				

....

4. The use of Technology and the demand for skilled workers

61. Firm demand for skilled workers: (please tick one box for each)

(a) In the last three years has the demand for skilled workers hired by your firm ……			(b) In the long run do you expect the demand for skilled workers needed in your firm to ……		
Increased	Decreased	Remained stable	Increase	Decrease	Remain stable
1	2	3	1	2	3

62. If the long run demand for skilled workers needed in your firm is expected to increase, decrease or remain stable, please give the reason(s) for the selected choice: increase, decrease or stable?

…………………………………………..

63. In the last three years, if your firm has used several new technologies, please name them and specify their various effects on the demand for skilled workers?

………………………………………………………………………………..

64. In the last three years, has the use of new technologies induced a significant effect/change on skill level and the demand for skilled workers? (Please choose the more appropriate description of the effect on the use of new technology)

(a) Change in skill level			(b) Change in the demand for skilled workers		
Increased	Decreased	Has no effect on the skill level of workers	Increased	Decreased	Has no effect on the demand for skilled workers
1	2	3	1	2	3

65. If any, in your opinion, how important is the use of new technologies in changing both the skill level and the demand for workers hired by your firm? Please tick the relevant answer(s) in the respective columns. (Multiple Answers Possible [MAP])

	Importance: Extremely 3	Moderately 2	Slightly 1	Not Relevant 0
Increasing the general skill level.				
Increasing the skill level mainly for unskilled workers.				
Increasing the demand for more educated, trained / experienced workers.				
Increasing the demand for more professional workers.				
Decreasing the demand for less educated, trained / experienced workers.				
Decreasing the demand for production workers.				
Substituting the demand for unskilled [less educated and production] workers.				
Others [please specify below].				

……………………………………………………………………………………………

66. If the use of new technologies reduces the demand for unskilled workers, in your opinion, how important are the following factors? (Please tick the relevant answer(s) in the respective columns. (Multiple Answers Possible [MAP]).

	Importance: Extremely 3	Moderately 2	Slightly 1	Not Relevant 0
Unskilled workers lack the skills required for filling the jobs.				
Unskilled workers are less productive.				
Unskilled workers failed to use technology effectively.				
The use of technology lead to reduction in some unskilled jobs.				
The use of technology lead to substitution/ elimination of some unskilled jobs.				
Others [please specify below].				

………………………………………………………………………………………………………

67. Does your firm have adequate availability of national skilled workers at this moment? (Please tick one box).

Yes	Yes, in restricted field(s)	No
1 → skip to question [70]	2 → skip to question [70]	3

68. If the answer is [3] for question [67], does your firm have a plan to rely on national skilled workers over the coming period? Please tick the relevant answer in the respective columns.

Yes	Yes, in restricted field(s)	No
1	2	3→ skip to question [70]

69. If the answer is [1] or [2] for question [68], what would be the percentage of national skilled workers in your firm in the short, medium and long term? Please approximate the percentage for each time period.

Short term (Up to three years)	Medium term (three to five years)	Long term (five to ten years)
.........%	.........%	.........%

70. How important are the effects of Upskilling [raising skill level] in fulfilling the following long run strategies? Please, tick the relevant answer(s) in the respective columns. (Multiple Answers Possible [MAP])

	Importance Extremely 3	Moderately 2	Slightly 1	**Not Relevant 0**
Facilitating an effective utilization & upgrading of technologies.				
Reinforcing the employment of national skills.				
Others [please specify below].				

....

5. **Training and short and long run plans for Skill Development**

71. How important are the following types of skill development activities in your firm? Please tick the relevant answer(s) in the respective columns. (Multiple Answers Possible [MAP])

	Importance Extremely 3	Moderately 2	Slightly 1	**Not Relevant 0**
Investing in training to train existing employees.				
Sending trainers and mentors abroad to acquire skills.				
Sending workers abroad to acquire skills.				
Bringing / attracting new foreign skills, scientists and engineers.				
Using ICT to upgrade skill level.				
Encouraging learning on the job.				
Supporting long distance learning.				
Others [please specify below].				

....

72. If any of the above types are important, please specify if these activities are to be pursued now or in the near future?

	To be Pursued now	**To be Pursued in the near future**
Investing in training to train existing employees.		
Sending trainers and mentors abroad to acquire skills.		
Sending workers abroad to acquire skills.		
Bringing/attracting new foreign skills, scientists and engineers.		
Using ICT to upgrade skill level.		
Encouraging learning on the job.		
Supporting long distance learning.		
Others [please specify].		

73. Does your firm have an in-house training unit? (Please tick one box).

Yes	No
1	2 → skip to question [76]

74. If any, how much did your firm spend on it in the year 2001?

....

75. How many staffs are there in the unit?

……………………………………………………………………………………

76. In the year 2001, what was the percentage of government subsidies offered to support training in your firm? (Please tick one box).

Zero	1% - 10%	11% – 20%	21% - 25%.	Over 25%
1	2	3	4	5

77. How does your firm find information about training opportunities? (Multiple Answers Possible [MAP])

Government departments or semi government institutions.	1
Chamber of Commerce.	2
Public education and training institutions [Universities and specialized colleges].	3
Information from other firms in your sector.	4
Foreign universities.	5
Private trainers [local and foreign companies].	6
Others [please specify below].	7

……………………………………………………………………………………

78. How important are the following functions for the training unit in your firm? Please tick the relevant answer(s) in the respective columns. (Multiple Answers Possible [MAP])

	Importance Extremely 3	Moderately 2	Slightly 1	**Not Relevant 0**
Encouraging technological/ organizational improvement.				
Upgrading skill level.				
Encouraging the acquisition of new knowledge.				
Monitoring skills and conducting a regular skill needs assessment.				
Others [please specify below].				

……………………………………………………………………………………

79. In the year 2001 did your firm provide a regular training to the following types of employees? (Please tick one box)

	Yes	No
Production workers.	1	2
Service workers.	1	2
Production engineering staffs.	1	2
Management staffs.	1	2
Other staffs not included above.	1	2

80. If your firm provide a regular training, how important are the following categories of training modes in maximizing the return / efficiency of training in your firm?

	Importance Extremely 3	Moderately 2	Slightly 1	**Not Relevant 0**
1. On– the job.				
2. On – the job and Off– the job combined.				
3. Off – the job within the firm [training center].				
4. Off– the job out side the firm [specialist training center in side the country].				
5. Off– the job out side the firm out side the country/abroad.				
6. Others [please specify below].				

……………………………………………………………………………………

81. Please rank the most important type of training against each of the occupation category listed below?

	Managerial	Professional/ scientists/technical and engineers	Clerical/administrative and skilled workers	Others
1. On– the job.				
2. On – the job and Off– the job combined.				

3. Off – the job within the firm [training center].				
4. Off– the job out side the firm [specialist training center in side the country]				
5. Off– the job out side the firm out side the country / abroad.				

82. If any of that training offered exclusively for the national workers, please rank the most important type of training offered exclusively for the national workers against each of the occupation category listed below?

	Managerial	Professional/ scientists/technical and engineers	Clerical/administrative and skilled workers	Others
1. On– the job.				
2. On – the job and Off– the job combined.				
3. Off – the job within the firm [training center].				
4. Off– the job out side the firm [specialist training center in side the country]				
5. Off– the job out side the firm out side the country / abroad.				

83. In the last three years, has the performance of training unit contributed significantly in raising skill level of workers hired at your firm? (Please tick one box).

Increased	Decreased	No notable change
1 ⟶ skip to question [86]	2	3

84. If the training provision did not contribute significantly in raising skill level of workers, how important are the following factors in making the training provision unsuccessful in your firm? Please tick the relevant answer(s) in the respective columns. (Multiple Answers Possible [MAP])

	Importance Extremely **3**	Moderately **2**	Slightly **1**	**Not Relevant 0**
Low educational qualifications of workers.				
Lack of appreciation of or information on the benefits of training.				
Lack of training materials and equipment.				
Lack of trainers and mentors.				
Low quality of trainers and mentors.				
In adequate / in accurate assessment of training needs.				
In adequate planning for training programmes.				
Mismatch between training programmes & changing skill needs.				
Mismatch between training programmes and changing technical needs.				
Lack of specialized training institutions.				
Lack of interactions between training institutions and firm.				
Lack of finance to cover the costs of training.				
Lack of full appropriability of the return from training investment				
High rate of mobility of trainees to leave for better – paid jobs after training.				
Lack of a system of training certification of skills acquired.				
Others [please specify below].				

………………………………………………………………………………………………

85. If any of the above problem(s) is /are important, how important are the following factors in making the training provision successful in your firm? Please tick the relevant answer(s) in the respective columns. (Multiple Answers Possible [MAP])

	Importance Extremely 3	 Moderately 2	 Slightly 1	Not Relevant 0
Enhancing the educational qualifications of workers.				
Increasing the appreciation of / information on the benefits of training.				
Enhancing the availability of training materials and equipment.				
Enhancing the availability of trainers and mentors				
Enhancing the quality of trainers and mentors.				
Enhancing better / accurate assessment of training needs.				
Enhancing adequate planning for training programmes.				
Enhancing training programmes to fit the changing skill needs.				
Enhancing training programmes to fit the changing technical needs.				
Enhancing the interactions between training institutions and firm.				
Enhancing the availability of finance to cover training costs.				
Enhancing the full appropriability of the return from training investment.				
Restriction the mobility of trainees.				
Enhancing a system of training certification of skills acquired.				
Others [please specify below].				

....

86. Would you be willing to participate in a follow – up interview as part of this research project?

Yes	No
1	2

We would like to extend to you sincere thanks for your kind cooperation and for finding the time in completing this questionnaire. Please return it by 21/ February / 2002.

Name of the person completing the questionnaire:
Telephone number:
Fax number:
Position in the company:
Date:

Appendix 2: Questionnaire of the Macro Survey (2002)

"Interview with Policy Makers in the Government and Experts: Skills Creation, Human Resources Development and Policy Intervention in the United Arab Emirates"

Please answer the following questions:

1. General assessment of upskilling efforts

1. In your opinion, which of the following statements give the more appropriate description / judgment of skills creation efforts in the UAE? (Please choose one answer)

Skills creation efforts have been fully / absolutely successful in all fields / sectors.	1
Skills creation efforts have been largely successful in all fields / sectors.	2
Skills creation efforts have been moderately successful in some fields / sectors.	3
Skills creation efforts have been slightly successful in some fields / sectors.	4
Skills creation efforts have been unsuccessful.	5

2. Please specify in what field(s)/ sector(s) the UAE has managed to create appropriate/ relevant skills and in what sectors/ fields it has made a relative progress to the development of local skills?

	UAE has made a relative progress to develop the local skills
Education and Higher Education sector.	
Information and Communication sector.	
Industrial sector.	
Manufacturing sector.	
Agriculture and Live Stock sector.	
Health and Medical Care sector.	
Services sector.	
Construction sector.	
Technical and Engineering field.	
Petroleum and Petrochemical field.	
Others [please specify below].	

....

2. Policies for enhancing skill creation and upgrading

3. How important are the following factors/ components in promoting and enhancing skills creation efforts in the UAE? Please tick the relevant answer(s) in the respective columns. (Multiple Answers Possible [MAP])

	Importance: Extremely 3	Moderately 2	Slightly 1	Not Relevant 0
Factors related to the trainee / educated workers.				
Education system.				
Training system.				
Resources allocation.				
Social partnership and collaboration between educational and training institutions, employers, workers and the state to determine skill needs and the most effective ways of meeting and financing them.				
Planning skills needs.				
Monitoring skill needs on a regular basis.				
Import skill from abroad.				
Others [please specify below].				

....

4. If skills creation is linked / related to the side of trainee/ educated workers, how important are the following factors in encouraging trainee/ educated workers to acquire skills/ enhancing skills creation? Please tick the relevant answer(s) in the respective columns. (Multiple Answers Possible [MAP])

	Importance Extremely 3	Moderately 2	Slightly 1	Not Relevant 0
Enhancing the positive external effects of both education and training.				
Increasing the information about future skill needs / trends				
Increasing the information on educational and training needs in the productive sectors and their demand for graduate students.				
Increasing the information about the future value of investments in education and training to minimize the risk aversion: preference of more certain short term returns to available jobs than long term skill investments				
Enhancing a system of certification of skills acquired.				
Minimization of education, learning and training costs.				
Providing adequate incentives for trainers.				
Increasing the interaction to market needs.				
Others [please specify below].				

……………………………………………………………………………………………

5. If skills creation is linked / related to enhancement of education system, how important / effective are the following factors / intervention policies in enhancing education system and so skills creation? Please tick the relevant answer(s) in the respective columns. (Multiple Answers Possible [MAP])

Factors / Possible Policies intervention	Importance Extremely 3	Moderately 2	Slightly 1	Not Relevant 0
Improve the internal efficiency/ quality of basic education.				
Improve the internal efficiency/ quality of tertiary education.				
Encourage the system of flexibility of educational institutions.				
Encourage the system of modernization and dynamism.				
Improve the quality of teachers or mentors.				
Improve the infrastructures.				
Monitoring educational needs on a regular basis.				
Better Planning for educational needs.				
Increase public spending on education.				
Increase private sector spending and involvement on education.				
Increase spending and incentives to encourage enrollment in technical education.				
Enhance the linkages [network] between universities, colleges, technical and training institutes and the productive sectors.				
Increase the harmony / consistency between education output and market needs by focusing on particular future skills needs.				
Increasing the motivation and incentives to attract/ change the attitudes of educated economically active population.				
Others [please specify below].				

……………………………………………………………………………………………

6. If skill creation is linked / related to enhancement of training system, how important/effective are the following factors / policies intervention in making training provision more successful and so enhancing skills in the UAE? Please tick the relevant answer(s) in the respective columns. (Multiple Answers Possible [MAP])

	Importance Extremely 3	 Moderately 2	 Slightly 1	Not Relevant 0
Enhancing the educational qualifications of workers.				
Increasing the appreciation of or information on the benefits of training.				
Enhancing the availability of training materials and equipment.				
Increasing the availability of trainers and mentors.				
Improving the quality of trainers and mentors.				
Regular / adequate assessment and monitoring of training needs.				
Enhancing adequate planning for training programmes/ needs.				
Enhancing training programmes to fit the changing skill needs.				
Enhancing training programmes to fit the changing technical needs.				
Enhancing/ encouraging the specialized training institutions.				
Enhancing the interactions between training institutions & firm.				
Enhancing the availability of finance to cover training costs.				
Enhancing the full appropriability of the return from investment in training.				
Decentralization of decision-making.				
Increasing the participation of private training institutions.				
Enhancing the system of training certification of skills acquired				
Others [please specify below].				

....

3. **Causes of low skill levels and failure of skill creation/upgrading efforts**

7. If there is some failure in skills creation, how important are the following factors / components in causing / explaining this failure? Please tick the relevant answer(s) in the respective columns. (Multiple Answers Possible [MAP])

	Importance Extremely 3	 Moderately 2	 Slightly 1	Not Relevant 0
Factors related to trainee / educated workers.				
Deficient education system.				
Deficient training system.				
Factors related to resources allocation.				
Others [please specify below].				

....

8. If there is some failure in skills creation linked / related to the side of trainee/ educated workers, how important are the following factors? Please tick the relevant answer(s) in the respective columns. (Multiple Answers Possible [MAP])

	Importance Extremely 3	Moderately 2	Slightly 1	Not Relevant 0
Externalities and failure to recoup all the benefits of educational investments.				
Lack of information on educational and training needs in the productive sectors and their demand for graduate students.				
Uncertainty about the future value of investments in education and training.				
Uncertainties about future skill needs / trends.				
Risk aversion: preference of more certain short – term returns to available jobs than long - term skill investments.				
Lack of a system of certification of skills acquired.				
High costs to finance education, learning and training.				
Inadequate incentives for trainers.				
Lack of interaction to market needs.				
10. Others [please specify below].				

………

9. If there is some failure in skills creation linked / related to education system, how important are the following reasons in lowering the returns from education? Please tick the relevant answer(s) in the respective columns. (Multiple Answers Possible [MAP])

	Importance Extremely 3	Moderately 2	Slightly 1	Not Relevant 0
A. Deficiency of basic education due to:				
Low quality / internal efficiency.				
Lack of flexibility of educational institutions.				
Lack of modernization and dynamism.				
Lack of teachers or mentors.				
Lack of infrastructures due to inadequate investment [public spending on education].				
Inadequate planning for educational needs				
Inadequate assessments and monitoring of educational needs.				
Low involvement and spending by private sector.				
Low spending in technical education.				
Weak incentives for enrollment in technical education.				
B. Deficiency of tertiary education				
Low quality / internal efficiency.				
Lack of flexibility of educational institutions.				
Lack of modernization and dynamism.				
Lack of teachers or mentors.				
Lack of infrastructures due to Inadequate investment [public spending on education].				
Inadequate planning for educational needs				
Inadequate assessments and monitoring of educational needs.				
Low involvement and spending by private sector.				
Low spending in technical education.				
Weak incentives for enrollment in technical education.				
Weak linkages [network] between universities, colleges, technical and training institutes and the productive sectors.				
C. Others [please specify below].				

………

10. If there is some deficiency in education system mainly attributed to low quality [internal efficiency] of education, how important are the following factors in reducing the internal efficiency/ quality of education? Please tick the relevant answer(s) in the respective columns. (Multiple Answers Possible [MAP])

	Importance Extremely 3	Moderately 2	Slightly 1	Not Relevant 0
Low quality at basic education level relative to international standard.				
Low rates of accomplishments and motivation at basic education level relative to international standard.				
Low rates of accomplishments and motivation at higher secondary education levels relative to international standard..				
Low quality at tertiary education level relative to international standard.				
Low rates of accomplishments and motivation at tertiary education level relative to international standard.				
Low survival rates and high drop –out.				
High repetition rates.				
High pupil / teacher ratios.				
Low public current expenditures per pupil.				
Low quality of teachers or mentors.				
Others [please specify below].				

....

11. If there is some deficiency in education system, did both deficiency of basic education system and deficiency of tertiary education system lead to mismatch between the output of education and market needs in the UAE? [Please tick one box for (a) and (b)].

(a) deficiency of basic education lead to mismatch between the output of education and market needs.		(b) deficiency of tertiary education lead to mismatch between the output of education and market needs.	
Yes	No	Yes	No
1	2	1	2

12. If there is some failure in skills creation linked / related to training system, how important are the following factors in making the training provision unsuccessful in the UAE? Please tick the relevant answer(s) in the respective columns. (Multiple Answers Possible [MAP])

	Importance Extremely 3	Moderately 2	Slightly 1	Not Relevant 0
Low educational qualifications of workers.				
Lack of appreciation of or information on the benefits of training.				
Lack of training materials and equipment				
Lack of trainers and mentors.				
Low quality of trainers and mentors.				
In adequate assessment of training needs.				
In adequate planning for training programmes.				
Mismatch between training programmes and changing skill needs.				
Mismatch between training programmes and changing technical needs.				
Lack of specialized training institutions.				
Lack of interactions between training institutions and firm.				
Lack of finance to cover the costs of training.				
Lack of full appropriability of investment in training.				
High rate of mobility of trainees to leave for better – paid jobs after training.				
Lack of a system of training certification of skills acquired.				
Others [please specify below].				

....

4. Short and Long terms mechanisms for skill upgrading and effects on technological upgrading and fulfilling socio-economic objectives

13. How important are the following types of skill formation in fulfilling / accelerating the long run economic growth strategies in the UAE? Please tick the relevant answer(s) in the respective columns. (Multiple Answers Possible [MAP])

	Importance			Not Relevant
	Extremely 3	Moderately 2	Slightly 1	0
Investing in formal education.				
Investing in vocational training.				
Investing in- firm training to train existing employees.				
Improving the quality of teachers, trainers and mentors.				
Sending teachers/instructors/ trainers abroad to acquire knowledge and skills.				
Sending students abroad to acquire knowledge and skills.				
Sending workers abroad to acquire knowledge and skills.				
Attracting new foreign skills, scientists & engineers.				
Using ICT to upgrade skill level.				
Encouraging learning on the job.				
Supporting long distance learning.				
Enhancing the system of accreditation and Licensing.				
Enhancing the system or programme of apprenticeship.				
Others [please specify below].				

………

14. If any of the above types are important, please specify if these activities have been already implemented, are to be pursued now or in the near future in the UAE? (Please tick one box for each statement below)

	Has been already implemented	To be Pursued now	To be Pursued in the near future
Investing in formal education.			
Investing in vocational training.			
Investing in training to train existing employees			
Improving the quality of teachers, trainers and mentors.			
Sending teachers/instructors/ trainers abroad to acquire knowledge and skills.			
Sending students abroad to acquire knowledge and skills.			
Sending worker abroad to acquire skills.			
Bringing /attracting new foreign skills, scientist and engineers.			
Using ICT to upgrade skill level.			
Encouraging Learning on the job.			
Supporting long distance learning.			
Enhancing the system of accreditation and Licensing.			
Enhancing the system or programme of apprenticeship.			
Others [please specify].			

15. How important are the effects of upskilling in fulfilling the following socio-economic goals? Please, tick the relevant answer(s) in the respective columns. (Multiple Answers Possible [MAP])

	Importance			Not Relevant
	Extremely 3	Moderately 2	Slightly 1	0
Increasing / reinforcing economic growth.				
Enhancing / accelerating technological upgrading.				
Solving imbalances in labour market: Reducing the future demand for foreign skilled labour.				
Reducing unemployment rate.				
Reinforcing self-reliance strategy.				

Others [please specify below].				

....

16. How important are the effects of upgrading of technologies in accelerating upskilling and fulfilling the following socio-economic goals? Please, tick the relevant answer(s) in the respective columns. (Multiple Answers Possible [MAP])

	Importance Extremely 3	Moderately 2	Slightly 1	**Not Relevant 0**
Increasing / reinforcing economic growth.				
Enhancing / accelerating upskilling.				
Solving imbalances in labour market: Reducing the future demand for foreign skilled labour.				
Reducing unemployment rate.				
Reinforcing self-reliance strategy.				
Others [please specify below].				

....

4. The incidence of external effect of schooling/ transfer of knowledge the hindering and other promoting factors

17. Does the external effect of schooling/education[13] occur and contribute to upskilling in the UAE? (Please tick one box).

Yes	No
1 → Skip to question [20]	2

If the answer is [2], please continue in answering questions [18] and [19].

18. If the external effect of schooling / education does not yet occur, how important are the following factors in reducing the external effect of schooling / education and in lowering its effects on upskilling? Please tick the relevant factors in the respective columns. (Multiple Answers Possible [MAP])

	Importance Extremely 3	Moderately 2	Slightly 1	**Not Relevant 0**
Skilled workers failed to deliver their knowledge and experiences to benefit unskilled workers.				
Unskilled workers were unable to acquire the knowledge and experiences from skilled workers.				
Low return from / quality of education.				
Low return from/ quality of training compared to international standard.				
Firm conditions do not encourage the external effects.				
Others [please specify below].				

....

19. If any of the above factor[s] is/ are important, how important are the following policies/solutions in inducing the external effect of schooling and in enhancing the upskilling? Please tick the relevant answer(s) in the respective columns. (Multiple Answers Possible [MAP])

	Importance Extremely 3	Moderately 2	Slightly 1	**Not Relevant** 0
Improves the qualifications of skilled workers to permit the positive effects on unskilled workers.				
Improves the qualifications and ability of unskilled workers to learn from skilled workers.				

13 This is a non-intentional external effect made by skilled worker and lead to an enhancement of the productivity of unskilled worker.

Improves the quality of education.				
Improves the quality of training to coincide with international standard.				
Improves firm conditions to encourage the external effects.				
Improves firm selection in both recruitment and termination.				
Sponsors education scholarship.				
Others [please specify below].				

....

5. Conclusions and further recommendations

20. Do you want to add any other general comments or suggestions for skill formation and human resources development in the UAE?
....
....

We would like to extend to you sincere thanks for your kind cooperation and for finding the time in completing this questionnaire.

Name of the person completing the questionnaire:

Telephone number:

Fax number:

Position in the institution:

Date:

About the Author

Dr. Samia Satti Osman Mohamed Nour obtained her first degree (B.Sc Hons. First Class) and second degree (M.Sc) in Economics from the University of Khartoum (Sudan) in 1994 and 1999 respectively, and her doctorate (Ph.D.) in Economics from the University of Maastricht (the Netherlands) in 2005. Currently, she is an affiliated researcher (and former visiting research fellow and fomer Ph.D. fellow) at UNU-MERIT, School of Business and Economics, Maastricht University, Maastricht, the Netherlands. She is also a Research Fellow at ASC, Leiden University, Leiden, the Netherlands Currently, she is an Associate Professor of Economics at the Department of Economics, Faculty of Economic and Social Studies, Khartoum University, Sudan, since January 2012. At the Department of Economics, Khartoum University, she teaches Macroeconomics, Labour Economics, Development Economics and Industrial Economics for the B.SC. (Undergraduate class) and Microeconomics for the M.Sc. (postgraduate class). She was employed as the coordinator of the Ph.D. programme in Economics (2006–2009), as Assistant Professor of Economics (December 2005–December 2011), and as a teaching assistant (April 1995–December 2005) at the Department of Economics, Faculty of Economic and Social Studies, Khartoum University. She received five different best student faculty prizes during her undergraduate studies and several research awards and grants during her postgraduate studies. She was recipient of the Arab Fund for Economic and Social Development Distinguished Scholar Award and Post-Doctoral Fellowship, the Arab Fund for Economic and Social Development, Kuwait (October 2010–December 2011). She was recipient of the University of Khartoum Scientific Excellence Award Prize in Humanities and Educational Studies (in the field of Economics) (February 2013). She completed several research projects supported by several regional and international institutions. Dr. Samia has worked as Economic Consultant for United Nations Population Fund and Organization for Economic Cooperation and Development (UNFPA-OECD) Joint Research project "Mobilising Migrants' Skills for Development in the MENA Region. Making the most out of young migrants skills" from Decmeber 2012 to May 2013. Dr. Samia has worked as Economic Consultant for European Investment Bank, (EIB, Luxemburg) Research Project "Overview of Knowledge Transfer in

S. Mohamed Nour, *Technological Change and Skill Development in Arab Gulf Countries*, Contributions to Economics, DOI 10.1007/978-3-319-01916-1,

MENA Countries-Egypt" from October 2011 to April 2012. She has worked as Economic Consultant for United Nations Economic Commission for Africa (UNECA, Ethiopia) Research Project "Assessment of MDGs in Africa-Sudan" from May to June 2010. She contributed two background papers for UNDP Third Arab Knowledge Report 2012–2013 (October 2012–March 2013). She stayed as a Ph.D. Fellow at Maastricht University and UNU-INTECH, now UNU-MERIT, Maastricht, the Netherlands from September 1999 to November 2005; as a Ph.D. Intern at UNU-WIDER, Helsinki, Finland from May to July 2002; as a visiting research fellow at ASC, Leiden University, Leiden, the Netherlands from May to July 2009 and as a visiting research fellow at UNU-MERIT, Maastricht University, Maastricht, the Netherlands from October 2010 to December 2011. Dr Samia's main research interests are in the fields of Economics, Economics of Technical Change, Macroeconomics, Microeconomics, Development Economics, Endogenous Growth, Human Capital and Labour Economics, and Knowledge Economy. She has published several reports, discussion and working papers and has contributed to ten articles published in international refereed journals. She is the author of the book "Technological Change and Skill Development in Sudan," (February 2013, Springer, Berlin, Heidelberg, Germany). She is also the author of the book "Technological Change and Skill Development in Arab Gulf Countries," (Forthcoming book: Springer Series Contributions to Economics, (forthcoming, November 30, 2013), Springer, Springer International Publishing Switzerland).

CPSIA information can be obtained at www.ICGtesting.com
Printed in the USA
LVOW10*1339221213

366435LV00002B/186/P

9 783319 019154